Nigel Cawthorne is the author of *A Brief History of Robin Hood* and *Jack the Ripper's Secret Confession*. His writing has appeared in over 150 newspapers, magazines and partworks – from the *Sun* to the *Financial Times*, and from *Flatbush Life* to *The New York Tribune*. He lives in London.

Recent titles in the series

A Brief History of Roman Britain
Joan P. Alcock

A Brief History of the Private Life of Elizabeth II
Michael Paterson

A Brief History of France
Cecil Jenkins

A Brief History of Slavery
Jeremy Black

A Brief History of Robin Hood
Nigel Cawthorne

A Brief Guide to Angels and Demons
Sarah Bartlett

A Brief History of How the Industrial Revolution Changed the World
Thomas Crump

A Brief History of King Arthur
Mike Ashley

A Brief History of the Universe
J. P. McEvoy

A Brief Guide to Secret Religions
David Barrett

His Finest Hour: A Brief Life of Winston Churchill
Christopher Catherwood

A Brief History of Witchcraft
Lois Martin

A Brief History of France
Cecil Jenkins

A BRIEF HISTORY OF

SHERLOCK ·HOLMES·

NIGEL CAWTHORNE

ROBINSON

RUNNING PRESS
PHILADELPHIA · LONDON

Constable & Robinson Ltd
55–56 Russell Square
WC1B 4HP
www.constablerobinson.com

First published in the UK by Robinson,
an imprint of Constable & Robinson, 2011

A copy of the British Library Cataloguing in Publication
Data is available from the British Library

UK ISBN 978-1-78033-012-9
3 5 7 9 10 8 6 4 2

First published in the United States in 2011 by Running Press Book Publishers,
A Member of the Perseus Books Group

Books published by Running Press are available at special discounts for bulk purchases in the
United States by corporations, institutions, and other organizations. For more information,
please contact the Special Markets Department at the Perseus Books Group, 2300 Chestnut
Street, Suite 200, Philadelphia, PA 19103, or call (800) 810-4145, ext. 5000, or e-mail
special.markets@perseusbooks.com.

US ISBN: 978-0-7624-4408-3
US Library of Congress Control Number: 2011928224

9 8 7 6 5 4 3 2 1
Digit on the right indicates the number of this printing

Running Press Book Publishers
2300 Chestnut Street
Philadelphia, PA 19103-4371

Visit us on the web!
www.runningpress.com

Printed and bound in the UK

Contents

Introduction

The Brains of Baker Street

Created by Sir Arthur Conan Doyle in 1887, the great detective Sherlock Holmes appears in four novels and fifty-six short stories, which first appeared in serial form in monthly magazines. All but four are narrated by Holmes's friend Dr John H. Watson.

Holmes was not the first detective in literature but he helped to establish the genre; from the beginning he had a huge following on both sides of the Atlantic. Sherlockians can now be found worldwide, and films and TV series are made about him to this day. Holmes's use of deductive reason affected real-life policing and inspired future generations of fictional detectives. It could be argued that every literary, film or TV detective is a direct descendent of Sherlock Holmes.

But Holmes remains rooted in the late Victorian and Edwardian eras, when the British Empire was at its zenith and when London, then the biggest city in the world, was shrouded in pea-souper fogs caused by the burning of wood and coal for heating, cooking and industry. It was a world of hansom cabs and gaslight. Telephones were rare; most communication was by letter and telegram. The railway had opened up the countryside, yet it would be years until the suburbs on the Surrey side of the Thames would begin to sprawl.

At that time, London was a major port and from London Bridge eastwards there was a massive complex of docks with its attendant poverty, slums, opium dens and prostitution, which also flourished in the West End. At night it would have been almost impossible to drive down the quadrant at the end of Regent Street into Piccadilly Circus for the crowds of working women.

London was home to political dissidents and Jews seeking refuge from persecution on the Continent. A Fenian bombing campaign had ended in 1885, though Irish home rule remained a major political issue. The unification of Germany had already led to the Franco-Prussian war. Ocean liners had begun to make travel to America, South Africa, India and Australia commonplace. A transatlantic cable laid in 1866 and supplemented with new cables in 1873, 1874, 1880 and 1894 made it easy for Holmes to telegraph police departments across North America. The invention of the steam-driven press and the abolition of stamp duty (the tax on learning) in 1855 made newspapers and magazines cheap and plentiful. The London underground system was being built and the construction of the sewerage system began to eradicate cholera.

Holmes arrived on the literary scene just when London needed a real-life detective: Jack the Ripper stalked the streets in 1888, but Scotland Yard seemed more concerned with prosecuting the clients of the male brothel in Cleveland Street, raided in 1889, and Oscar Wilde, who was imprisoned in 1895.

Holmes's last case is set in the year 1914. Conan Doyle had continued to publish the stories until 1927, but placed them in the era before the Great War swept away Holmes's world forever.

Doyle did not like Holmes and thought his historical novels to be more important. He famously tried to kill off Holmes in 1893 by plunging him over the Reichenbach Falls with Professor Moriarty, but was forced revive him in 1901 with *The Hound of the Baskervilles*. It would be no more possible to kill Holmes now.

Nigel Cawthorne
Bloomsbury, 2011

Chapter 1

Sir Arthur Conan Doyle

At a dinner in the Balmoral Ballroom of London's Trocadero on 28 September 1928, the creator of Sherlock Holmes, Sir Arthur Conan Doyle, complained that he suffered sometimes 'from some little confusion between the author and the character'. He was, he said, more like Dr Watson, the fictional author of the Sherlock Holmes stories; however, according to psychologists, he noted, we are 'multiplex' and conceded that 'there may be represented in my being some strand of Sherlock'.

Arthur Ignatius Conan Doyle was born in Edinburgh on 22 May 1859. In 1820, his grandfather John Doyle had moved from Dublin to London, where he became a political cartoonist and a friend of the writers Charles Dickens, Walter Scott and William Makepeace Thackeray, the artist Edwin Landseer and the politician Benjamin Disraeli.

John Doyle's surviving children inherited their father's gift for the arts. But the youngest, Charles, lagged behind the others and moved to Edinburgh where he became a draughtsman in the Office of Works, though he continued to work as an artist and illustrator in his spare time. In Edinburgh he met Mary Foyle, whose widowed mother had been forced to move to the city from Kilkenny to escape the Potato Famine. They were married in 1855.

As their family grew Charles's ambitions became circumscribed and by the time Arthur was born Charles had become an alcoholic. Arthur grew close to his mother, who filled him with stories of medieval derring-do. Mary, from an Anglo-Irish family, had been educated in France and, following the deaths of two of her daughters, she joined the Philosophical Institution, a literary and debating society, and made use of its extensive library. Her voracious reading was joked about by family and friends, many of whom also mixed in literary circles. For a while, Arthur and his mother lodged with the historiographer-royal for Scotland, John Hill Burton, who was then revising the manuscript of John Hanning Speke's account of his quest to find the source of the Nile. At the age of six, Conan Doyle began writing adventure stories of his own. At seven, he was taken to stay with his mother's well-to-do relatives in Ireland, where he witnessed a confrontation with the Fenians, who began a bombing campaign in England the following year.

When Conan Doyle and his mother returned to Scotland, his parents got back together again and moved into an overcrowded house in the suburb of Newington. There Arthur became the leader of a street gang that would later see literary incarnation as Holmes's youthful allies, the Baker Street Irregulars. He briefly attended the local school, Newington Academy, where years later the French teacher, Eugene Marie Chantrelle, seduced one of his pupils, married her and later murdered her for the insurance money by poisoning her with an overdose of raw opium. By then, Conan Doyle was a medical student and several of his teachers provided forensic and pharmacological evidence at Chantrelle's trial.

At the age of nine and with the aid of his uncles – particularly Michael Conan, Paris correspondent for the *Art Journal* – Arthur was packed off to Hodder, a Catholic prep school in Preston, Lancashire, where he was taught by Jesuits. He was unhappy there, but fell under the wing of a young priest who comforted him by telling him stories. He also found solace in reading, particularly the adventure novels and Westerns of the American Captain Mayne Reid and the Scot R.M. Ballantyne. Later he became an avid reader of Walter Scott, James Fenimore Cooper and the writer of romances Charles Reade, who was a friend of his Uncle Dicky and something of an expert on violins.

At the age of eleven, Conan Doyle moved up to the related senior school, Stonyhurst, which had recently invested in a new chemistry lab. The school also boasted a number of Old Masters, a Shakespeare first folio, Henry VII's cope and Eleanor of Aquitaine's reliquary. It also had a yew alley, like that in *The Hound of the Baskervilles*. The food was poor and the Jesuits strict. Boys were never left alone together so that, according to Conan Doyle, they could not practise 'the immorality which is rife in public schools'. Stonyhurst did imbue him with a life-long love of cricket, though he never made the first eleven. Even though he was beaten and bullied, he did not look forward to returning to the domestic strife of his overcrowded home during the vacations.

Arthur's older sister Annette was educated in France, as their mother had been. During the Franco-Prussian War of 1870; her school was overrun. Her letters home were published under a pseudonym in *The Scotsman*. Meanwhile, the youthful Arthur told stories at school, demanding payment in the form of cakes and tarts. At the age of fourteen, he began a magazine called *Wasp* with his classmates, contributing cartoons as well as stories. Subsequently, he started his own short-lived *Stonyhurst Figaro* and had begun to devour French novels, particularly those written by Jules Verne. School plays instilled in him a love of the theatre, though his poor elocution kept him out of speaking roles.

During Conan Doyle's time at Stonyhurst, an old boy hit the headlines: Roger Tichborne, the son of baronet, travelled the world after leaving the school and went missing, presumed dead. When his father died, an unemployed Australian butcher named Arthur Orton turned up, presenting himself as the missing 'Tichborne claimant', represented by his solicitor, John Holmes. In court, under cross-examination, his knowledge of Stonyhurst proved pitiful, causing much mirth among the school's pupils and Conan Doyle begged his parents to send him accounts of the trial.

For Christmas 1874 when he was fifteen, Conan Doyle went to stay with relatives in London, the first time he had visited the capital. The journey was almost postponed when a blanket of snow fell and the temperature dropped to 18°F (−8°C). Nevertheless a brief thaw allowed him to take a train to Euston then a cab to the home of Uncle Dicky and Aunt Annette in Earls Court. He went to the theatre, courtesy of Uncle Dicky's boss, Tom Taylor, the editor of *Punch*. He saw *Our American Cousin*, the play Abraham Lincoln had been watching when he had been assassinated nine years earlier, and Henry Irving playing *Hamlet* – though Conan Doyle was less than complimentary about the performance of the celebrated actor. He also visited the Tower of London, London Zoo, Hengler's Grand Cirque on the site of today's London Palladium and Madame Tussaud's, which was then above the Bazaar in Baker Street and which was complete with a separate section relating to famous crimes dubbed the 'Chamber of Horrors' by *Punch* in 1845.

After matriculating in 1875, Conan Doyle went to a secondary school at Feldkirch in the Austrian Alps to improve his German. There he edited the *Feldkirchian Gazette*, which carried a presumably fictitious account of a cricket match between the college and town and featured his own high-scoring innings. He endured a winter that he found even colder than those he had known in Edinburgh but in the spring he enjoyed walks in the mountains and good Austrian beer, and he developed a taste for German culture.

While Conan Doyle was away, his family took in a lodger, a young doctor named Bryan Waller who had literary connections of his own. By letter Waller urged Arthur to follow in his own footsteps and study medicine in Edinburgh. He even sent textbooks out to Austria. Waller was also a Freemason. Conan Doyle later became a Mason himself, a calling that is mentioned frequently in the Holmes stories.

In June 1876, Conan Doyle travelled home via Lake Constance, Basel, Strasbourg and Paris, where he stayed with his great-uncle Michael, who encouraged him to read Edgar Allan Poe. When Arthur arrived back in Edinburgh, he discovered that his mother was staying on Waller's family estate in Yorkshire. The following April she gave birth to a daughter, christened Bryan Mary Julia Josephine Doyle.

In the autumn of that same year, Arthur enrolled in Edinburgh University's Medical School, where he came into contact with some remarkable characters. One of them was Sir Robert Christison, who had retired the year before but, as professor of medical jurisprudence and medical police, had been a pioneer of forensic medicine. He published *A Treatise on Poisons* in 1829, taking a particular interest in curare, and would demonstrate in lectures how South American Indians fired poison darts from blowpipes. Conan Doyle used this in 'The Adventure of the Sussex Vampire'.

Christison published *Suggestions for the Medico-Legal Examination of Dead Bodies* ten years later. His expertise on the bruising of corpses had helped secure the conviction of William Burke after his accomplice William Hare turned King's evidence, and showed that the two men had murdered their victims to provide corpses for anatomical dissection. Some of Christison's forensic techniques are referred to at the beginning of *A Study in Scarlet* and, like Christison, Holmes also publishes monograms on forensic science.

Christison used his students as guinea pigs in his study of the cocoa leaf and its extract, cocaine, and he climbed the 3,232 feet (985 metres) of Ben Vorlich while chewing cocoa, noting that it not only cured fatigue but actually prevented it. This may have been the origin of Holmes's use of cocaine. Both Christison and his successor Professor Thomas Fraser tested dangerous drugs on themselves, as did Conan Doyle and his characters Holmes and Watson in 'The Adventure of the Devil's Foot'.

Another of Conan Doyle's lecturers was the Surgeon of Police and Medical Officer of Health for Edinburgh, Dr Henry Littlejohn, who introduced modern scientific advances – including photography and fingerprinting – to the Scottish courts.

One of Littlejohn's students and Conan Doyle's mentor, Dr Joseph Bell, perfected the use of acute observation to make rapid diagnoses from minimal evidence. According to Conan Doyle's autobiography *Memories and Adventures*, Bell could deduce from a man's appearance in civilian clothes that he had once been a non-commissioned officer in a Highland regiment stationed in Barbados, a feat Holmes would emulate. Bell also taught his students to pay close attention to the smells and tastes of various substances he would ply them with in his lab.

One day a week, Conan Doyle would forego his midday meal to spend his lunch money on a second-hand book. He favoured eighteenth-century authors such as Joseph Addison and Jonathan Swift. He also devoured the *Essays* of historian Thomas Babington Macaulay, who he praised for his 'short, vivid sentences, the broad sweep of allusion [and] the exact detail' and was influenced by the American Oliver Wendell Holmes, another doctor-turned-writer and known among his mother's literary circle.

Conan Doyle moved to Birmingham to train in a practice in 1879, shortly after his father finally went into a care home for alcoholics. Despite working long hours, he found time to write and sent a story called 'The Haunted Grange at Goresthorpe' to *Blackwood's Edinburgh Magazine*, where it excited no inter-est. But he was paid £3 by another Edinburgh periodical, *Chambers's Journal*, which published 'The Mystery of Sasassa Valley', a story set in South Africa, topical at the time due to the Zulu Wars. He followed this with a piece published in the *British Medical Journal* (*BMJ*) about his experimentation with the drug gelseminum.

In 1880, Conan Doyle took six months off from his medical studies to join a whaling fleet for an expedition into the Arctic. It was a toughening experience. While culling seals, he fell into the freezing water five times in four days. He kept a journal of the trip and penned the short stories 'A Journey to the Pole' and 'A Modern Parable', which have not survived, and he drew on this Arctic experience and the characters he met on board in later stories, including the Holmes tale 'The Adventure of Black Peter'. While he was away, the British were defeated at the Battle of Maiwand in Afghanistan where, he would later report, Dr Watson was injured. Conan Doyle returned to his studies, graduated with honours in June 1881, then headed to Ireland for a holiday. While there he wrote another mystery story, 'The Gully of Bluemansdyke', which was published in *London Society* magazine.

When he returned to Scotland he became interested in photography and began writing for the *British Journal of Photography* (*BJP*) but then went on a trip to West Africa as a ship's surgeon. On board, he enjoyed flirting with the female passengers, one of whom would not let him examine her, fearing the young doctor might take liberties. He filled his time with reading or discussing literature with Henry Highland Garnet, a former slave who was travelling to Liberia to take up his post as US Consul. Despite his friendship with Garnet, he wrote later of his dislike of Africans, though elsewhere he said he found them 'quiet and inoffensive', an ambivalence that surfaces in the Holmes stories.

Back in Scotland he wrote more stories for *London Society* and medical articles for *The Lancet*. He applied for jobs, including a staff position in Buenos Aires, but was determined not to go to sea again; there was more money in writing. Eventually, he joined George Budd, his friend from university, in Budd's prosperous practice in Plymouth but the two fell out over letters from Conan Doyle's mother, who was suspicious of Budd. A girlfriend from Ireland offered Conan Doyle £100 (over £7,000 in today's money) to see him though his difficulties but instead he moved to Portsmouth to set up his own practice. It did not go well and he decided to change course, to make writing his career and he set about studying the market by reading popular novels. His initial attempts were unsuccessful, and rejections began to pile up. Then finally, after rejection from *London Society* and *Temple Bar*, 'The Winning Shot' was accepted by *Bow Bells*. The story, set on Dartmoor, anticipated *The Hound of the Baskervilles*. Along with his writing, he began to indulge his interest in the paranormal, which was newly fashionable and even infected the pages of the *BJP*. It also chimed with his passion for the Gothic, which he had brought with him from the Edinburgh of Robert Louis Stevenson and Walter Scott.

More supernatural stories followed, though he received lower fees for these than for his earlier work. But slowly he began to prosper and hankered for female company. At a dance, he got as 'drunk as an owl' and proposed to half the women, both single and married. In 1872, he wrote 'J. Habakuk Jephson's Statement' ,about the mysterious disappearance that year of the crew of the *Mary Celeste*, mistakenly calling the brigantine the *Marie Céleste*. The name stuck. The story was published by the *Cornhill*, London's most influential literary magazine and home to Thackeray and George Eliot. A critical notice in the *Illustrated London News* compared Conan Doyle to Stevenson, then at the height of his powers.

He continued writing medical articles, including one where he uses the science-fiction device of notionally reducing a man to a height of a thousandth of an inch and introducing him to the bloodstream, where he illustrated the recent advances in bacteriology and vaccination. He also wrote an article for the *Daily Telegraph* in support of the Contagious Diseases Act that allowed the arrest and forcible examination of women for sexually transmitted diseases in ports and army towns. This made him the scourge of feminists. He further fuelled the controversy with articles in the *BMJ* and *The Lancet*. During this period, he wrote *The Narrative of John Smith*, where the eponymous Smith gives voice to Conan Doyle's scientific, spiritualist and religions passions. The novel went unpublished. He claimed later that the manuscript had been lost in the post. However, ideas from this early work would recur in the Holmes stories.

Although he played cricket and bowls, and attended parties and balls, Conan Doyle remained a serious-minded young man. He joined the Portsmouth Literary and Scientific Society and gave a lecture on his Arctic travels, attended by an audience of 250. President of the Society was Major-General Alfred Drayson, a prolific writer, theosophist and committed spiritualist, who encouraged Conan Doyle's interest in esoteric matters. Even so, Conan Doyle still found time to become a founder member of Portsmouth Association Football Club, the amateur forerunner of today's Portsmouth FC, and played for them as goalkeeper and occasionally full-back under the pseudonym AC Smith.

Confined to bed with a bladder infection – which he claimed were a recurrence of an old African fever – he surrounded himself with books, paper and pencils. He found writing easier in the prone position and worried that if he became a full-time writer, he would spend his entire life in bed.

In 1884 his Uncle Dicky died leaving little money, but Conan Doyle benefitted from the posthumous publication of Dicky's youthful journals and an exhibition of his work. He spent the money on a new bookcase and volumes of Samuel Johnson, James Boswell and Alexander Pope.

That year, *Cornhill* hired Conan Doyle and halved its price from a shilling to sixpence in an effort to gain a broader audience. The magazine held an annual dinner which offered him the opportunity to rub shoulders with the established novelist George du Maurier and F. Anstey, author of *Vice Versa*. Conan Doyle wrote not just for *Cornhill*, who rejected two of his stories, but also for *Cassell's Saturday Journal*, *Belgravia* magazine and the *Boy's Own Paper*, which published 'The Fate of the *Evangeline*' in their Christmas 1885 edition. The story quotes Edgar Allan Poe's fictional detective, Auguste Dupin: 'Exclude the impossible . . . and what is left, however improbable, must be the truth.' In fact, Auguste Dupin – who appears in 'The Murders in the Rue Morgue' (1841), 'The Mystery of Marie Rogêt' (1842), and 'The Purloined Letter' (1844) – never said that. So it was perhaps, permissible for Sherlock Holmes to make the sentiment his own in *The Sign of the Four* (1890), 'The Adventure of the Beryl Coronet' (1892), 'The Adventure of the

Bruce-Partington Plan' (1912) and 'The Adventure of the Blanched Soldier' (1926).

Conan Doyle then began work on a semi-autobiographical novel, *The Firm of Girdlestone*, about the life and loves of an Edinburgh medical student. But it did not find a publisher until 1890 when Conan Doyle's literary fame was on the ascendant.

In March 1885 he took in twenty-five-year-old Jack Hawkins as a resident patient, who he looked after with the help of his housekeeper, Mrs Smith. Hawkins was suffering from cerebral meningitis – a type of 'brain fever' incurable at the time – and Hawkins died soon after. In a second semi-autobiographical novel, *The Stark Munro Letters* published in 1895, Conan Doyle records a scene where a detective comes round to enquire about the death of young resident patient taken in by Dr Munro. And in 1893, he published the Holmes story 'The Resident Patient'.

Conan Doyle married Hawkins's sister, Louise, soon after her brother's death. In place of a honeymoon, Conan Doyle went off on a tour of Ireland with the Stonyhurst Wanderers, the school's old boys' cricket team. It is not clear whether Louise, who was technically in mourning over the death of her brother, went with him or if she stayed with Conan Doyle's mother, who was now living permanently in a cottage on the Waller family estate. Afterwards Louise and her mother moved into Conan Doyle's house in Southsea, leaving no room for Conan Doyle's twelve-year-old brother, who had been living with him up until that point. He was then despatched as a boarder to school in Richmond, Yorkshire, the alma mater of Bryan Waller.

Marriage did not help his writing career. The only thing he produced in 1885 was the short story 'The Mystery of Uncle Jeremy's Household', which features a detective, a medical student named Hugh Lawrence, who can be seen as a prototype Sherlock Holmes, and an 'Oriental' coming to Britain to carry out a ritualistic murder – a theme echoed in a number of Holmes's stories. Initially, it was rejected by *Blackwood's*, then published by the *Boy's Own Paper* in 1887. Six more of his stories were then published in a three-volume anthology called

Dreamland and Ghostland: An Original Collection of Tales and Warnings from the Borderland of Substance and Shadow. Nevertheless, Conan Doyle toyed with the idea of writing 'The Autobiography of a Failure'.

Instead, in the spring of 1886, he sat down to write *A Study in Scarlet,* the first of the Sherlock Holmes novels, which he completed in just over a month.

Chapter 2

The Birth and Death of Sherlock Holmes

The detective story has a long history. One can argue that it begins in the Book of Daniel in the Old Testament, where Daniel halts Susanna's execution for adultery, demanding an investigation to establish the evidence against her. He then cross-examines the two elders, who say they saw her lying with a young stranger. But their testimony is conflicting, Susanna is spared and the elders are put to death for perjury. The detective story could also be said to begin with Voltaire's *Zadig* (1747), whose eponymous hero shows off his Enlightenment reasoning by describing the king's horse and queen's dog from the clues they'd left behind.

The British had always enjoyed reading about crime. The five-volume *Newgate Calendar* of 1774, which detailed the life and death of notorious criminals. It sat alongside the Bible and John Bunyan's *The Pilgrim's Progress* in many homes. Conan Doyle certainly read *Calendar*, it competed with the Gothic novel, with its thrilling tales of the macabre, another area Conan Doyle strayed into. But it was Thomas de Quincey who gave the genre of crime fiction its literary cache with 'On Murder Considered as One of the Fine Arts', published in *Blackwood's Magazine* in 1827. That, and its follow-ups 'A Second Paper on Murder Considered as One of the Fine Arts' in 1839 and 'Postscript' in 1854, were later lauded by such critics as G.K. Chesterton, Wyndham Lewis and George Orwell, who wrote *The Decline of English Murder* in 1946.

Conan Doyle acknowledged the popularity of 'sensational stories' in 'The Fate of the *Evangeline*'. He was, of course, familiar with Poe and the French pioneer of detective fiction Émile Gaboriau, whose protagonist, thief-turned-policeman Monsieur Lecoq, was based on the real-life Eugène Vodocq of the Paris Sûreté. In Gaboriau's books we get to follow Lecoq's deductive process and he gets a mention in *A Study in Scarlet* along with Gaboriau, Poe and Poe's detective Dupin. In his autobiography, Conan Doyle says that after *The Firm of Girdlestone*, 'I felt now that I was capable of something fresher and crisper and more workmanlike. Gaboriau had rather attracted me by the neat dovetailing of his plots, and Poe's masterful detective, Monsieur Dupin, had from boyhood been one of my heroes.'

Alexander Dumas and Honoré de Balzac had also strayed into crime fiction, along with Charles Dickens, who in *Bleak House* introduced the unflappable Inspector Bucket, thought to be based on Inspector Charles Frederick Fields of Scotland Yard's recently formed Detective Department. Then in *The Moonstone* – which, like several Holmes's stories, introduces a little oriental colour – Wilkie Collins gave us Sergeant Cuff.

'But could I bring an addition of my own?' asked Conan Doyle. 'I thought of my old teacher Joe Bell, of his eagle face, of his curious ways, of his eerie trick of spotting details. If he were a detective he would surely reduce this fascinating but unorganized business to something nearer to an exact science.'

This was topical: science – in the form of photography, fingerprints, toxicology and the forensic autopsy – was only just beginning to enhance the art of investigation.

'I would try if I could get this effect,' said Conan Doyle. 'It was surely possible in real life, so why should I not make it plausible in fiction?'

It was not enough for Conan Doyle to say that his detective was clever; he wanted to give the reader examples of his cleverness, the sort of examples that Dr Bell gave his students every day. First, he had to come up with a name. He filled a leaf of a notebook with possibilities, deciding against those that gave some hint of his character, so out went Mr Sharps and Mr Ferrets. Then he came up with Sherringford Holmes, which then became Sherlock Holmes.

Holmes, Conan Doyle said, was a simple name and Conan Doyle had been brought up in a household all too familiar with Oliver Wendell Holmes. As for Sherlock, Conan Doyle claimed that the forename came from the MCC bowler Frank Shacklock; however, at school he had a friend called Patrick Sherlock.

Conan Doyle says that it was clear that Sherlock Holmes 'could not tell his own exploits, so he must have a commonplace comrade as a foil – an uneducated man of action who could both join in the exploits and narrate them'. He wanted a drab, quiet name for this unostentatious man – 'Watson would do,' said Conan Doyle. 'And so I [had] my puppets and wrote my *Study in Scarlet*.'

This is not entirely true. Watson was not originally named Watson, but Ormond Sacker. And *A Study in Scarlet* was originally *A Tangled Skein*. It begins with a terrified woman rushing up to a cabbie. The two of them fetch a policeman who turns out to be John Reeves, who had been with the force for seven years, and it was Reeves who was originally the protagonist. A 'consulting detective' called Sherrinford or Sherringford Holmes only appears in a later draft. Reeves shares rooms with Slacker, who had seen action in the Sudan, not in Afghanistan as in the final version. The name Watson seems to have been taken from Dr James Watson, who lived near Conan Doyle in Southsea and had recently returned from China.

When *A Study in Scarlet* was finished, it was a short novel running to just over 43,000 words, or 200 pages. Conan Doyle sent it to *Cornhill* and, though the editor James Payn claimed to be enthusiastic, he rejected it, as did the publishers Arrowsmith's and Frederick Warne. At Ward Lock, a publisher of cheap, sensationalist fiction, the editor-in-chief's wife Jeannie Gwynne Bettany plucked the manuscript from the slush pile. Conan Doyle accepted mere £25 for the full copyright. That was the only money he ever received for the work.

Conan Doyle then threw himself into politics, supporting the new Liberal Unionists, who opposed Gladstone's proposal to give home rule to Ireland. He wrote parodies of Dickens, Defoe, Scott, Smollett and Swift in 'Cyprian Overbeck Wells (A Literary Mosaic)' which was accepted by *Boy's Own*, but when other freelance work dried up he was reduced to translating a German piece on gas pipes for *Gas and Water Review*. Meanwhile, he was becoming increasingly interested in spiritualism, which was popular even among men of science at the time. He also took an interest in hypnotism.

Disappointed by the fate of *A Study in Scarlet*, Conan Doyle began to write *Micah Clarke*, a historical novel set during the 1685 Monmouth Rebellion. The tale, of a Puritan protagonist supporting a Protestant rebellion, might seen an odd choice for a Catholic but Conan Doyle saw the Monmouth Rebellion as a fight for intellectual liberty. Before he had finished it, *A Study in Scarlet* came out in *Beeton's Christmas Annual*. It was an instant success, and praised by *The Times*. The *Annual* sold out within two weeks and Ward Lock were soon planning a new edition, this time with illustrations. Some were commissioned from Conan Doyle's father, Charles, still confined to an asylum. First though he had to trace his father's work before blocks had been made. Then there was a fight for money.

He did finish *Micah Clarke*, which ran to 670 closely researched pages and was repeatedly rejected. Conan Doyle then turned down a commission for a boy's adventure story so that he could toy with ideas that would be used in *The Sign of the Four* and *The Hound of the Baskervilles*. He also planned to give up on his failed practice in Southsea and become an ophthalmic surgeon in London so he would have more time to write. But such a move depended on the success of *Micah Clarke*.

He continued to write, *The Mystery of Cloomber*, reflected his interest in the occult was and the play *Angels of Darkness*, a dramatization of the second section of *A Study in Scarlet*, set in Utah, where Sherlock Holmes does not appear and Dr Watson only turns up in a cameo at the very end. He also wrote the short stories 'The Bravoes of Market Drayton' and contributed the scientific article 'The Geographical Distribution of British Intellect' to the conservative magazine *The Nineteenth Century*. The article concluded, naturally, that the best brains came from Scotland, notably Edinburgh.

Micah Clarke was finally accepted by Longman's on the recommendation of the reader who had discovered Rider Haggard. However, they thought it too long and that it had to be cut.

Louise fell pregnant, while Conan Doyle busied himself becoming the vice-president of the Hampshire Psychical Society and taking a trip to Paris, where he visited the Louvre, used as a backdrop for 'The Ring of Thoth', a short story published by *Cornhill* and credited as the source for Boris Karloff's film *The Mummy*. He then contributed an article on Robert Louis Stevenson's writing to *National Review*. He frequently borrowed from Stevenson but considered *Micah Clarke* superior to anything Stevenson had written – it was George Meredith Conan Doyle looked up to. His ambition was to create great literature but he saw no harm in popularity; it was a democratic age and he reasoned that the people were the final arbiter, not the critics. Yet while he was becoming a well-known literary figure in London, a Portsmouth paper took a sideswipe at him: Conan Doyle had by then become a well known psychic, and the paper asked why he didn't use his powers to track down Jack the Ripper, who was then on the rampage?

On 28 January 1889, Conan Doyle delivered his first daughter, Mary Louise. A few hours later, he was back at his desk cutting the manuscript of *Micah Clarke*, which received generally favourable reviews and sold out its first print run of 1,000 within a month; another 2,000 were sold later in the year. That August he began *The White Company*, another historical adventure, this time set during the Hundred Years' War.

Soon after, he was invited to dinner by the managing editor of Philadelphia's *Lippincott's Monthly Magazine*, Joseph Marshall Stoddart, who was in London to sign up British authors. At the dinner, Conan Doyle met fellow Irishman Oscar Wilde and the two got on well. Stoddart commissioned *The Picture of Dorian Gray* from Wilde and signed Conan Doyle to £100 contract for a work of not less than 40,000 words. Within days, Conan Doyle said he would give Sherlock Holmes, from *A Study in Scarlet*, another tricky problem to unravel. The new work was originally called 'The Sign of Sixteen Oyster Shells', then 'The Sign of Six' or 'The Problem of the Sholtos' and finally *The Sign of the Four*, which was published in *Lippincott's* in February 1890. There are indications that Conan Doyle meant this to be the last of Holmes: at the end of the story, Watson is preparing to marry and leave 221B Baker Street – without his amanuensis there could be no more Holmes.

Capitalizing on his success, Conan Doyle managed to sell the serialization rights to *The Firm of Girdlestone* for £240 and then he sold the volume rights in the UK and US. With the proceeds, he made investments in property and shares that would eventually make him a wealthy man.

An anthology of his short stories appeared, competing with reprints of the stories he had sold outright early in his career. With the acclaim that greeted *The Sign of the Four*, *The Firm of Girdlestone* and *The Captain of the Polestar and Other Stories*, and sales of *Micah Clarke* topping 10,000, Conan Doyle went back to work on *The White Company*, and found time to lecture on 'Witches and Witchcraft'.

Novelist and founder of the Society of Authors, Walter Besant recommended Conan Doyle to literary agent A.P. Watt, who had recently taken on Rudyard Kipling. Kipling credited Watt with doubling his income. Watt placed *The White Company* with *Cornhill*, getting £200 for the serialization rights, plus another £250 for the volume rights from the magazine's sister company. There followed the short story 'A Straggler of '15', an old man's recollection of the Battle of Waterloo that Watt placed with *Black and White* magazine. Conan Doyle was now so flush that he splashed out on second-hand Remington typewriter and devised a schedule for his sisters to type up his stories.

All the while he was still practising medicine and travelled to Berlin to learn more about a new cure for tuberculosis. He was to write about this for the *BMJ* and W.T. Stead, the crusading editor of the *Pall Mall Gazette* and now the *Review of Reviews*, had promised to take an article. Finally, Conan Doyle decided it was time to give up his medical practice and was given a going away party by fellow Southsea doctor James Watson. Leaving their baby daughter with her grandmother on the Isle of Wight, Conan Doyle and his wife headed for Vienna, where he would study ophthalmology and write the short novel *The Doings of Raffles Haw*, about a man who cannot find happiness even though he has discovered how to make gold. This had been commissioned by Alfred Harmsworth for his new penny paper, *Answers*.

He also wrote the first draft of *The Refugees*, commissioned for £800 by the American magazine *Harper's*, a novel set on both sides of the Atlantic during the reign of Louis XIV. His short story 'The Voice of Science', which pokes fun at fellow members of the Southsea Literary Society, was placed by Watt with *Strand Magazine*.

When he returned to London he set up home in Montague Place in Bloomsbury, near the British Museum's Reading Room, where he continued his research for *The Refugees*. Adjoining Montague Street is Sherlock Holmes's initial address before he moved to Baker Street, and Conan Doyle's ophthalmology surgery was fifteen-minutes walk away in Upper Wimpole Street, near Queen Anne Street, where Dr Watson would later live.

Less than a week after returning to England, Conan Doyle sent 'A Scandal in Bohemia' to Watt. It would be the first of a series of six individual short stories featuring Holmes and Watson, each to be published in a single issue of a magazine. He explained that they were no longer living in a leisurely age and readers could not be expected to wait while longer stories unfolded over a number of issues. What they wanted was instant gratification featuring characters they were already familiar with. Watt took the story to *Strand Magazine*, one of the few publications that would take a story of over 8,500 words and, at a rate of £4 per 1,000 words, it was a good deal better than his usual flat fee of three guineas.

Less than two weeks later, Conan Doyle delivered 'A Case of Identity'. Nine days after that, 'The Red-Headed League' hit Watt's desk. By then, Watt has sold the US rights for £50 to Sam McClure, the owner of a New York-based newspaper syndicate. McClure also took the US rights to *The Doings of Raffles Haw*, but publication had to be held back on both sides of the Atlantic until that July, when the Chace Act came into force to protect the copyright of British authors in the US.

'The Boscombe Valley Mystery' reached Watt before the end of April. Further work was halted by a bout of influenza, but Conan Doyle decided once and for all to give up medicine and closed his Upper Wimpole Street surgery. Flu over, he sent in 'The Adventure of the Five Orange Pips'. Then the family moved from Montague Place to a large house in the suburb of Upper Norwood.

In addition to the Sherlock Holmes series, he wrote the 40,000 word novella *Beyond the City* in time for the Christmas issue of *Good Words*. The novella, a satire on suburban living and the 'new woman' hankering for sexual equality, would have been longer but the religious magazine could not afford the wordage.

When 'A Scandal in Bohemia' appeared it was accompanied by line drawings by Sidney Paget, whose image of Holmes is the one that endures, despite Conan Doyle's complaint that Holmes looks too handsome. It was Paget who first put Holmes in a deerstalker and Inverness cape, which do not appear in the stories; instead Holmes wears a 'long grey travelling-cloak and close-fitting cloth cap' in 'The Boscombe Valley Mystery' and an 'ear-flapped travelling-cap' in 'The Adventure of the Silver Blaze'.

With the first Sherlock Holmes story, *Strand Magazine* sold 300,000 copies and within a week Conan Doyle had bought 250 shares in the magazine's holding company. Soon after, on

10 August 1891, he delivered 'The Adventure of the Man with the Twisted Lip', the last of the series of six. He then closed his study door and went on a cricketing tour of Holland with his local Norwood team.

When he returned, he refused to write a preface for a new edition of *A Study in Scarlet*, or even let Ward Lock use the name Sherlock Holmes in the subtitle; after all, he was not making any money out of it. By then *Strand Magazine* were begging him for more Sherlock Holmes stories, but he held out for a fee of £50 – he had been averaging £35 up till then. The *Strand* paid up and Conan Doyle got to work on another six stories in rapid succession: 'The Adventure of the Blue Carbuncle'; 'The Adventure of the Speckled Band'; 'The Adventure of the Nobel Bachelor'; 'The Adventure of the Engineer's Thumb'; and 'The Adventure of the Beryl Coronet' were finished by 11 November. However, by then, it seems that Conan Doyle was planning to kill off the series so that he could get on with 'better things'. He was eager to get back to *The Refugees*, which he had left off earlier in the year. It was his historical novels that were important, he thought, not the endless adventures of this detective. When *The White Company* was published to disappointing reviews he pulled strings. A dinner was arranged with the editor of *The Times* who then said that it was the best book of its kind since *Ivanhoe*. By end of 1891, Conan Doyle had earned £1,616 largely by his pen – five times what he had earned as a doctor in Southsea. But any idea that he would kill off Sherlock Holmes was quashed by Conan Doyle's mother, who came up with the idea for 'The Adventure of the Copper Beeches'. When he finished it, he wrote to his mother: 'So now a long farewell to Sherlock. He still lives, however, thanks to your entreaties.' Meanwhile he went back to *The Refugees* and took a commission to write *The Great Shadow*, a book about the Napoleonic Wars, for *Arrowsmith's Christmas Annual*.

He also participated with other popular authors in the writing of a serialized novel called *The Fate of Fenella* for *Gentlewoman* magazine. The episode he penned concerned jealousy in marriage, a subject he would return to, notably in 'The Adventure of the Cardboard Box' which, after publication in the *Strand Magazine*, he had removed from the collection *The Memoirs of Sherlock Holmes* in 1894. It did not appear between hard covers until *His Last Bow* in 1917. Meanwhile he began to spend time with Jeannie Bettany, who had rescued *A Study in Scarlet* from the slush pile and had been recently widowed. At the time, he wrote a poem about a man torn between an old familiar love and a new entrancing one.

Conan Doyle spent time in the theatre, watching the new plays of Emile Zola and Henrik Ibsen, whose *Thérèse Raquin* and *Ghosts* dealt with adultery and syphilis. He joined the Reform Club and a bohemian group who called themselves the Idlers. He contributed to their magazine, *The Idler* – a bitter rival of *Strand Magazine* – and made friends with its editor Jerome K. Jerome and fellow cricket-lover J.M. Barrie.

Conan Doyle turned his short story 'The Straggler of '15' into a play, initially as a curtain-raiser for Barrie's *Walker, London*. It was read by Bram Stoker, the business manager of Henry Irving, who paid him £100 for it. Stoker later found fame as the author of *Dracula*.

The Refugees was now finished. *The Doings of Raffles Haw* had been published and, messing with the likes of George Meredith and Arthur Quiller-Couch, Conan Doyle thought his Sherlock Holmes days were behind him. But the editor of the *Strand*, Herbert Greenhough Smith, pestered him for more. Conan Doyle demanded £1,000 for twelve new stories, thinking the price would put Smith off; instead, he accepted.

Fortunately, Conan Doyle had a ready source of new plot lines – the sackfulls of mail that now arrived both for the author and the great detective. One letter came from Dr Joseph Bell, who Conan Doyle openly acknowledged as the model for Holmes. Bell suggested a plot involving a 'bacteriological criminal'. Conan Doyle replied that he wanted to keep Holmes out of the laboratory for fear science would alienate the reader. However, he did use some of Bell's ideas and Bell's correspondence concerning Holmesian methodology was published in the *Strand*.

Notebooks from the time show how hard Conan Doyle worked on his stories. He would jot down ideas and phrases, then tick them off as he used them, either in the finished story or in other notes where he had worked them out in more detail before transferring them to the final script. The notebooks also contain metaphysical musings, speculation on the future of the Empire and ideas for new plays.

In the early summer of 1892, Conan Doyle wrote 'Silver Blaze', 'The Adventure of the Cardboard Box' and 'The Yellow Face'; then he took off on a trip to Norway with a party that included Jerome K. Jerome. Conan Doyle learnt a little Norwegian and insisted on visiting the hospital in Bergen where the leprosy bacillus had been isolated twenty years before. He was back in England in time to captain the Idlers' eleven, which included E.W. Hornung, creator of gentleman-thief Raffles, in a cricket match against the Norwood team.

That October, the collection *The Adventures of Sherlock Holmes* was published. It was dedicated 'To my old teacher Joseph Bell MD'. A month later, Louise gave birth to their second child, a son named Arthur Alleyne Kingsley – Arthur after his father, Alleyne for the hero of *The White Company* and Kingsley after family friend Kingsley Milbourne and his uncle Charles Kingsley, author of *The Water-Babies*.

Conan Doyle was by now only thirty-three and longed to branch into the theatre, but as the head of a growing family he needed to continue on the Holmesian treadmill. So, after two Holmes novels and fifteen short stories, Conan Doyle decided to do some research. Until then, accuracy had not bothered him much; his Holmes stories were fantasy, unlike his historical works where precision was paramount. He managed to get an entrée into the Black Museum, the crime archive in the basement of Scotland Yard's new headquarters on Victoria Embankment. He went with Jerome K. Jerome and Willie Hornung, who was now engaged to Conan Doyle's sister. They were shown a letter that had allegedly come from Jack the Ripper and Conan Doyle wondered why Scotland Yard had not taken more trouble to investigate the handwriting. This seems to have inspired one of his next tales, 'The Adventure of the Reigate Squire' which followed correspondence with Alexander Cargill, a handwriting expert in Edinburgh.

The December issue of *Strand Magazine* carried 'Silver Blaze' where, for the first time, Holmes leaves London and heads for the wilds of Dartmoor, which was familiar to Conan Doyle from his time in Plymouth. Over then next four months, he polished off the remaining Holmes stories and wrote a series of medical tales concerning blood, childbirth and syphilis for *The Idler*. The editor, Jerome K. Jerome, thought they might emulate the success of Holmes, though they were so explicit that only three out of the eight Conan Doyle produced could be used. Conan Doyle was then struck down with a cold and took the opportunity to read Jane Austen for the first time.

During 1892, Conan Doyle earned £2,729; he was fast becoming rich man. But he worked hard. In the year, he turned out some 214,000 words. Notably, only 7,000 of them concerned Sherlock Holmes, but these were the most lucrative.

The following year Conan Doyle returned to the theatre, collaborating with J.M. Barrie on the libretto of the comic opera *Jane Annie, or, The Good Conduct Prize* for Richard D'Oyly Carte, the impresario behind Gilbert and Sullivan. George Bernard Shaw called *Jane Annie* 'the most unblushing piece of tomfoolery that two respectable citizens could conceivably indulge in public'; nevertheless, it ran for six weeks at the Savoy Theatre. As a result Conan Doyle was invited to write a one-act Holmes play but he refused. Instead he dramatized his short story 'A Question of Diplomacy', which appeared as *Foreign Policy*.

Then Conan Doyle decided to make a career on the lecture circuit, beginning with a talk on George Meredith at the Edinburgh Philosophical Institute, where his mother had been a leading light, which earned him eighteen guineas.

Amongst Conan Doyle's circle of literary acquaintances was

Robert Louis Stevenson, who wrote in correspondence that he enjoyed the Sherlock Holmes stories and addressed him as a fellow 'spookist' as they were both members of the Society for Psychical Research. Conan Doyle replied that he never hoped to write another one and sent him a copy of *The White Company*.

That August Conan Doyle travelled to Switzerland to give another talk on George Meredith, and there expressed his intention to kill off Holmes once and for all – 'He is becoming such a burden to me.' He even visited the scene of the crime: the Reichenbach Falls. When he got back to Norwood, he despatched Holmes in 'The Final Problem', which was published in *Strand Magazine* in December 1893. It is said that clerks in the City of London donned black armbands and the *Strand* lost 20,000 subscriptions. It was then that he asked that 'The Adventure of the Cardboard Box' be left out of the second collection of Holmes stories, *The Memoirs of Sherlock Holmes*, to make room for 'The Final Problem'.

An entry in Conan Doyle's diary remarks curtly: 'Killed Holmes.'

Chapter 3

Holmes Resurrected

Two months before Sherlock Holmes disappeared over the Reichenbach Falls, Charles Doyle, Arthur's father, died in an asylum in Dumfries. Conan Doyle did not attend the funeral, preferring to remain in Norwood to give a talk on 'Recent Evidences as to Man's Survival of Death'. Also, his wife was ill, showing the early symptoms of tuberculosis. She was attended by the Queen's physician, Sir Douglas Powell. The prognosis was not good and she was sent to Switzerland to recuperate. With no further money coming in from Sherlock Holmes – and a subsequent falling out with A.P. Watt – Conan Doyle undertook a nationwide lecture tour to cover the expense. Nevertheless he forked out £40 to help Liberal MP Henry Labouchère defend a libel suit. Labouchère's amendment to the Criminal Law Amendment Act of 1885 led to the downfall of Oscar Wilde.

He went to Davos to visit his wife and he found that she had put on weight. He used his time there to complete *The Threshold*, an autobiographical novel about the travails of a young doctor for which Jerome K. Jerome had offered £1,000 for the serial rights. It was, in fact, a reworking of *The Narrative of John Smith*, which he had claimed had been lost in the post and was eventually published as *The Stark Munro Letters*. Meanwhile, his earlier medical tales, now toned down, had been sold as a collection for publication in the UK and the US under the title *Round the Red Lamp*.

Straightaway, he began another novel, *The Parasite*, the tale of a female hypnotist who enslaves a physiology professor. After completing 100,000 words, he tried to learn to ski, a pastime that had just arrived in Switzerland from Norway. He was unsuccessful in his attempts but is credited with helping popularize the sport among the British.

Back in England, he made his peace with A.P. Watt and, on behalf of the Society of Psychical Research, he answered the summons of a veteran of the Second Afghan War who complained about mysterious noises in his house in Charmouth in Dorset. He spent the rest of the summer playing cricket and writing a series of articles about his favourite authors for *Great Thoughts* magazine. These were collected as *Through the Magic Door* and provided material for his forthcoming lecture tour of the US.

'The Straggler of '15' eventually graced the stage as *Waterloo*. Henry Irving took eight curtain calls and Bram Stoker declared it 'an enormous success'. Irving's leading lady and mistress Ellen Terry visited Conan Doyle to congratulate the author personally and begged for a copy of his poem 'The Storming Party', which tells story of two soldiers who are going into battle when one discovers that the other is in love with his wife. Meanwhile Conan Doyle advanced Hornung £50 to collaborate on a play about prizefighting in the Regency era, which he hoped would co-star Terry, but they abandoned it after one act. Conan Doyle continued to give financial support to Hornung, who had married his sister Connie in 1893.

Conan Doyle had a passion for America and believed in the reunion of the English-speaking peoples – a sentiment voiced by Holmes. In September 1894, he set sail for his first visit to the United States. He was met by a huddle of pressmen when his ship docked in the Hudson River. *The New York Times*, particularly, was impressed by his energy and athleticism and he made forty appearances up and down the East Coast and across the Midwest. He intended to speak on Meredith and other contemporary writers. But all anybody wanted to hear about was Sherlock Holmes.

Conan Doyle was captivated by everything he saw in the US, except copies of his books that had been pirated and cheaply produced. When faced with anti-British audiences, he good-naturedly preached the kinship of their two nations, quelling any hostility. In Cambridge, Massachusetts, he visited the grave of Oliver Wendell Holmes, who had died only a month before. Back in New York, he was visited by Sam McClure, whose eponymous magazine was on the brink of bankruptcy and owed $5,000 to British authors. Conan Doyle wrote a cheque for $5,000. In return, he took a stake in the magazine, whose circulation soared to 250,000 within a year.

He spent Thanksgiving with Rudyard Kipling, who was then living with his American wife in Vermont and when he returned home he was even more enthusiastic about the US. His only gripe was how little he had been paid – just £500 – which made him decide to give up lecturing and return to writing short stories.

'A Foreign Office Romance' featured a suave French diplomat. Then came 'The Recollections of Captain Wilkie' where a doctor, again based on Joseph Bell, comes up against a supposedly reformed thief. He indulged his interest in the Napoleonic wars with a series of stories concerning Brigadier Gerard that found a lucrative outlet in the US and were also published in the *Strand*. He failed, though, to find a protagonist with the standing of Holmes

He returned to Davos, and set to work on *Rodney Stone*, a novel that drew on his earlier dramatic collaboration on Regency prizefighting – Conan Doyle was a boxing fan – and borrowed the name of one of his characters, Bunbury, from *The Importance of Being Earnest*, when Oscar Wilde was in the midst of his downfall. *Rodney Stone* was a commercial success, and brought him £7,000.

He headed for Cairo in November 1895, when General Kitchener was preparing to avenge General Gordon, who had been killed in Khartoum ten years earlier. Conan Doyle considered writing a popular history of the British involvement in

Egypt since 1882, claiming that the British had done more for the country in thirteen years than the pharaohs ever had. He travelled down the Nile to the borders of Sudan where he met the forward parties building the railroad that would support Kitchener's invading force. He used his experience, not to write a popular history, but as a basis for his novel *The Tragedy of the Korosko*, where a party of European tourists are kidnapped by Dervishes. The following year Conan Doyle set out with Kitchener's punitive expedition as a war correspondent for the *Westminster Gazette* but after a month was persuaded to turn back, having seen no action. This gave him material for the story 'The Three Correspondents'.

A competent horseman, Conan Doyle bought himself a steed he called 'Brigadier' after his fictional Napoleonic hero. Then he became embroiled in Anglo-Irish politics, proposing a loyalist toast at a dinner of the Irish Literary Society, despite the presence of W.B. Yeats and Parnell's biographer Barry O'Brien, who said that such a toast would only go ahead over his dead body.

While waiting to move into his new home, Undershaw in Hindhead, Surrey, near the natural amphitheatre of the Devil's Punchbowl, Conan Doyle considered adapting Sherlock Holmes for the stage. He also began more stories in his series about the pirate Captain Sharkey, published as *The Dealings of Captain and Other Tales of Pirates* in New York in 1905. At the time, he was having difficulties with his novel *Uncle Bernac*, set again in the Napoleonic Wars.

In March 1897, the thirty-seven-year-old Conan Doyle fell passionately in love with Jean Leckie, who was just twenty-three. She became a regular visitor at Undershaw, despite the presence of Conan Doyle's wife, accompanying him on walks and rides. That autumn he wrote 'The Confession', a short story about illicit love.

Superficially, life at Undershaw continued in high Victorian style, with servants, meals inspired by Mrs Beeton and the attendance of Sidney Paget, who had been commissioned to paint Conan Doyle's portrait. This shows him as stern patriarch with a bushy moustache twisted at the ends and with a notebook and pencil in hand.

The household expenses and his munificence to the Society for Physical Research were putting a strain on his finances, and he sat down to write a series of mystery and suspense tales for *Strand Magazine* that were collected as *Round the Fire Stories*. They were not detective stories, he insisted, and the editor should not mention Holmes in connection with them. Instead, they reflected his continued interest in the paranormal and dealt with contemporary themes such as the certification of the mentally incompetent, alcoholism, incarceration, homosexuality, cross-dressing, gambling, debauchery and murder.

After another play he had co-written was rejected, he went to Rome, where he met the novelists George Gissing and H.G. Wells, who were both, coincidentally, escaping tangled love affairs at home. It is thought that Conan Doyle knew Wells, who had now just published *The War of the Worlds* from the time he had been an assistant in a grocery store in Southsea. Conan Doyle seems to have been influenced by Wells when he wrote *A Duet*, a novel about modern marriage and what was then called 'the woman question', while Wells began writing stories about the paranormal for the *Strand*. By then Conan Doyle was so famous that, at a fancy dress party, a friend turned up as Conan Doyle himself.

A Duet did not do well and Conan Doyle reimbursed the publisher by buying up half the copies of his sister's novel, which had flopped. He considered returning to writing novels set during the medieval period, but a young American actor named William Gillette persuaded him that money was to be made from putting Holmes on the stage in the US.

Unfortunately, the theatre in San Francisco where it was going to debut burnt down and a copyright performance was staged at the Duke of York's theatre in London on 12 June 1899. Conan Doyle thoroughly approved of Gillette's addition of the line 'Oh, this is elementary, my dear Watson' which, pared down, became Holmes's cinematic catchphrase. It never appeared in any of the books, though Holmes remarks uses the word 'elementary' as a slight.

Conan Doyle returned to the prizefighting ring for 'The Croxley Master' and to Gerard for 'The Crime of the Brigadier', both published in *Strand Magazine*. He continued to play cricket and helped his neighbour, the writer Grant Allen, who was dying of cancer, complete the final two instalments of *Hilda Wade*, the eponymous tale of a female Sherlock Holmes that was being published by *Strand*. Then he went back on the lecture circuit after a trip to South Africa was cancelled due to the outbreak of the Boer war

On 6 November 1899, Gillette's *Sherlock Holmes* opened to a rapturous reception at the Garrick Theater on Broadway. Now convinced of the continued financial security of his family, Conan Doyle determined to do his bit in South Africa. He was talked out of volunteering for active service, but was persuaded that, as a doctor, he would be much more use in a field hospital. Nevertheless, he took time to see the action and came under fire. While he was away, *The Green Flag and Other Stories* was published.

Back home, he defended British policy, if not always British practice, in *The Great Boer War*, and stood in support of the war as a Liberal Unionist in the 1900 general election in Edinburgh Central. He lost – though the coalition of Conservatives and Liberal Unionists won nationwide – possibly due to anti-Catholic sentiment in the city. But his views brought him to the attention of the rising star Winston Churchill, who sought out his support and invited him to join his club, the Athenaeum. Conan Doyle responded patriotically and set up an armed militia. But he took time off to play cricket for the Marylebone Cricket Club (MCC), even taking the wicket of the aging W.G. Grace on his first outing, though Grace reciprocated later in the summer.

Bertram Fletcher Robinson, a journalist he had met on the way back from South Africa, drew Conan Doyle's attention to the legend of a giant hound that terrorized the inhabitants of Dartmoor, near Robinson's family seat in Devon. He immediately wrote to *Strand Magazine* proposing a serial of not less than 40,000 words based on the tale that would become *The Hound of the Baskervilles*. At the time, the *Strand* was publishing his three-part crime series 'Strange Studies from Life', based on real-life cases and illustrated by Sidney Paget.

As *The Hound of the Baskervilles* began to take shape, Conan Doyle realized that it needed a strong central character and began toying with the idea of resurrecting Sherlock Holmes, though the literary world was now full of cheap imitations of the great detective. Greenhough Smith at the *Strand* was keen, planning to publish when Gillette's *Sherlock Holmes* opened in London, but he was not keen to credit Robinson as co-author. However, Conan Doyle negotiated him up to an unprecedented £100 per 1,000 words, and handed a flat fee of £500 for the serialization on to Robinson. He then began to prepare the ground for a Holmes revival by telling the *Strand*'s downmarket sister publication *Tit-Bits* that there was 'no limit to the number of papers he [had] left behind or the reminiscences in the brain of his biographer'; the story of *The Hound of the Baskervilles* clearly predates Holmes's death at the Reichenbach Falls. On 25 May 1901, *Tit-Bits* announced that Sherlock Holmes was about to make a comeback. Meanwhile, Conan Doyle and Robinson were tramping Dartmoor, studying its prehistoric dwellings and visiting Fox Tor Mire, which becomes Grimpen Mire in the book. They were visited by the governor of Dartmoor prison and three members of his staff, who sent a note saying that they were coming to 'call on Sherlock Holmes'. At the Robinson family home they met the coachman, Henry Baskerville, who later received a copy of the book inscribed with an apology for the use of his name. There may have been another origin for the name though: Conan Doyle owned a property in Hereford where there was a neighbour called Baskerville and where there is also a tale involving a large hound – as there is elsewhere in Britain.

Other names in the book are also borrowed from family friends, and the Northumberland Hotel in seems to have been based on an amalgam of the hotels near Trafalgar Square – the Grand, Morley's or the Golden Cross – where Conan Doyle would stay when he came to London.

Now a pillar of the establishment, Conan Doyle sat next to Edward VII at a dinner in March 1901, shortly after the death of Queen Victoria. That August, *The Hound of the Baskervilles* began its serialization in *Strand Magazine*, with Gillette's *Sherlock Holmes* opening on 9 September. The series ran until the following April when 25,000 copies of the book went on sale. Both the play and the book were a great success.

In January, to coincide with the opening of parliament, Conan Doyle published 250,000 copies of the 60,000 word sixpenny pamphlet *The War in South Africa: Its Cause and Conduct*, which by the end of March had gone through sixteen editions, including one in Welsh. A knighthood was proffered, but Conan Doyle knew that other writers, such as Rudyard Kipling, had turned down honours as unbefitting to their trade but his mother pressured him to accept.

He published another tale of the paranormal, 'The Leather Funnel', which also involved crime and torture. He then went on holiday to Italy, where he visited the writer Norman Douglas, a hedonist and paedophile in the Oscar-Wilde mould (his last words were said to have been 'Get these fucking nuns away from me'), and the former Prime Minister Lord Rosebery (also rumoured to have been homosexual) who was a fan of *The Hound of the Baskervilles*. On his Scottish estate there was also a legend about a baying hound that Conan Doyle may have heard during his childhood in Edinburgh.

When Edward VII suffered appendicitis, delaying his coronation, he took to his bed and read *The Hound of the Baskervilles*. Though he seems not to have enjoyed it, he knighted the author that October and got Sir Henry Irving to perform *Waterloo* at Sandringham for the visiting Kaiser Wilhelm.

Conan Doyle returned to his Brigadier Gerard stories, hoping to get him on the stage, too. He also threw himself into good works – though, confusingly, supported both the Zionists and the British Brothers' League, an anti-Semitic organization that opposed immigration. He also opposed King Leopold's brutal rule in the Congo and supported protectionism to the extent that he bought a run-down Wolseley rather than a better French car he had been offered.

He refused a retainer from *Strand*, who were hoping for more Holmes stories and said that 'Sherlock . . . won't come up as far as I can see.' But then *Collier's Weekly*, who had just published the Raffles stories in the US, offered $25,000 for six new tales of Sherlock, Conan Doyle replied resignedly: 'Very well.' He eventually accepted £6,000 ($29,000 at the 1903 exchange rate) but for US rights only. He would get another £3,000 from *Strand*. It was for this series that he came up with the ingenious tale of Sherlock Holmes escaping death in 'The Adventure of the Empty House'.

The other stories, including 'The Adventure of the Norwood Builder', 'The Dancing Men' and 'The Solitary Cyclist' borrow some of their settings and ideas from events in Conan Doyle's private life: his relationship with young Jean Leckie, now living in South London; his encounter with the seven-year-old son of a hotel landlady; and reading of Poe's '*The Gold Bug*'. When Greenhough Smith complained that the stories lacked originally Conan Doyle said this was inevitable. That's why he had been reluctant to return to Sherlock Holmes.

Such was the anticipation of their publication that the young P.G. Woodhouse, a life-long fan, wrote a satirical song about the return of Sherlock Holmes for *Punch* magazine. He and Conan Doyle later became friends and cricket teammates. To garner publicity for the return of Sherlock Holmes in the US, the *Evening News* carried the story that Conan Doyle had leased a hotel in Montauk on Long Island to seek out local colour. President Roosevelt, who had a home there, wrote to *Collier's* asking when Conan Doyle would be there because he wanted to meet him.

At first, Conan Doyle wrote eight stories for the series, then extended it to twelve. Afterwards, he talked of retiring Holmes once more. But Sam McClure offered him $75,000 for another twelve stories or $25,000 for a novella to run in his magazine. Conan Doyle turned him down, thinking he had run out of plots, but Arthur Barlett Maurice, an editor at the New York literary magazine *The Bookman*, pointed out that he had mentioned 'The Adventure of the Second Stain' in 'The Naval Treaty' published back in 1893. Watt offered it to McClure for £1,000. He refused, so the story went to *Collier's*, who were happy to take a thirteenth story in the series. At the beginning of 'The Adventure of the Second Stain', Watson reports that Holmes has retired to take up bee-keeping in Sussex. Consequently, *Collier's* trumpeted that this would be 'the last Sherlock Holmes store ever to be written'.

While he researched the later Holmes stories, Conan Doyle made an effort to learn about real-life criminal detection, police procedure and the law and by 1903 he had joined Our Society, a group of writers and lawyers that included the famous forensic pathologist Bernard Spilsbury. Together he and Spilsbury toured the Jack-the-Ripper murder sites in Whitechapel. He also knew William Melville, thought to be one of the models for M in the James Bond novels and the former head of Special Branch who foiled the Jubilee Plot to assassinate Queen Victoria in 1887. He went on to run the Secret Security Bureau, later MI5.

Even when the economy turned flat, Conan Doyle continued making enough money to support his extended family members and buy a couturier's to supply dresses for his young mistress. He became an enthusiastic, though reckless, motorist and boxed with athletic visitors in the ring he had installed at Undershaw, where the visitors' book was filling with names of foreign fans.

He returned to medieval novels with *Sir Nigel*, a prequel to *The White Company*, and he stood again in Scotland in the 1906 general election, though he was rejected once more. His play, *Brigadier General*, was finally accepted for the stage. This period was only marred by the suicide of his theatrical agent, who had stolen £9,000 of Conan Doyle's money, along with over £13,000 from J.M. Barrie and some from Willie Hornung, whose *Raffles* went on stage in the US.

On 4 July 1906, his wife Louise died. Despite his belief in spiritualism he made no effort to contact her after death. After a suitable interlude, Jean Leckie returned to Undershaw and Conan Doyle soon visited the former Prime Minister Arthur Balfour and went on a fact-finding visit to Parkhurst Prison on the Isle of Wight.

Conan Doyle then took up the case of George Edalji, the son of a Parsee who had become an Anglican vicar. Edalji had been convicted of maiming animals around the Staffordshire village of Great Wyrley although he had a watertight alibi. Conan Doyle's investigative work and petitioning of the home office got Edalji freed and eventually exonerated.

In March 1907, he and Jean Leckie were engaged and were married in September. Guests included George Edalji. They honeymooned in Italy, Greece and Turkey, where he was summoned by the Sultan, who was a fan but who could not receive him because of Ramadan, but invested him with the Order of Mejidie anyway. Returning to England, the couple moved into a house that Conan Doyle had bought in Crowborough in Sussex, where he soon added two chapters to his marriage primer, *A Duet*, which became *A Duet with Occasional Chorus*.

He wrote 'A Pot of Caviare', set during the Boxer Rebellion, adapted *The Tragedy of the Korosko* for the stage as *The Fires of Fate* and resumed the Regency boxing play he had been writing with Willie Hornung and which was now called *The House of Temperley*. But getting these staged proved difficult and, after another story failed, he returned to Sherlock Holmes. He did not envisage writing another series but agreed to provide *Strand Magazine* with a story for its mid-summer issue and another at Christmas, under the general title of the *Reminiscences of Sherlock Holmes*. He came up with 'The Adventure of Wisteria Lodge', a two-parter that was published in both *Collier's* in August, and the *Strand* in September and October.

That year saw the publication of Robert Baden-Powell's *Scouting for Boys*, which recommended *The Adventures of Sherlock Holmes* and *The Memoirs of Sherlock Holmes* to boys to improve observational skills, and *The White Company* to inspire chivalry. The founder of the Boy Scouts had already lauded the there observational skills of Sherlock Holmes and Dr Joseph Bell in his Boer War manual *Aids to Scouting for NCOs and Men*, published in 1901.

Conan Doyle returned to the paranormal with 'The Silver Mirror' and, in November, a stage version of 'The Pot of Caviare' was produced at the Jersey Opera House. He finished 'The Adventure of the Bruce-Partington Plans' for *Strand Magazine*'s Christmas issue and the December issue of *Collier's*, who offered £750 per story for a series.

Jean gave him a new son on St Patrick's Day, the first of their three children. That summer King Leopold gave up his private fiefdom of the Congo. To keep up the propaganda effort, Conan Doyle wrote *The Crime of the Congo*, which sold 60,000 copies in the UK alone. It was also published in the US, and in French, German and Portuguese. He also urged an international effort to prevent further atrocities in the Congo, which was still under Belgian control. At a dinner given by the Anti-Slavery and Aborigines' Protection Society in honour of the African-American civil rights leader Booker T. Washington, Conan Doyle gave a speech on race. Later he went to the Old Bailey to watch the trial of Dr Crippen.

The Fires of Fates opened to a critical mauling and closed after four months, and Conan Doyle used his own money to stage *The House of Temperley*, which also bombed. But he had paid the rental on the theatre and put on a stage version of *The Speckled Band* instead. It was a success, but did not recoup his earlier losses. He then claimed he was giving up on theatre, but wrote at least three more pieces, including a one-act play, probably *The Crown Diamond*, featuring Sherlock Holmes.

It was then he decide to move into the emerging world of cinema. American Mutoscope & Biograph had produced *Sherlock Holmes Baffled* as early as 1900 and Holmes had appeared in other films, including a series in Denmark, but none of them used material from Conan Doyle's stories. It was only in 1912 that the Anglo-French company began filming Conan Doyle's original tales, with his cooperation, but there were copyright problems to be overcome as the early Holmes stories had been sold outright before movie versions had been envisioned. Eventually though *The Copper Beeches* was made, along with the non-Holmesian *The House of Temperley* which Conan-Doyle declared was far better than his own play. But he was in no hurry, cinema was clearly in its infancy and he knew that the movie rights in his work were bound to rise.

Jean was expecting again and the couple took a holiday in the Cormsh village of Poldhu, where Holmes reappears in 'the Adventure of the Devil's Foot'. This was followed by 'The Adventure of the Red Circle' and 'The Disappearance of Lady Frances Carfax'. Conan Doyle reworked a couple of Brigadier Gerard and Captain Sharkey stories, and wrote the underground horror story 'The Terror of Blue John Gap'. He then wrote a series of stories set in the Roman Empire for the *London Magazine* and which, he admitted, were really about British Imperialism. He produced another paranormal story and *Songs of the Road*, a book of poetry.

The Edwardian era was now over and Conan Doyle found himself out of step with the new literary and artistic world. Yet he embraced the new era, going up in a biplane, investing in a company that made motorcycle engines and advocating divorce reform. However, he took against the Suffragettes when they were accused of burning down the cricket pavilion in Tunbridge Wells. They had, he said, set their cause back by a generation. The Suffragettes responded by putting noxious black fluid through his letter box.

Added to Conan Doyle's numerous other interests was

palaeontology and, in 1911, he sat down to write *The Lost World*, which introduced Professor Challenger, who reappears in a series of novels and short stories by Conan Doyle and other authors.

Following the loss of the *Titanic*, on which his old colleague W.T. Stead died, Conan Doyle wrote the poem 'Ragtime' which appeared in the programme of a fund-raising event at London's Hippodrome for the families of the victims. The disaster caused a public falling-out between Conan Doyle and George Bernard Shaw, who had sarcastically called the loss of the *Titanic* 'a triumph of British navigation'. He then took up the case of Oscar Slater, a German-born Jew who had fled to New York under an assumed name after the murder of a rich widow in Glasgow. When apprehended, he returned to Britain voluntarily and was convicted on the flimsiest of evidence and condemned to death, a sentence later commuted to life at penal servitude. Conan Doyle rushed out a pamphlet, *The Case of Oscar Slater* and, with the help of the great advocate Edward Marshall Hall, Slater was eventually released in 1925.

Although *The Lost World* took Conan Doyle to the fringes of the controversy over the Piltdown Man, he continued his Professor Challenger science-fantasy series with *The Poison Belt*. Fearing German aggression, he wrote 'Great Britain and the Next War' for the *Fortnightly Review* and advocated building a Channel Tunnel to ensure Britain's food supply. His friend Roger Casement answered with 'Ireland, Germany and the Next World War', advocating the Nationalist cause.

A bout of illness impelled him to write 'The Adventure of the Dying Detective', thought to be a homage Dr Bell, who had first suggested the idea and had died eighteen months previously.

For years, Willie Hornung had been trying to persuade Conan Doyle to pit Holmes against Raffles. William Gillette was also keen and the editor of *Everybody's Magazine* claimed he could guarantee Conan Doyle $100,000. He refused and instead produced 'The Horror of Heights' about strange creatures that live high in the atmosphere. Other stories followed. None involved Holmes. Then, early in 1914, he began *The Valley of Fear*, which he again indicated would be Holmes' last outing.

In May 1917, he sailed for New York on the *Titanic*'s sister ship, SS *Olympic*, at a time when he was being satirized in a poem in *Life* magazine for so obviously drawing on Poe and Gaboriau when Holmes was so dismissive of the detectives Dupin and Lecoq. Conan Doyle answered his critic in verse in 'To an Undiscerning Critic'.

By then, Conan Doyle was a household name in the US and the *Olympic* was greeted by a cutter carrying a film crew eager for footage of the arrival of the famous British author. Said to be more widely known in the US than any other Englishman, he was treated with visits to New York's notorious prison, the Tombs, and Sing Sing, where he sat in the electric chair.

The detective William J. Burns, who had visited Conan Doyle in Sussex the previous year, entertained him at a restaurant in Coney Island, where the band played 'God Save the King' and after asking for Conan Doyle's opinion of the suffragettes, the *New York World* ran the headline: 'Sherlock's Here; Expects Lynching of "Wild Women"'.

He headed next to Canada then to the Rocky Mountains, where he wrote the poem 'The Athabesca Trail', whose verses were thereafter used to promote local railroads and wildlife parks. He returned home in July, shortly before North Atlantic shipping would be menaced by U-boats, and wrote *Western Wanderings* about his trip.

When war was declared, Conan Doyle was recruited to the Propaganda Bureau, where he wrote *To Arms!*, explaining why Britain had gone to war. Anti-German articles he had written for the *Daily Chronicle* were repackaged as *The World War Conspiracy* and *The German War*. He kept a war diary, hoping to be commissioned to write the official account of the conflict. But there were other contenders: Hilaire Belloc turned down the job, which went to John Buchan, though Conan Doyle continued to petition the prime minister, Herbert Asquith, for the position. In the meantime he wrote articles that predicted a British victory for American papers. He also wrote the obituary of W.G. Grace and the first part of his account of the Great War began appearing in *Strand Magazine* in April 1916. He then donned a uniform and went to the Western Front, where he was asked what Sherlock Holmes was doing for the war effort. So he sat down and wrote 'His Last Bow' where Holmes comes out of retirement to foil a German spymaster about to flee with British secrets on the eve of war. After this was published in *Strand Magazine* there were enough stories to make another collection, which John Murray published as *His Last Bow* in 1917.

The slaughter of the First World War, not least among Conan Doyle's own family, increased his interest in spiritualism. He became involved in séances and continued to write patriotic articles and poems. Along with other authors, he signed an open letter praising the Russian Revolution for ridding the country of its autocracy and introducing democracy. He had regular conversations with the new prime minister, Lloyd George, who asked him to go on an official mission to Russia, which he declined.

When the war was over, Conan Doyle threw himself wholeheartedly into spiritualism, though he still found time to call for Germans to be tried for war crimes, to rail against British greengrocers for profiteering, and to finish his history of the Great War, *The British Campaign in France and Flanders*, which was now dismissed as propagandist.

On a visit from America, the magician Harry Houdini attended a number of séances with Conan Doyle, later exposing his mediums as frauds. This did not shake Conan Doyle's spiritualist beliefs. Indeed, he even came to believe in fairies after being taken in by a photograph faked by two little girls in Cottingley, Yorkshire. He travelled to Australia to lecture on the paranormal and, later, tried to photograph fairies himself.

By 1920, more than fifty films had been made about Sherlock Holmes and Conan Doyle was determined to cash in. After checking the copyright, he approached the Stoll Film Company, who went on to make *The Yellow Face*, *The Dying Detective* and *The Devil's Foot*, with Eille Norwood playing Holmes.

In 1921, Conan Doyle dusted off the script for *The Crown Diamond*, which Stoll filmed and premiered at the London Coliseum that May. Conan Doyle then rewrote it as the short story 'The Adventure of the Mazarin Stone', which was published in the *Strand* in October. It was the first of an occasional series that would be published collectively as *The Case-Book of Sherlock Holmes* in 1927.

On 28 September 1921, Conan Doyle was fêted at the Trocadero restaurant on Shaftesbury Avenue and even Prime Minister Lloyd George sent at telegram praising his latest story. He travelled back to New York, where he drew an audience of 3,500 in Carnegie Hall, but had to contend with frivolous questions about marital relations in the spirit world. On his lecture trip, otherwise confined to spiritualism, he took time to pay another visit the grave of Oliver Wendell Holmes and was received well even in Salt Lake City, despite his less than flattering depiction of Mormonism in *A Study in Scarlet* and the Mormons' antipathy to spiritualism. He went on to Los Angeles where, after a court case concerning rights, a major Sherlock Holmes' film starring John Barrymore went into production.

Back in England, Conan Doyle talked of a creating a new character that would 'break new ground' and got on with his autobiography *Memories and Adventures*. He wrote more about spiritualism and the Holmes story 'The Problem of Thor Bridge', which was published in the *Strand* in February and March 1922. Then came 'The Adventure of the Creeping Man', 'The Adventure of the Sussex Vampire' and 'The Adventure of the Three Garridebs', which first appeared in *Collier's*. After that, he returned to Professor Challenger with *The Land of Mist*.

Now over sixty, Conan Doyle began to spend more time alone in a flat he had taken in Victoria, where he was looked after by a housekeeper in proper Holmesian style. He returned to Holmes in 1924, producing 'The Adventure of the Illustrious

Client', 'The Adventure of the Three Gables', 'The Adventure of the Blanched Soldier', 'The Adventure of the Lion's Mane', 'The Adventure of the Retired Colourman', 'The Adventure of the Veiled Lodger' and 'The Adventure of Shoscombe Old Place'. He told Beverley Nichols that it was 'too easy' – he had written 'The Adventure of the Veiled Lodger' and played two rounds of golf on the same day. However, he admitted to Greenhough Smith that these Holmes's stories were not 'of the first flight' and once again bore 'farewell to him forever'.

Conan Doyle informed the readers of the *Strand* of this and invited them to come up with their choice of the twelve best Holmes stories to match his list which ran: 1. 'The Speckled Band'; 2. 'The Red-Headed League'; 3 'The Dancing Men'; 4. 'The Final Problem'; 5. 'A Scandal in Bohemia'; 6. 'The Empty House'; 7. 'The Five Orange Pips'; 8. 'The Second Stain'; 9. 'The Devil's Foot'; 10. 'The Priory School'; 11. 'The Musgrave Ritual'; and 12. 'The Reigate Squires'.

His last collection was published as *The Case-Book of Sherlock Holmes* on 16 June 1927, with a print run of 15,150 copies, the longest print run since *The Hound of the Baskervilles*.

Conan Doyle was also in demand as an amateur sleuth and was called in by the police when Agatha Christie went missing in 1926. He then called in a medium who said that Christie was not dead and would be heard from the following Wednesday. In fact, she was found that Sunday, staying at a hotel in Harrogate under an assumed name.

He travelled to Australia, New Zealand, South Africa and Rhodesia, drawing large audiences for his talks on spiritualism. He also recorded interviews with the Gramophone Company and Movietone News that delved into the background of Sherlock Holmes as well as spiritualism and he wrote travel books and more science-fantasy stories, some featuring Professor Challenger.

In 1929, he went to see a German film version of *The Hound of the Baskervilles* and after travelling to Stockholm to give a lecture he grew ill. He returned to Sussex and updated *Memories and Adventures* and published *The Edge of the Unknown*, a collection of pieces about the paranormal. But the Conan Doyle name was not the draw it had once been and the print run was less than 1,000. In America, Doubleday balked at publishing his account of his African trip, *Our African Winter*.

He died on 7 July 1930. Six days later, 6,000 people packed the Albert Hall in London for a séance, where medium Estelle Roberts claimed to have contacted Sir Arthur.

'He gave me a message,' she said, 'a personal one, which I gave to Lady Doyle, but am unable to repeat publicly. I saw him distinctly. He was wearing evening dress.'

Chapter 4

A Study in Scarlet and The Sign of the Four

Conan Doyle wrote four Sherlock Holmes novels, which appeared initially as stories in magazines. The first, *A Study in Scarlet*, was followed by *The Sign of the Four*.

A Study in Scarlet

A Study in Scarlet was the cover story in the November 1887 issue of *Beeton's Christmas Annual* and in July 1888 it was published by Ward Lock & Co. as a book, with illustrations by Conan Doyle's father, Charles. A second edition, published in 1898, was illustrated by George Hutchinson and in 1890 the first American edition was published by J.B. Lippincott & Co.

A Study in Scarlet is a novel in two parts. Part one announces itself as: 'Being a reprint from the reminiscences of John H. Watson, MD, late of the Army Medical Department.' The first chapter begins with Dr Watson explaining that, after being injured in the Second Anglo-Afghan War, he had returned to England and was now looking for a place to live. An old friend named Stamford introduced him to Sherlock Holmes, who immediately deduces that Watson has been in Afghanistan.

Holmes is looking for someone to split the rent of rooms at 221B Baker Street and the two move in together. Watson is amazed by Holmes, who has a good knowledge of practical science, criminology and the law. He also plays the violin well

and is good fencer and boxer. But he knows nothing of literature, philosophy and politics. Soon he has a bewildering array of
visitors. He reveals that he is a consulting detective and that
these visitors are his clients. When a retired Marine sergeant
turns up with a letter from Tobias Gregson of Scotland Yard
asking for his help in the investigation of a recent murder,
Holmes invites Watson to accompany him to the crime scene.

They head to an address off Brixton Road in south London.
Holmes takes time to examine the pavement and the garden
path leading to the house, where he meets Gregson and another
policeman named Lestrade. On the floor is a dead man. There
is blood in the room, but no wound on the body. A card in his
pocket, a letter and the monogram on his linen identify the dead
man as Enoch J. Drebber of Cleveland and an engraving on his
ring indicates that he is a Freemason. A second letter and a
pocket edition of Boccaccio's *Decameron* carry the name of
Joseph Stangerson. When they move the body, a woman's
wedding ring tinkles to the floor.

On the wall is the word 'RACHE' written in blood. Holmes
points out that this is German for 'revenge'. Holmes deduces
from the smell on the victim's lips that he had been poisoned.
He goes on to describe the appearance of the as of yet unseen
murderer: he is six feet tall, with small feet for his height, a florid
complexion, square-toed boots, long fingernails on his right
hand; he'd been smoking a Trichinopoly cigar and arrived with
the victim in a cab that had been drawn by a horse with three
old shoes and one new one on his fore-leg.

On their way to interview the constable who had found the
body, Holmes explains how he knows all this. The constable tells
Holmes that a man who appeared to be very drunk had been
near the house that night and Holmes says that this was, in fact,
the murderer, who had come back to the scene of the crime to
retrieve the wedding ring. The investigation, Holmes says, was
one of the finest he had ever come across: 'a study in scarlet'.

Holmes places a classified advertisement in all the newspapers saying that a wedding ring had been found in Brixton Road

that morning. The ad is answered by an old lady who claims the ring belongs to her daughter. When she leaves, Holmes follows her and when he returns he tells Watson that the old lady had taken a cab which he hopped onto the back of. When the cab arrives at what the old lady had given as her home address she was nowhere to be seen. Nor does she live there. He believes she must have got out of the cab on the way. Holmes then tells Watson that the old lady was, in fact, a male actor who must be, at the very least, the murderer's accomplice.

The next day, Watson finds Holmes briefing six street urchins who he is employing on the case. He calls them the 'Baker Street division of the detective police force', elsewhere 'The Baker Street Irregulars'. Then, Gregson visits Baker Street and tells Holmes that he has arrested the murderer. He had found the boarding house where Drebber had been staying with his secretary Stangerson. The landlady, Mrs Charpentier, told him that Drebber had been a drunk and had attempted to molest her daughter, Alice. She had thrown both lodgers out, but Drebber had come back that night and tried to abduct Alice. Her older brother Arthur, a violent man, defended his sister, then chased after Drebber with a cudgel. So Gregson arrested Arthur Charpentier.

Then Lestrade turns up. He has tracked down the hotel Stangerson had moved to, but found him dead. His body was lying near the window and he had been stabbed through the heart. Again the word 'RACHE' was written in blood on the wall. The only things Stangerson had with him were a novel, a pipe and a small box containing two pills. Holmes cuts one of the pills in half and feeds it to the landlady's terrier, which is old and ill. The pill has no effect. Then he cuts the other pill in half and feeds it to the dog, who dies instantly. One of the pills is harmless; the other a deadly poison.

Next, Wiggins, the leader of the Baker Street Irregulars, turns up, having fetched a cab for Holmes, who asks for the cabman to come up to help him with his luggage. When the cabby reaches for a portmanteau, Holmes handcuffs him, then introduces him to Gregson and Lestrade as Jefferson Hope, the murderer of Drebber and Stangerson.

Part Two, 'The Country of Saints', takes place far from London. It flashes back Utah in 1847 and seems to have borrowed from 'Story of the Destroying Angel' published by Robert Louis Stevenson and his wife Fanny in the collection *The Dynamiter* in 1885.

John Ferrier and a five-year-old girl named Lucy, the only survivors of a party of twenty-one pioneers, are dying of hunger and thirst. They are rescued by a group of Mormons migrating to Salt Lake City. An Elder named Stangerson leads a forward party to investigate and their leader Brigham Young agrees to help Ferrier and Lucy provided they adopt the Mormon faith.

Ferrier proves himself to be a useful guide and hunter, and is given a generous land grant, where he builds a farm. He and Lucy, whom he adopts, become rich. However, Ferrier has not adopted the Mormon practice of polygamy and remains inexplicably celibate. Meanwhile Lucy has grown into a beautiful woman who is one day saved from an attacking bullock by a young man named Jefferson Hope. They become engaged with Ferrier's consent, provided Hope's silver claim prove profitable.

While Hope is away at his mine, Brigham Young calls on Ferrier and tells him that it is against the religion for Lucy to marry someone who is not a Mormon. She must marry one of the sons of the ruling Council of Four, either Joseph Stangerson or Enoch Drebber. She is given a month to choose. But Ferrier has secretly sworn that his daughter will never be a Mormon. He sends word to Hope but Drebber and Stangerson arrive. They argue over who should marry Lucy and Ferrier eventually throws them out. Then, each day a number appears daubed somewhere on the farm, counting down the of days until Lucy must marry.

On the eve of the last day, Hope finally arrives. He, Lucy and Ferrier flee to Salt Lake City. After two days, they begin to run short of food. They make camp and Hope goes out hunting. He returns to find John Ferrier's freshly dug grave and Lucy gone. He tracks her abductors back to Salt Lake City, where he discovers that, the day before, Lucy has been married to Drebber.

Hope retires to the wilderness and Lucy dies of a broken heart. When she is laid out in her coffin, a weather-beaten man in tattered garments turns up, kisses her forehead and removes the wedding ring from her finger, saying: 'She shall not be buried in that.'

Attempts are made on the lives of Drebber and Stangerson. But Hope eventually realizes that the hardship of living in the wilderness is weakening him and if he dies like a dog in the hills he will have no revenge. So he returns to his mine and works there for five years before returning to Salt Lake City in disguise. He learns of a split among the Mormons. Drebber and Stangerson have left. Drebber, who had inherited Ferrier's farm, is wealthy; Stangerson is poor.

Hope combs the US, looking for the two lapsed Mormons. In Cleveland, Ohio, he spots Drebber. But Drebber has seen him too and he and Stangerson, who is now Drebber's private secretary, go to a justice of the peace. Hope is arrested and by the time he is released Drebber and Stangerson have left for Europe. Again Hope follows them, pursuing them from city to city until they arrive in London.

The narrative then switches back to the reminiscences of Dr Watson.

After his arrest, Hope is taken to Scotland Yard, where he volunteers his story. He has an aortic aneurysm and fears he will die before his trial.

Hope contends that, as Drebber and Stangerson had killed Ferrier and Lucy, they had forfeited their own lives. But so much time had passed that he feared they would never be convicted and sentenced by a court, and so he decided to be judge, jury and executioner. He had also vowed that Drebber would see the wedding ring as he was dying so that his last thoughts would be of the crime for which he was being punished.

Hope dies before he comes to trial. Holmes then explains to Watson each step of his deduction. He had sent a telegram to the head of the Cleveland police, who revealed that Drebber had applied for protection against an old love rival named Jefferson Hope.

Credit for Hope's arrest goes to Gregson and Lestrade, though the newspaper accounts do mention that he was apprehended in the rooms of 'a certain Mr Sherlock Holmes'.

'Never mind,' says Watson. 'I have all the facts in my journal, and then the public shall know them.'

A Sign of the Four

A Sign of the Four was published in February 1890 in *Lippincott's Magazine* in Philadelphia and London. The first book edition was published by Spencer Blackett in London in October that year.

Chapter 1, 'The Science of Deduction', is incidentally the same title as Chapter 2 of *A Study in Scarlet*, where Holmes first shows off his powers as a 'consulting detective', but this time the chapter opens with Holmes injecting himself.

'Which is it today?' asks Watson. 'Morphine or cocaine?'

'It is cocaine, a seven-per-cent solution,' said Holmes. Watson declines his offer to try it and warns Holmes of its effects. Holmes maintains that he only uses it when he has no intellectual problem to stimulate the brain.

Holmes then takes a moment to criticize Watson's account of *A Study in Scarlet*, which he thinks to be too romanticized: 'Detection is, or ought to be, an exact science and should be treated in the same cold and unemotional manner.'

The action begins when an attractive young lady named Mary Morstan arrives to consult Holmes. Her father had returned to London from India ten years before and had sent word for her to meet him at the Langham Hotel. When she arrived there, staff confirmed that her father was staying there but he had gone out the night before. He never returned and her subsequent enquiries led nowhere.

Her father had only one friend she knew of in England, a Major Sholto who lived in Norwood. But he had retired and claimed to be unaware that Morstan was in the country.

Four years after her father's disappearance *The Times* posted an advertisement looking for Miss Morstan. She replied. That day she received a valuable pearl in the post and, since then, has received a similar pearl every year for the last six years.

But then that morning she had received an anonymous letter that read: 'Be at the third pillar from the left outside the Lyceum Theatre tonight at seven o'clock. If you are distrustful bring two friends. You are a wronged woman and shall have justice. Do not bring police.' Holmes and Watson volunteer to accompany her and, in the meantime, Holmes goes through the back files of *The Times* and discovers that Major Sholto had died a week before Miss Morstan received the first pearl.

On the way to the Lyceum, Miss Morstan tells Holmes that Sholto and her father were in charge of troops guarding convicts on the Andaman Islands in the Bay of Bengal. She also shows Holmes a strange paper that was found in her father's desk after he disappeared. The document appears to be a map and written on it are the words 'the sign of the four' along with the names Jonathan Small, Mahomet Singh, Abdullah Khan and Dost Akbar.

At the rendezvous, Miss Morstan, Holmes and Watson are met by a coachman and taken to the south London home of Thaddeus Sholto and are ushered in by an Indian servant. Thaddeus says his father Major Sholto had returned to England a wealthy man; however, he was afraid for his personal safety and had a fear of men with wooden legs.

On his deathbed the Major told Thaddeus and his twin brother Bartholomew that in India he and Captain Morstan had come into possession of a large quantity of treasure. When Morstan returned to England, he went to Sholto's house in Norwood to demand his share. While the two men argued over the division of the spoils, Morstan suffered a fatal heart attack. Fearing that he would be implicated in his death, Sholto disposed of the body.

Major Sholto urged his sons to give Miss Morstan the half share of the treasure that was rightfully her father's but he was suddenly scared by the sight of a man at the window and died without divulging the whereabouts of the goods. Later an intruder searched his room and left a note that merely said: 'The sign of the four.'

Before he died, Major Sholto had recovered a string of pearls that he had intended to send to Miss Morstan. Thaddeus thought they should send it, but Bartholomew was against it. As a compromise, they agreed to send her one pearl a year. But Bartholomew had now found the treasure in a low garret under the roof and Thaddeus had contacted Miss Morstan so that they could go to Pondicherry Lodge in Norwood to claim their respective shares.

When they arrive they find Bartholomew Sholto dead in a locked room, poisoned by a thorn lodged in his head. The box of treasure has been stolen and a note has been left behind that reads: 'The sign of the four.'

Holmes examines the room and works out how two people got in and out and that one had a wooden leg and the other, a small and agile accomplice, had killed Batholomew with a poisoned dart.

Inspector Athelney Jones arrives, dismisses Holmes's 'theorizing' and arrests Thaddeus for the murder of his brother. Holmes assures Sholto that he can clear him of the charge, names one of the killers as Jonathan Small and gives a detailed description of him.

Watson takes Miss Morstan home and Holmes then sends him to get a sniffer dog named Toby, which they use to follow the trail of Small and his companion. On the way, Holmes explains that Sholto and Morstan learnt of the hidden treasure and that Jonathan Small had drawn a map of where it was hidden and signed it on behalf of himself and his accomplices – the sign of the four. As Small was a convict and could not get the treasure himself, Sholto had taken it but when Small was freed he came to reclaim the treasure.

The dog leads Holmes and Watson to a wharf where they learn that a steam launch named the *Aurora* was hired by a wooden-legged man and a 'brown, monkey-faced chap', who Holmes concludes is an Andaman Island aboriginal. The Baker Street Irregulars are then despatched with the task of finding the *Aurora*. Later, disguised as a sailor, Holmes joins the search.

Inspector Jones turns up at Baker Street and Holmes asks him to provide a fast police launch. He had deduced that Small must have a lair downriver where they were waiting until they can arrange for passage to America or the Colonies. Holmes has found the *Aurora* in boatyard and has discovered that she is to sail at eight that night.

The police launch, with Holmes and Watson on board, arrives at the boatyard in time to see the *Aurora* depart. They give chase. The Aborigine is shot dead and Small is captured. The treasure chest turns out to be empty. Small says that he threw the treasure overboard during the chase as no one has a right to it except himself and his three fellow convicts.

Small explains that he'd met the others when he was on guard duty in the city of Agra during the Indian Mutiny (or Great Rebellion) of 1857–8. One night two Sikh men under Small's command threatened to kill him if he didn't join their scheme: to kill a rich merchant who was transporting the rajah's treasure. He did join them and the four men swore an oath that they should always act for each other. Small drew four maps, one for each of them, showing where the stolen treasure was hidden.

The murder was discovered after the Mutiny and the four were arrested and sentenced to life of penal servitude. Small was sent to the Andaman Islands, where he offered Sholto and Morstan a deal: if they could secure freedom for him and the other three they would cut them in for an equal share of the treasure. He drew two more copies of the map but Sholto cheated them all by recovering the treasure alone and taking it back to England.

Luckily Small saved the life of an Andaman Islander named Tonga, who helped him escape. Together they made their way to England. Small found Sholto only just in time to witness his death through the window. He bided his time and eventually heard from Sholto's Indian butler that the treasure had been found. They stole the treasure, but Tonga had then killed Bartholomew Sholto.

With Small in custody, Watson tells Holmes that he has become engaged to Miss Morstan and as Watson gets a wife and Jones takes credit for breaking the case, Holmes turns back to cocaine.

Chapter 5

The Adventures of Sherlock Holmes

After *A Study in Scarlet* and *A Sign of the Four* Conan Doyle began writing short stories about Sherlock Holmes which appeared in the *Strand* and other magazines. The fifty-six stories were then collected into five volumes. The first, *The Adventures of Sherlock Holmes*, was published on 14 October 1892 by G. Newnes Ltd and contained twelve stories that had appeared in the *Strand* in 1891 and 1892.

A Scandal in Bohemia

'A Scandal in Bohemia' was first published in *Strand Magazine* in July 1891 with ten illustrations by Sidney Paget. The story begins with Watson musing on the curious effect one woman – Irene Alder – has on Holmes. Watson is by now married and has moved out of 221B Baker Street to set up home elsewhere. Occasionally he hears of the doings of the great detective but on 20 March 1888 he decides to drop in on Holmes, who offers him a drink and a cigar and proceeds to deduce the details of Watson's private life from his appearance.

Holmes has received an anonymous note saying that a gentleman will call at eight that evening in a matter that concerns one of the royal families of Europe. He deduces that is was written by a German who turns up wearing a mask. The visitor introduces himself as Count Von Kramm and says he is the agent for a wealthy client, but Holmes quickly realizes that he is in fact the King of Bohemia. The king admits this and tears off his mask.

Five years before, the King had an affair with the opera singer Irene Adler. He is now engaged to a Scandinavian princess but Irene has letters of his and a compromising photograph showing them together. She threatens to ruin the wedding, which is three days way. He has tried to buy the letters and photograph, but she will not sell. His agents have broken into her house, diverted her luggage and waylaid her, but have still failed to retrieve them.

The king gives Holmes £300 in gold and £700 in notes (worth £83,000 at today's prices) to cover present expenses, and declares that he would give one of the provinces of his kingdom to have the photograph back. The image is a 'cabinet' – usually around 6.5 by 4.5 inches – too large to be carried around, so it must be in her home.

Watson returns to Baker Street at three o'clock the following afternoon at Holmes's request but Holmes had gone out at eight that morning and has not yet returned. Watson waits. At nearly four, a drunken-looking groom comes in; it is Holmes in disguise. He has been to Irene Alder's house and he spoke with stable workers in a nearby mews. She has a gentleman caller, a lawyer named Godfrey Norton. He turned up and, after a short visit, took a cab to the Church of St Monica in Edgware Road, via a shop in Regent street. Minutes later, Irene got in her landau and told the driver to take her to St Monica's. Holmes follows and when he arrive, found himself dragged into the church to be a witness to Norton's and Adler's wedding, though they then go their separate ways.

Holmes disguises himself as a Nonconformist clergyman, and he and Watson return to Irene Adler's house. Soon after, they hear her arriving home after her evening drive. As her landau comes to a halt, one of the loafers in the street opens the door in the hope of earning a copper. Another pushes him out of the way. A fight breaks out. Holmes intervenes. In the ensuing scuffle, he cries out and falls to the ground with blood running down his face. He is carried into the house and laid on a sofa in the sitting room.

Watson looks through the sitting-room window and on Holmes's signal, throws a plumber's smoke-rocket through the window and yells 'fire!'. Watson slips through the crowd to the corner, where Holmes joins him a few minutes later.

Holmes then explains that everyone in the street was an accomplice hired for the occasion. When the cry of 'fire!' went up Irene had rushed to save the photograph, which was hidden behind a sliding panel, but replaced it once she realized that it was a false alarm. The plan is now to return early the following morning with the king, giving him the chance to recover the photograph by his own hand.

Returning to Baker Street, Holmes and Watson are just about to go in the front door, when someone in the street says: 'Good-night, Mister Sherlock Holmes.'

Next morning, they arrive at Irene's house with the king the following morning. The housekeeper informs them that Irene and her husband had left for the Continent on the 5.15 from Charing Cross. When they slide back the panel in the sitting room, they find the compromising photograph gone, with another in its place. This one shows Irene on her own in an evening dress and with it is a letter addressed to Sherlock Holmes. It says that after the fire proved to be a false alarm she quickly changed into men's clothes and followed Holmes and Watson back to Baker Street, where she had bid him 'good-night'. The king, she says, may now marry whom he wishes, but she will keep the photograph for her own protection.

What a queen she would have made, rues the king, if only she had been of the right social class. He offers Holmes a valuable ring as a reward, but Holmes asks instead to have the photograph of Irene – the woman who had outsmarted him.

The Red-Headed League

'The Red-Headed League' was first published in the *Strand Magazine* in August 1891, with ten illustrations by Sidney Paget. Again, the story begins with Watson dropping round to see his old friend in Baker Street. With Holmes is a red-haired, elderly gentleman named Jabez Wilson.

He produces a newspaper advertisement headed 'The Red-Headed League'. It offers £4 a week for purely nominal services; only red-headed men need apply.

Wilson owns a pawnbrokers in Coburg Square, near the City, where he has a clever young assistant named Vincent Spaulding who is willing to work for half pay to learn the business. Spaulding also has a passion for photography and is always disappearing into the cellar, which he uses as a darkroom. It was Spaulding who had brought the advertisement to Wilson's attention, urged him to answer it, and accompanied him to the interview. Wilson was hired over all the other red-heads and was set to work copying out the *Encyclopaedia Britannica*. This continued for eight weeks until he turned up to find the door locked and a sign that read: 'THE RED-HEADED LEAGUE IS DISSOLVED.'

It was then that he consulted Holmes, who says he will solve the case by the following Monday. After Wilson leaves, Holmes begs Watson not to speak to him for fifty minutes. This is, he says, 'a three-pipe problem'.

Afterwards, Holmes and Watson visit the pawnbrokers, where Holmes uses his stick to beat on the pavement outside. They meet Spaulding, whom Holmes notices has dirt on the knees of his trousers. After a quick survey of the surrounding streets, Holmes calls Inspector Jones and Mr Merryweather, director of the bank in the next street.

Armed, the four hide themselves in the bank vault where Merryweather has stored 30,000 gold Napoleons. Notorious criminal John Clay (aka Spaulding) and his accomplice Archie break through the wall. 'The Red-Headed League' had been contrived to keep Wilson out of the way while they tunnelled from his basement to the bank vault.

A Case of Identity

'A Case of Identity' was first published in *Strand Magazine* in September 1891 with seven illustrations by Sidney Paget.

Watson has visited Holmes and they are sitting by the fire in Baker Street, discussing crime. Holmes offers Watson some snuff from a gold box given to him by the King of Bohemia after the Irene Adler case. Enter Miss Mary Sutherland, who comes to consult Holmes. Her fiancé, Hosmer Angel, has disappeared and her stepfather Mr Windibank will not go to the police. During the conversation, she reveals she has an income from New Zealand stock, but her stepfather draws the interest and hands it over to her mother while she earns a living copy typing.

Her stepfather does not want her to go anywhere where she might meet a husband. But while he was away in France on business Miss Sutherland and her mother went to a ball where she met Hosmer Angel. After that, they met again, but only when Windibank was away.

She knows little about him, only that he worked in Leadenhall Street. Her letters to him were addressed to the post office there, while his letters to her were always typewritten. Holmes notes that even the signature is typewritten. Nevertheless, the affair continued apace. Angel proposed and made her swear on the Bible that, whatever happened, she would always be true.

Although they intended to marry before her stepfather returned, Miss Sutherland thought she should write to him. Her letter was returned from Bordeaux on the morning of her wedding as he had already left to return to England.

On the day of their wedding Miss Sutherland and Angel travelled to the church in separate carriages but, when they arrived, Angel's carriage was empty. She has not seen or heard from him since. However, when she told her stepfather, he reassured her that she would hear of her fiancé again.

Miss Sutherland is clearly distressed. She cannot sleep and sobs as she tells her story. Holmes agrees to look into the matter, but tells her to forget about Angel. She will never see him again.

'Let the whole incident be a sealed book,' says Holmes, 'and do not allow it to affect your life.'

'You are very kind, Mr Holmes,' says Miss Sutherland, 'but I cannot do that. I shall be true to Hosmer. He shall find me ready when he comes back.'

Holmes tells Watson that he will know the identity of Miss Sutherland's fiancé by the following evening. When Watson returns, Holmes tells him that Windibank has sent a note agreeing to come to Baker Street at six.

When Windibank arrives, Holmes tells him that he has found Hosmer Angel.

Windibank grows angry and says: 'If you can catch the man, catch him . . .'

Holmes locks the door and says: 'I have caught him.' He points out that a typewriter is as individual as a man's handwriting and that Windibank's note and Angel's letters were written on the same machine.

Windibank confesses. He married an older woman for her money and can make use of her daughter's money as long as she remains single. He disguised himself as Hosmer Angel then made her swear on the Bible to be true, figuring that she would then not entertain another suitor for at least ten years.

Windibank points out that he has not broken the law but that Holmes, by locking the door, has opened himself to an action for assault and illegal constraint. Holmes unlocks the door, then decides to administer a sound thrashing with a riding crop. Windibank flees.

'And Miss Sutherland?' asks Watson.

'If I tell her she will not believe me,' says Holmes. 'You may remember the old Persian saying, "There is danger for him who taketh the tiger cub, and danger also for who so snatches a delusion from a woman."'

The Boscombe Valley Mystery

'The Boscombe Valley Mystery' was first published in *Strand Magazine* in October 1891 with ten illustrations by Sidney Paget.

Watson is having breakfast with his wife when a telegram arrives from Holmes asking Watson to accompany him to the west of England to investigate the 'Boscombe Valley tragedy'. The train leaves from Paddington at 11.15 a.m. Watson's wife encourages him to go.

On the train, Holmes explains that the local landowner, John Turner, had made his money in Australia. One of his tenants was Charles McCarthy, who Turner had known in Australia. McCarthy's only son James is eighteen; Turner has a daughter of the same age.

The previous Monday McCarthy had hurried to a small lake in a wood called Boscombe Pool, where he said he had an important meeting at three. Witnesses saw his son James heading towards the pool with a gun soon after. Another witness, the young daughter of the lodgekeeper, saw the two men having a row and James raise his hand as if to strike his father. Frightened, she ran away. James McCarthy then came running up to the lodge saying that his father was dead. He was not carrying the gun and had blood on his sleeve. His father went back with McCarthy and they found his father's dead body. The head had been beaten in by a heavy, blunt object. The gun was found nearby and James McCarthy was arrested.

McCarthy claimed that he had only just returned from Bristol and had taken his gun to go out hunting. He had no idea his father was in front of him and was about a hundred yards from the water when he heard the cry 'Cooee!', the signal he and his father used. They met by the pool and an argument ensued. His father's temper was ungovernable, so he left, but after he had gone just a hundred and fifty yards he heard an altercation. He returned to find his father dying. He dropped his gun, knelt down and held as father as he died. Then he went to the lodge to get help.

The coroner had asked McCarthy whether his father had said anything before he died. Yes, McCarthy said he had made some allusion to 'a rat'. McCarthy refused to say what the row with his father had been about, insisting it had nothing to do with the murder. However, he did have an impression that a coat had been lying on the ground when he ran back to his father, but it had gone by the time he had returned with the lodgekeeper.

Miss Turner and others in the area believed James McCarthy's innocence and called in Inspector Lestrade, who made little headway and so referred the case to Holmes. Holmes and Watson are met from the train by Lestrade and Miss Turner at the nearby town of Ross.

Holmes tells her that he thinks McCarthy is innocent and she rebukes Lestrade.

'He gives me hopes,' she says.

She thinks the row between James and his father was about her. McCarthy wanted his son to marry Miss Turner while her father was opposed to the match. Holmes asks to see her father but she says this is impossible. He is ill and, although he had never been strong, his health had now completely broken down.

Holmes and Lestrade go to Hereford to see the prisoners, while Watson stays behind to read the coroner's report. He concludes that the fatal blow had been struck from behind. Holmes returns to report that James McCarthy was in love with Miss Turner but two years before had secretly married a barmaid in Bristol. When his father upbraided him for not proposing to Miss Turner he held up his hands in exasperation. But now that he is about to be hanged the barmaid has told him she already had a husband in Bermuda Dockyard.

Holmes then tells Watson why he is convinced that James is innocent: his father had been on his way to meet someone. It could not have been his son, as McCarthy senior thought he was away in Bristol.

Before visiting Boscombe Pool the following day, Holmes examines the boots McCarthy senior had been wearing when he was killed. He then inspects the scene of the crime. In the wood, he picks up a stone. This is the murder weapon discarded by the killer, he says, noting that the grass was growing under it. He goes on to give a detailed description of the murderer and, later, explains his reasoning to Watson. 'Cooee!' he says, is a distinctively Australian cry, so McCarthy was expecting to meet someone from Australia. Holmes opens a map of Victoria and points out the town of Ballarat – James had only caught the last two syllables.

The killer is John Turner.

Confronted, Turner confesses that, in Australia, he had robbed a gold convoy. McCarthy had been the wagon driver. When Turner returned to England a rich man he met McCarthy, who was then destitute. As McCarthy knew the secret of Turner's wealth, he let him live rent free in a farm on his estate, but would not let his daughter marry McCarthy's son. The two were to meet at Boscombe Pool to talk it over. There he over-heard the father and son rowing over his daughter. He grew angry and seized his chance to kill McCarthy.

Turner says he will come forward if James were sentenced to hang, otherwise, as he was suffering a terminal illness, he would rather die in his bed. Holmes promises to use Turner's confession only if McCarthy is condemned. As it is, the evidence he presents at the assizes is enough to secure an acquittal.

The Five Orange Pips

'The Five Orange Pips' was first published in *Strand Magazine* in November 1891 with six illustrations by Sidney Paget. It begins with Watson reviewing Holmes's cases from the years between 1882 and 1890. He fixes on one from September 1887 when he was staying with Holmes while his wife was visiting her mother.

A young man from Horsham in Sussex visits. His name is John Openshaw and he has a strange story. His uncle Elias Openshaw had been a planter in Florida, served as a colonel in the Confederate Army and had returned to England after the American Civil War.

John lived on his uncle's estate in Horsham and was allowed to go anywhere in the house except for one locked room. On 10

March 1883 a letter arrived, postmarked Pondicherry, India. It contained five orange pips. When Elias opened it, he cried out 'K.K.K.' When asked what it meant, he said: 'Death.' Later that day he burnt his papers and drew up a will.

He began to drink heavily and ran around brandishing a pistol. Then on 2 May 1883 he was found dead in the garden pond.

On 4 January 1885 Elias's brother Joseph received another letter containing five orange pips. The letters 'K.K.K.' were written on the envelope, which was postmarked Dundee. The letter inside instructed him to leave 'the papers' on the sundial in the garden. Three days later, Joseph Openshaw is found dead in a nearby chalk-pit.

For the next two years and eight months, John Openshaw lived happily on his uncle's estate but when a similar letter arrived for him, postmarked east London, he took it to the police, who would not take the matter seriously, so he came to see Holmes. He has a single clue: after his uncle had burnt his papers, John found an unburnt page from his uncle's diary. Headed March 1869, it mentioned that three men had been sent pips. Two were 'cleared' and the third 'visited'.

Holmes deduces from the time between the letters and their postmarks that whomever is writing them is on a sailing ship.

It seems that his uncle had returned to England with some papers belonging to the Ku Klux Klan – the orange pips were their warning.

The following day, the newspaper reports that the body of John Openshaw has been found in the Thames. Though his pride is hurt, Holmes is determined to avenge him. When Watson returns that evening, Holmes declares that he has the killers in the palm of his hand. He puts five pips in an envelope, addressing it to Captain James Calhoun of the *Lone Star*, Savannah, Georgia and marks it 'S.H. for J.O.'. He had spent the day studying *Lloyd's Register* and found that the *Lone Star* had been in Pondicherry in January and February 1883 and at Dundee in January 1885. She had been in London the week before and is now on her way back to the US. Of the crew only the captain and the two mates were Americans.

However, they never receive the pips. The *Lone Star* sank in the North Atlantic.

The Man with the Twisted Lip

'The Man with the Twisted Lip' was first published in *Strand Magazine* in December 1891 with ten illustrations by Sidney Paget.

Late one night, a friend of Watson's wife calls. Her husband has been missing for two days. He is an opium addict and she is sure he is on a drug binge in the East End. Watson goes to fetch him home and in the opium den he finds Holmes, disguised as an old man, looking for respectable family man Neville St Clair, who has also disappeared. On the day he went missing, his wife saw him at an upstairs window above the opium den. He was not wearing his usual City attire.

She entered the building but her way was blocked by the opium den's owner. She fetched the police and in the room where Mrs St Clair had seen her husband they found instead a beggar. However, Mrs St Clair noticed a box of wooden bricks that her husband said he would buy for their son. A search turned up some of her husband's clothes. Blood was found on the windowsill and, when the tide went out, his coat was found in the Thames. Its pockets were weighed down with pennies and ha'pennies, and the beggar with the twisted lip was arrested.

At first Holmes thinks that Mr St Clair has died,. but then Mrs St Clair receives a letter from her husband. After a night of thought – and an ounce of shag – Holmes goes to the police station where the beggar is sleeping. He washes the beggar's face to reveal – Neville St Clair.

St Clair explains that he had been a journalist and had disguised himself to write a story about the life of a beggar, only to discover that he could make more money begging than as a journalist. When debt forced him to make a living out of it, he took a room above the opium den to change clothes. When his wife saw him, he quickly disguised himself, intending to throw his clothes out of the window. In the rush he accidentally cut himself and only managed to throw out his coat.

As no crime was committed St Clair is freed, after promising not to return to begging.

The Adventure of the Blue Carbuncle

'The Adventure of the Blue Carbuncle' was first published in *Strand Magazine* in January 1892 with eight illustrations by Sidney Paget.

Watson visits Holmes after Christmastime and finds him contemplating a battered hat. It had been dropped, along with a Christmas goose, by a man who had been attacked in the street by ruffians and rescued by a uniformed commissionaire named Peterson. But the man ran away leaving the hat and goose, which Peterson took home. The goose has a tag tied to its leg that reads: 'For Mrs Henry Baker. The hat has the initials 'H.B.' in the lining. When Mrs Peterson prepares the bird for the oven she finds in a jewel in its crop. It is the Countess of Morcar's blue carbuncle, which five days earlier a plumber named John Horner had been accused of stealing from the Countess's jewellery case in the Hotel Cosmopolitan. A £1,000 reward is being advertised for its return in *The Times*.

An advertisement is placed in the evening papers and Henry Baker turns up at Baker Street. Holmes has bought him another goose, but offers him the feathers, legs and crop of the other one, which he says they had been forced to eat on it would have gone to waste. Baker is happy with the fresh goose, which indicates that he knows nothing of the blue carbuncle.

It transpires that the original goose had been provided by the landlord of the Alpha Inn near the British Museum. The landlord tells Holmes and Watson that he bought the goose from a Mr Breckinridge in Covent Garden. They duly go to Covent Garden, where Breckinridge opens his ledger and shows Holmes that he bought twenty-four geese from a Mrs Oakshott of 117 Brixton Road. But before they leave another man turns up asking about the goose. This is James Ryder, an attendant at the Hotel Cosmopolitan.

They take him to Baker Street where they force a confession from him: the countess's maid had told him about the blue carbuncle and, after he called Horner to fix something in the countess's room, he rifled through the jewellery case, raised the alarm and had Horner arrested.

Ryder then went to Mrs Oakshott, his sister, who has promised him one of her geese for Christmas. He fed the jewel to one of the birds to conceal it but the bind broke free and when he went to retrieve it he picked the wrong one. He took the bird to a fence who opens up the goose, but cannot find the jewel. Ryder returns to his sister's only to find that she has sold the rest of the goose to Breckinridge.

Ryder breaks down. Holmes takes pity on him and lets him go.

'I am not retained by the police to supply their deficiencies,' he says.

The Adventure of the Speckled Band

'The Adventure of the Speckled Band' was first published in *Strand Magazine* in February 1892 with nine illustrations by Sidney Paget.

Watson looks back to the days when he was a bachelor and sharing rooms with Holmes in Baker Street, in particular to April 1883, when a young woman named Helen Stoner arrived at 221B in a state of agitation. She and her twin sister Julia lived with their stepfather, Dr Grimesby Roylott, who benefited from an income left by their dead mother, but only if they lived with him and did not marry.

Two years earlier, Julia got engaged. Shortly before her wedding she left her bedroom one evening because of the smell of strong Indian cigars Roylott had been smoking in his room next door. She went to talk to her sister and happened to ask her if she had ever heard anyone whistle in the night. Later, Helen heard her sister scream, then a low whistle. Julia appeared at her bedroom door and said, 'It was the band, the speckled band!' She collapsed dead while stabbing her finger in the air in the direction of Roylott's room. No sign of poison was found and the coroner concluded that she had died of fright.

Helen is now engaged and, as work is being done on her bedroom, she had moved into her sister's room. Last night she heard the same low whistle and, terrified, she dressed and made her way to London to consult the great detective.

After Helen leaves, Dr Roylott visits Holmes and demands to know what Helen has said. Holmes refuses to say and later he and Watson visit Helen Stoner at home, where they examine her sister's bedroom. Holmes notices that the bed is fixed to the floor and, recently, a bell-pull and a ventilator that led to the next-door room had been installed. He already suspected this because Julia had smelt her stepfather's cigars. By then, Holmes has seen their mother's will and discovered that the marriage of his stepdaughters would leave Roylott penniless. Holmes tells Watson that he has already solved the mystery. The next stage is to put his theory to the test.

That night, Helen helps Holmes and Watson sneak into Julia's bedroom and retires to her own room. After three, they see a gleam of light in the ventilator and hear a hissing sound. Holmes strikes a match and lashes at the bell-pull with his cane.

'You see it, Watson?' he yelled. But Watson had seen nothing.

Then from the room next door came a scream. They enter Roylott's bedroom to find him dead. Around his brow is a speckled band.

'It is a swamp adder,' says Holmes, 'the deadliest snake in India.'

Roylott had put it through the ventilator so that it would bite Julia first, then Helen. The whistling was used to call off the snake, which then climbed back up the bell-pull. (There are no adders in India. Had this, say, been a poisonous cobra, that too would have been ineffective as cobras are deaf.) But this time the snake, agitated by Holmes's attack, had bitten Roylott. Holmes admits he was indirectly responsible for Roylott's death, but says it is unlikely to weigh very heavily upon his conscience.

The Adventure of the Engineer's Thumb

'The Adventure of the Engineer's Thumb' was first published in *Strand Magazine* in March 1892 with eight illustrations by Sidney Paget.

Dr Watson notes that this is one of only two cases which he personally brought to the attention of Sherlock Holmes. In the summer of 1889, a guard from Paddington Station brings a patient to Watson's surgery nearby. The patient is a hydraulic engineer named Victor Hatherley. Watson bandages his hand – his thumb had been torn out by the roots. He had fainted when it happened. When he came to, he staunched the bleeding by binding the wound tightly with his handkerchief: it was a matter of hydraulics – his field – he says.

Watson asks about the accident. Hatherley says it was no accident, but a 'murderous attack'. Together they go to Baker Street to see Holmes.

The previous day Hatherley had been visited by a man who called himself Colonel Lysander Stark, though he had a trace of a German accent. He asked if Hatherley would examine the hydraulic press he used to compress Fuller's earth into bricks. The job was to be kept strictly confidential and Stark offered him fifty guineas (worth over £4,000 at today's prices) for the work. Hatherley agreed and took the last train to Eyford in Berkshire, where he was met by the Colonel. Arriving at a darkened house, they were met by a woman who spoke with Stark in a foreign tongue. Hatherley was left in a room full of books in German. The woman then appeared at the door, put her finger to her lips and warned him to leave. But the thought of the fifty guineas kept him there.

Stark then introduced Hatherley to his secretary and manager, Mr Ferguson. They negotiated the labyrinthine staircases and corridors of the old house until they reached a small chamber which, he was told, was the cylinder of the hydraulic press.

When he examined the mechanism by lamplight, it was obvious that the machine was not being used to compress fuller's earth at all and he said: 'I should be better able to advise you as to your machine if I knew what the exact purpose was for which it was used.'

As a result of these rash words, Hatherley found himself locked in the cylinder. The piston then began to descend. He was about to be crushed to death when, at the last moment, he saw a small panel being opened. He threw himself out and was helped to escape by the same woman who had warned him earlier. But before he could jump through an opened window, Stark arrived brandishing a cleaver. By then Hatherley was hanging from the window sill and Stark severed his thumb. Hatherley fell to the ground and made his escape.

Holmes shows him the notice of his disappearance that has already appeared in the newspaper. He deduces that Stark and his gang were using the press to make counterfeit coins.

They travel to Eyford to find the house burnt down and no sign of Stark. It turned out that the house belonged to a Dr Becher, a German who matches Stark's description. Holmes tells Hatherley that he has had his revenge: the oil lamp he left in the press had caused the fire.

The Adventure of the Noble Bachelor

'The Adventure of the Noble Bachelor' was first published in *Strand Magazine* in April 1892 with eight illustrations by Sidney Paget.

Holmes is consulted by Lord Robert St Simon, whose wife, an American heiress named Hatty Doran, disappeared at their wedding reception. His bride had seemed delighted with the match but her demeanour suddenly changed when, in church, she dropped her bouquet, which was handed back to her by an unknown man. At the reception, a former acquaintance of Lord Robert's, a *danseuse* at the Allegro named Flora Miller, caused a disturbance and was arrested. Beforehand, she had been seen walking in Hyde Park with Lord Robert's wife.

When Lord Robert finishes telling the tale, Holmes says he has solved the case. He later tells Watson that he had achieved this before Lord Robert even arrived, from the press coverage alone.

Lestrade turns up. The police have been dragging the Serpentine for Mrs St Simon's body. Holmes says they might as well drag the fountain in Trafalgar Square. Lestrade takes offence and produces her wedding dress. It was found near the lake with the rest of her clothes with the wedding ring on top of the pile. Lestrade thinks he has found evidence that links Flora Miller to the disappearance. In the pocket of the discarded dress is a note that says: 'You will see me when all is ready. Come at once. F.H.M.'

Turning the note over, Holmes sees that it is part of a hotel bill. He then declares: 'Lady St Simon is a myth. There is not, and there never has been, any such person.'

The evening, Holmes invites Lord Robert to dinner, along with Mr and Mrs Francis Hay Moulton.

'The lady, I think, you have already met,' says Holmes to Lord Robert. It is, of course, Hatty Doran.

She explains that she had met Frank in a mining camp in the Rockies before her father struck gold. They married secretly and Frank returned to prospecting. The mining camp he was in was attacked by Indians and he was listed among the dead. Then Hatty met Lord Robert, believing herself free to marry again.

But Frank was not dead. He had been captured by Apaches and eventually escaped. He followed her to London, where he saw a notice in the newspaper announcing her wedding. He went to the church and, when she saw him writing a note, she dropped her bouquet, giving him the opportunity to hand the missive to her.

At the reception she saw Frank through the window and went out to see him but was accosted by Flora Miller. It seemed she was not the only one who had a secret. She then caught up with Frank. They dumped her wedding clothes and made off. They would have left for Paris if Sherlock Holmes had not tracked them down and given them the opportunity to meet Lord Robert privately to explain the situation.

Watson wants to know how Holmes tracked the couple down. Holmes explains that the prices on the bill meant that it came from one of the more expensive hotels in London. He had the initials from the note. From the hotel register, he discovered that a Francis H. Moulton had left the day before and had given a forwarding address.

The Adventure of the Beryl Coronet

'The Adventure of the Beryl Coronet' was first published in *Strand Magazine* in May 1892 with nine illustrations by Sidney Paget.

Alexander Holding, a City banker, arrives as Baker Street to consult Holmes. A prominent member of society has borrowed £50,000, leaving as collateral a valuable beryl coronet. He does not feel safe leaving it in the office at night and takes it home with him. He awakes to find the coronet in the hands of his son Arthur, a ne'er-do-well who has been lured into gambling by the notorious rake Sir George Burnwell. The coronet is damaged, with a piece carrying three beryls missing. They could not be found. Holding accuses his son of being a thief and calls the police. But Arthur will neither confess nor explain his actions even though he has been caught red-handed. Holmes, however, is convinced of his innocence.

Holding had been awoken by noise in the house; if his son had truly wanted to steal the coronet he would have kept quiet. And if he had stolen the jewels and hidden them so successfully that a thorough search of the house and garden had not unearthed them, why had he not stolen the other thirty-six? And why would he remain silent rather than come up with some inventive lie?

Holmes goes to Holding's house in Streatham and examines footprints in the snow outside. Indoors he meets Holding's niece, Mary, who has been crying and soon after runs away.

Holding's priority is to get the beryls back. Their loss would cause a national scandal. Holmes gets him to write a cheque for £4,000. He has deduced that Mary had stolen the coronet and handed it out of the window to her lover Sir George Burnwell. Arthur, who could not sleep for worrying about his gambling debts, saw them. He intercepted Burnwell in the garden. In the ensuing struggle a piece broke off, and Burnwell made off with it. When his father caught him, Arthur was returning the damaged coronet. Holmes catches up with Burnwell and pays him for the return of the beryls.

Holding is saved from scandal and reconciled with his son. Mary has run off with Burnwell.

'Whatever her sins are,' says Holmes, 'they will soon receive a more than sufficient punishment.'

The Adventure of the Copper Beeches
'The Adventure of the Copper Beeches' was first published in the *Strand Magazine* in June 1892, with nine illustrations by Sidney Paget.

A young woman named Violet Hunter visits Holmes, asking whether she should accept a job as governess. She is attracted by the salary – £120 a year, more than four times what she currently earns. However, a number of strange conditions come with the job, one of which is to have her long cut hair short.

She agrees to take the job, on the understanding that Holmes would come to Copper Beeches in Hampshire, the home of her new employer, Jephro Rucastle, if required. A telegram summoning him arrives after a fortnight. Holmes and Watson travel to Winchester to meet her and she tells Holmes that, along with looking after Rucastle's children, she is required to wear a blue dress and sit in the front room with her back to the window. She began to suspect there was something she was not supposed to see outside, so she hid a shard of a broken mirror in her hand-kerchief and saw a man standing on the road looking towards the house.

During these sessions, Mr Rucastle sometimes told funny

stories that made Miss Hunter laugh. But Mrs Rucastle does not laugh; she does not even smile.

Rucastle keeps a hungry mastiff that the drunken groom, Toller, lets run free in the gardens at night. Miss Hunter is warned not to go out for fear of the dog. In a drawer she found a coil of hair identical to the tresses shorn from her own head. Then she saw Rucastle coming out of a room that is kept locked. The windows are permanently shuttered. Rucastle claimed that his hobby is photography and she has seen him coming out of his darkroom. She is not convinced.

When the drunken Toller left the keys in the door, Miss Hunter seized the opportunity to enter. Beyond is another door that is barred. She saw a light under the door and heard footsteps from within. Terrified, she ran out – straight into the arms of Mr Rucastle. He sought to comfort her, but overdid it, leaving Miss Hunter more frightened than before. It was then that she wired Holmes.

The Rucastles are going out that night. Toller, Holmes assumes, will be drunk. To give Holmes and Watson free access to the house, all Miss Hunter has to do is lock Toller's wife in the cellar. Holmes has deduced that Miss Hunter has been hired to impersonate someone imprisoned behind the barred door. That person, he believes is her employer's daughter by his first marriage, Alice Rucastle, who is said to have moved to Philadelphia. The man in the road is her friend – or possibly her fiancé – who is thrown off the scent by her untroubled appearance in the window.

That evening Holmes and Watson enter Copper Beeches. They break into the barred room to find the skylight open and the prisoner gone. Rucastle catches them and fetches his mastiff. When the dog attacks him, Watson shoots it with his revolver.

Mrs Toller then explains that Alice had been left money in a will, but left it in Rucastle's hands. When she met a man and seemed likely to marry, Rucastle tried to get her to sign the inheritance over to him. Under pressure, she became ill with brain fever and her hair was cut off. Rucastle then imprisoned her and hired Miss Hunter to unknowingly impersonate Alice.

But Alice's fiancé was not fooled. He climbed up to the roof and rescued her though the skylight. They married the following day. Watson notes, at the end of the story, that Holmes appeared to have been drawn to Miss Hunter but that 'As to Miss Violet Hunter, my friend Holmes, rather to my disappointment, manifested no further interest in her.' She went on to become the headmistress of a girls' school.

Chapter 6

The Memoirs of Sherlock Holmes

The Memoirs of Sherlock Holmes was published on 13 December 1893 by G. Newnes Ltd. It was the third volume of The Strand Library and contained eleven stories published in *Strand* in 1892 and 1893 as further episodes of *The Adventures of Sherlock Holmes*. The first American edition, published by Harper & Brothers in February 1894, also included 'The Adventure of the Cardboard Box', which had been removed from English editions.

Silver Blaze
'Silver Blaze' was first published in *Strand Magazine* on December 1892 with nine illustrations by Sidney Paget.

Holmes and Watson head for the racing stables at King's Pyland on Dartmoor. The trainer John Straker has been found dead and the racehorse named Silver Blaze, the favourite in the forthcoming Wessex Cup, is missing. The owner of the horse, Colonel Ross, and the police officer in charge of the case, Inspector Gregory, have asked for Holmes's help.

A former jockey, Straker lived with his wife and a maidservant two hundred yards from the stables, which were locked at nine o'clock, two of the boys walked to the trainer's house to eat. The third, Ned Hunter stayed behind on guard. When the maid bought him his supper, a dish of curried mutton, they were approached by a stranger who asked Ned about the horses the stable had entered in the Wessex Cup. Ned threatened to set the dog on him but by the time he unleashed the hound, the man was gone.

When Straker heard the story, he appeared anxious. At one in the morning, he went to check on the horses. His wife awoke at seven to find he had not returned. She dressed and went to the stables to find Ned unconscious and Silver Blaze's stall empty. A search of the area found Straker's coat on a bush around a quarter of a mile away and, in a dip below, his body was found. His head had been struck by a blunt instrument and there was a cut on his thigh. In his right hand he held a small knife with blood stains up to the handle; in his left was a silk cravat the maid identified as belonging to the man she had seen the night before.

Ned Hunter, who had recovered, also identified the cravat. Analysis of the curry he had eaten showed it contained powdered opium. Inspector Gregory found and arrested the stranger. A gambling man named Fitzroy Simpson, he admitted to being in the area to learn what he could about Silver Blaze and the second favourite, Desborough, which was being trained by Silas Brown at the nearby Mapleton stables owned by Lord Blackwater. Simpson owned a heavy walking stick that could have been responsible for Straker's head injury but as he had no wound himself, Holmes dismissed his involvement.

Among the dead man's possessions were a small candle, some matches and milliner's bill. Examining the scene of the crime, Holmes finds a burnt match. He then tells Colonel Ross not to remove Silver Blaze's name from the entries to the Wessex Cup. Then Holmes and Watson follow the tracks of the horse across the moor to Mapleton.

Holmes confronts Silas Brown, who admits to having Silver Blaze. He is an experienced 'horse-faker' who has disguised the favourite and was intending to hide him until the race was over. Back in King's Pyland, Holmes announces that he is returning to London.

'So you despair of arresting the murderer of poor Straker?' says Gregory.

As Holmes and Watson head for the station, one of the stable-lads tells Holmes that three sheep in a nearby paddock have gone lame. Holmes tells Gregory this is significant. Gregory asks Holmes if there is any other detail he would like to draw to his attention. Holmes replies: 'To the curious incident of the dog in the night-time.'

'The dog did nothing in the night-time,' says Gregory.

'That was the curious incident,' says Holmes.

Four days later, Holmes and Watson arrive at Winchester to watch the Wessex Cup. In the weighing enclosure, Holmes has the winning horse washed with spirits of wine, revealing Silver Blaze's distinctive markings. But where is the killer of John Straker? asks Ross.

'In my company at the present moment,' says Holmes.

Holmes explains that Silver Blaze had killed Straker. His reasoning is this: Straker got his wife to cook curry to disguise the taste of the opium he would slip in the dish set aside for Ned. When Silver Blaze was taken, the dog did not bark waking the two stable-lads in the loft. So whoever took the horse was known to the dog. Hence it was Straker himself.

The trainer needed money to maintain a mistress who had expensive tastes in clothes as revealed by the milliner's bill in his pocket. His plan was to hobble the horse. This had to be done on the moor in case the horse made a noise. On the way, he picked up the cravat that Simpson had dropped when he ran away. Straker took off his coat and lit a candle, intending to nick the horse's tendon with his knife. Sensing danger Silver Blaze reared up. His hoof struck Straker on the head and the knife gashed his thigh as he fell. As to the lame sheep, Straker had been using them for practice.

The Yellow Face

'The Yellow Face' was first published in *Strand Magazine* in February 1893 with seven illustrations by Sidney Paget.

The story begins with an apology from Watson. Normally, he reports only Holmes's successes. This time he is to relate one of his rare failures.

Holmes is bored and goes for a walk in the park with Watson. When they return, a gentleman has called, but has since departed, leaving behind a pipe. From it, Holmes deduces that he is anxious, he values the pipe highly, he is muscular, left-handed, has excellent teeth, is careless and well-off.

The man returns. Holmes surprises him by addressing him by name, Grant Munro – explaining that his name is written in the lining of his hat. Munro explains that he has been happily married for three years, but now his wife Effie is keeping a secret from him.

She had been married once before in Atlanta and had one child. But then yellow fever struck. She was a widow when Munro married her and they moved to the countryside near Norbury. Recently, she had asked him for £100 (£8,000 at today's prices) and would not explain what she wanted it for.

New tenants moved into a nearby cottage. From an upstairs window, Munro saw a strange face looking at him that was then plucked away. When he knocked on the front door, it was answered by a tall, gaunt woman with a forbidding expression. He asked if he could render any assistance to his new neighbours but was rudely rebuffed.

Then, at three in the morning, he woke to find his wife dressing to go out. When she returned twenty minutes later, she said she had felt faint and stood outside the door to take the air. The following day, he returned early to catch his wife coming out of their new-neighbours' cottage. She refused to explain what she was doing there and he made for the door. She stopped him, saying that if he forced his way into the cottage, everything would be over between them. He said he would only trust her if she did not go there again. She promised. As they left, he turned back to see the strange face looking at him from the upstairs window.

Three days later, when he returned home early, it was clear that she had broken her promise. He rushed to the cottage, burst in but found no one there. However, in the comfortably furnished room upstairs he found a picture of his wife. When confronted, his wife refused to explain and the following day Munro went to see Holmes.

Holmes sends Munro home, telling him to wire if he sees anyone at the cottage. Holmes then tells Watson that blackmail is involved.

Just after tea, a wire arrives and Holmes and Watson take the train to Norbury. They accompany Munro to the cottage but before he can force his way in, his wife appears at the front door. He pushes her aside and upstairs they find a little girl. She is wearing a strange pale mask which Holmes removes to reveal that she is black. Munro's wife reveals that the child is her daughter.

She opens her locket and shows Munro a picture of her first husband, a black man. After he had died, she left the child with a servant in America and when she married Munro, she was afraid to tell him her secret. She used the £100 he gave her to pay for the child and servant to come to England. They were to stay in the nearby cottage so that she could see her daughter and, to prevent local gossip about a black child, the daughter would wear a mask. Then Mrs Munro asks: 'What is to become of us, my child and me?'

Munro's answer is to pick up the little girl and kiss her.

Back at Baker Street, Holmes says that if he ever seems to become over-confident in his powers, Watson should whisper 'Norbury' in his ear.

The Stockbroker's Clerk

'The Stockbroker's Clerk' was first published in *Strand Magazine* in March 1893 with seven illustrations by Sidney Paget.

Holmes arrives at Watson's surgery in Paddington and asks him to go with him to Birmingham. They are to accompany a young stockbroker's clerk named Hall Pycroft. Having been made redundant, Pycroft has been offered a job with another City firm: Mawson & Williams. But before he took up the offer, he was visited by a man named Arthur Pinner, who offered him a job as manager of a new hardware distribution company in

France at a much higher salary. First, though, he would need to meet Pinner's brother, Harry, in Birmingham. Pinner handed over £100 and asked him to sign a letter saying he is willing to take the job. But when Pycroft said that he intended to write to Mawson's to resign his post there, Pinner told him not to, saying he had a bet with the manager there that he would never hear from Pycroft again.

When Pycroft reached Birmingham he went to the address he had been given. There was no company plate on the door but Pinner's brother was there. He told Pycroft to go through the directories of Paris and extract the names and addresses of all hardware sellers. That took all week. Then Pycroft was asked to make a list of furniture shops as they also sell crockery. Pycroft noticed that Pinner's brother had a gold tooth identical to the man he had met in London. He became suspicious and then went to consult Holmes.

In Birmingham, Pycroft introduces Holmes and Watson to his new employer as potential recruits. Harry Pinner then tries to hang himself, but Watson revives him. Holmes concludes that Arthur and Harry Pinner are the same man and that the whole point of the exercise was to obtain Pycroft's signature so that someone pretending to be him could take his place at Mawson's.

From the newspaper, they learn that there has been a robbery at Mawson & Williams. But a forger and cracksman named Beddington had been stopped leaving the building with £100,000 worth of railway bonds. The paper says: 'His brother, who usually works with him, has not appeared in this job as far as can at present be ascertained, although the police are making energetic inquiries as to his whereabouts.' 'We may save the police some little trouble in that direction,' says Holmes.

The *Gloria Scott*

'The *Gloria Scott*' was first published in *Strand Magazine* in April 1893 with seven illustrations by Sidney Paget.

One winter's evening Holmes gives Watson some papers to look over concerning the case of the *Gloria Scott*, including a message that, he says, 'struck Justice of the Peace Trevor dead'. It reads: 'The supply of game for London is going steadily up. Head-keeper Hudson, we believe, has been now told to receive all orders for fly-paper and for preservation of your hen-pheasant's life.'

Watson is puzzled and asks Holmes why, in particular, he should study this case. Holmes replies: 'Because it was the first in which I was ever engaged.'

Victor Trevor had been Holmes's only close friend at college. At the beginning of one long vacation he invited Holmes to stay at his father's place in Donnithorpe, Norfolk. His father was a Justice of the Peace with a reputation for leniency.

After dinner, Mr Trevor asked the young Holmes to deduce something about him. Holmes remarks that he was once intimately associated with someone with the initials 'J.A.'. The old man almost had a heart attack. Earlier Holmes had spotted the letters tattooed in the crook of his elbow.

A sailor arrived at the house. Mr Trevor recognized him as Hudson, whom he had known thirty years before, and told him to help himself to food and drink in the kitchen. An hour later, he was found passed out, completely drunk, on the dining-room sofa.

Holmes returned to his rooms in London to do some experiments in organic chemistry. Seven weeks later he was invited back to Donnithorpe by Victor, who said he needed Holmes's advice and assistance. His father was a death's door and Victor blamed Hudson.

Mr Trevor had taken Hudson on as gardener, then butler, despite his drunken ways. Hudson took advantage of Victor's generosity, and went on shooting trips with his father's boat and best gun. When Victor upbraided Hudson for his insolence, his father forced Victor to apologize. Then, Hudson announced he was moving on to Mr Beddoes in Hampshire.

Shortly after, the fatal letter came. When he read it, Mr Trevor had a stroke and died, saying only that there were papers in the back drawer of a Japanese cabinet. Holmes studied the note and realized that, by taking every third word, you got the message: 'The game is up. Hudson has told all. Fly for your life.'

Victor then handed Holmes the papers from the Japanese cabinet. They told of the voyage of the *Gloria Scott* after leaving Falmouth on 8 October 1855 to her destruction on 6 November. Among the papers was a letter from Trevor to his son, revealing that his real name was James Armitage and he was a criminal who had been sentenced to transportation. He was held below decks on the *Gloria Scott* with Jack Prendergast, a notorious thief whose haul had not been recovered. He had an accomplice on board who bribed the crew and armed the prisoners. They then took over the ship.

Armitage, his friend named Evans and a few others balked at killing their guards in cold blood. Prendergast offered the objectors the small boat and they set off on their own. As they headed towards the African coast, they saw the *Gloria Scott* blow up. They returned to rescue the sole survivor – Hudson. They were picked up the next day by the *Hotspur*, bound for Australia, and they pretended to be the survivors of a passenger ship that had foundered.

In Sydney, Armitage and Evans changed their names. They prospered, returned to England and bought country estates. Then Hudson turned up. At the bottom of the letter, as *post scriptum*, a shaky hand had written: 'Beddoes writes in cipher to say H. has told all. Sweet Lord, have mercy on our souls!'

Afterwards Victor became a tea planter in India, and Hudson and Beddoes disappeared. The police believed Hudson had killed Beddoes and had fled. Holmes thought it was Beddoes who had killed Hudson and made off with as much money as he could lay his hands on.

The Musgrave Ritual

'The Musgrave Ritual' was first published in *Strand Magazine* in May 1893 with six illustrations by Sidney Paget. Conan Doyle had referred to this case earlier in the preamble to 'The Yellow Face' as one of the half-dozen cases where Holmes had make a mistake.

Watson encourages Holmes to tidy up the records of earlier cases that litter their rooms, which prompts Holmes to begin reminiscing about his third case. It involved another fellow student, Reginald Musgrave. Holmes had not seen him for four years when Musgrave arrived at the rooms Holmes then occupied in Montague Street, Bloomsbury.

Musgrave's father had died and he had taken over the family estates in Hurlstone, West Sussex. But something strange was going on there that the police could not unravel. It concerned the family butler of twenty years, Brunton. He was a Don Juan who had become engaged to the housemaid, Rachel Howells, but had then dumped her for Janet Tregellis, the daughter of the head gamekeeper.

One night Musgrave caught Brunton reading a family paper concerning a strange observance dating from the seventeenth century called the Musgrave Ritual. He fired him but Brunton begged to be allowed to stay a month. Musgrave gave him a week's notice, but after two days he disappeared, leaving all his possessions behind.

Then Rachel disappeared too. Her footprints led to the edge of a lake, which was dragged. No trace of her was found, only a linen bag containing some rusty metal and dull-coloured pieces of pebble or glass. Holmes then asked to read the paper concerning the ritual. It was in the form of questions and answers:

'Whose was it?'
'His who is gone.'
'Who shall have it?'
'He who will come.'
'Where was the sun?'
'Over the oak.'
'Where was the shadow?'
'Under the elm.'
'How was it stepped?'
'North by ten and by ten, east by five and by five, south by two and by two, west by one and by one, and so under.'

'What shall we give for it?'
'All that is ours.'
'Why should we give it?'
'For the sake of the trust.'

Holmes deduced the ritual was a set of instructions which, if followed step by step, would lead them to a passageway. Musgrave then pointed out that Holmes had omitted the final instruction 'and so under'. Eventually, in the cellar, they found a large flagstone with an iron ring attached to it.

As Brunton had clearly followed the same trail, Holmes called in the police. With the aid of a burly Sussex constable, Holmes raised the slab. Underneath they found a small chamber containing a rotting chest, which was open and empty. Beside it was Brunton. He had been dead for some days, though there was not a mark on him.

Holmes reasoned that, as it had taken two of them to raise the slab, Brunton had also needed help. He had called on Rachel. When they had lifted the slab, Brunton went down and handed up the contents of the chest. The slab then fell back – whether by accident or design, Holmes could not say – and Brunton suffocated.

Rachel had fled, leaving her faithless lover to his fate. Holmes believes that the relics found in the chest – and later in the lake – were the battered remains of Charles I's crown, the Crown of St Edward thought to have been destroyed by order of Parliament after the Civil War in 1649. It had been hidden under the family home in the hope that Charles II would come and reclaim it, and the Musgrave Ritual had been handed down as the way to find its hiding place.

Rachel Howells had thrown the relics from the chest in the lake, thinking then worthless. She was never heard of again. Holmes thinks she went abroad.

The Reigate Puzzle

'The Reigate Puzzle' was first published in *Strand Magazine* in June 1893 with seven illustrations by Sidney Paget. It has also appeared with the alternative titles 'The Reigate Squire' and 'The Reigate Squires'.

On 14 April 1887, Watson receives a wire telling him that Holmes has fallen ill in Lyons. Watson retrieves Holmes and takes him to recuperate at a house in Reigate, Surrey, belonging to a friend named Colonel Hayter.

Hayter takes a gun to bed with him as a nearby house belonging to 'Old Acton' had been broken into recently and those responsible are still at large. There is another incident after Holmes arrives. At the Cunningham's, William Kirwan the coachman has been shot dead. According to Hayter's butler, he had been killed defending his master's property against a burglar who escaped. Hayter then mentions that Acton and Cunningham had been involved in a lawsuit, with Acton claiming on half of Cunningham's estate.

Inspector Forrester, the investigating officer, asks Holmes to help him with his enquiries. Cunningham says that from a window upstairs he had seen the man who had shot the coachman. His son Alec says he had seen the two men struggling from the back door. After the fatal shot, he says, the assailant instantly fled.

A torn fragment of paper was found in the dead man's hand. The words remaining say: '. . . at quarter to twelve . . . learn what . . . may. . . .' Holmes is suspicious that a burglar would attempt to break into the house while the Cunninghams were still awake and the lights on. He asks Cunningham to post a reward. Holmes has already written it out, but has made a mistake. Cunningham corrects it, inadvertently giving a sample of his handwriting.

Holmes then asks the Cunninghams to show him the house. In Cunningham Senior's bedroom, Holmes knocks over a glass and a bowl of oranges. In the confusion, he slips into Alec Cunningham's room. The Cunninghams follow. Then Watson hears the cry: 'Help! Help! Murder!' and rushes into the next room to find Holmes on the floor with the Cunninghams attacking him. When the Cunninghams are restrained, Holmes tells Forrester to arrest them for killing the coachman. Alec Cunningham draws a gun but Forrester knocks it from his hand. Holmes then flourishes the rest of the coachman's note.

Later Holmes explained that if, as Alec Cunningham said, the assailant had fled instantly, he could not have torn the rest of the note from the dead man's hand. In that case, Alec must have done it himself. He noted that the handwriting on the note was irregular and, upon analysing it, deduced that each alternate word had been written by a different hand. But there was a family resemblance between the two scripts, which led him to believe they belonged to the Cunninghams, father and son.

As there was no black powder on the clothes, William Kirwan had to have been shot from some distance, not by a man struggling with him. Plus, there were no footprints in the muddy ditch the assailant would have had to cross if he had escaped as the Cunninghams had described.

The Cunninghams had broken into Acton's house to retrieve a document that his lawsuit depended on. They sought to divert suspicion by making it look like an ordinary burglary. But Kirwan the coachman had followed them and was now blackmailing them. The note lured him to the house, where they shot him.

Upstairs, Holmes had seen Alec Cunningham's dressing gown hanging behind the door. He knocked over the fruit to give him a chance to examine it and found the remains of the note in the pocket.

The Crooked Man

'The Crooked Man' was first published in *Strand Magazine* in July 1893 with seven illustrations by Sidney Paget.

The story starts shortly after Watson's marriage. Holmes turns up late at night and asks to stay. He wants Watson to accompany him to Aldershot the following day and begins outlining the case he is investigating. Colonel James Barclay of the Royal Munsters has been found dead.

Barclay had risen from the ranks. Commissioned for bravery during the Indian Mutiny, he went on to lead the regiment. Along the way, he married Miss Nancy Devoy, the daughter of a colour-sergeant. They had been happily married for thirty years. Though he was sometimes vicious and vindictive with others, he was never that way towards her. He was also known to get depressed and did not like to be left alone in the dark.

Mrs Barclay was going to a meeting at eight one evening. She took Miss Morrison, a next door neighbour, with her. After dropping off Miss Morrison on the way home, she returned home at a quarter past nine. She then went into the morning room and asked the housemaid to bring her a cup of tea. Colonel Barclay joined her there. When the housemaid arrived with the tea, she heard them rowing. But she knocked and tried the door. It was locked. She called the cook and coachman, who also heard the altercation. While the colonel's remarks were subdued and inaudible, Mrs Barclay was heard to say: 'You coward! What can be done now? Give me back my life. I will never so much as breathe the same air with you again! You coward! You coward!'

Then they heard a cry, a crash and a woman's scream. Unable to break down the door, the coachman ran around to the French window. He found Mrs Barclay unconscious on the couch, while the colonel lay dead in a pool of blood. He went to open the door, but key was, and remained, missing.

When Holmes reaches Aldershot, the housemaid told him she had heard her mistress say the name David twice during the quarrel. Both the servants and the police remarked that there was a look of terror on the colonel's face.

As the key could not have been taken out of the room by either Colonel or Mrs Barclay, Holmes concluded that a third person must have been present. He finds the footprints of a man on the lawn outside and faint ones on the board where he had entered. There are also the footprints of a small animal on the curtains.

Holmes interviews Miss Morrison, who says that on their

way home Mrs Barclay's carriage passed a crooked man, bent over as if deformed. He cried out: 'My God, it's Nancy!'

Mrs Barclay turned white and would have collapsed if the stranger had not caught hold of her. Miss Morrison wanted to call the police but Mrs Barclay then spoke quite civilly to the man.

'I thought you had been dead this thirty years, Henry,' she said. She then asked Miss Morrison to leave them so they could have a private word.

Miss Morrison did as she was asked, but when Mrs Barclay caught up with her, her eyes were blazing and the man was waving his fist as if mad with rage. Mrs Barclay told Miss Morrison to tell no one.

Holmes traces the man. His name is Henry Wood and he is lodging nearby. According to his landlady, he carries a small animal in a box, sometimes speaks in a strange language, and moans and groans as if in pain. He had tried to pay her with what Holmes recognizes as an Indian rupee. Holmes goes to interview him and takes Watson as a witness.

Although it is a warm day, they find Wood crouching over a fire. Fearing that the police might arrest Mrs Barclay for murder, he is prepared to talk. Once, he had been the smartest man in the regiment; he and Barclay had competed for the hand of Nancy but while she loved him, her father wanted her to marry Barclay.

Cut off during the Indian Mutiny, Wood had gone out to summon help, but Barclay betrayed him to the enemy and Wood was tortured and left crippled. After the Rebellion had been put down he continued to live among the natives. Eventually, he earned enough money by entertaining the troops to return home.

After meeting Nancy in the road, his feelings overcame him and he broke into the villa. At the sight of him, the colonel keeled over and cracked his head on the fireplace. Nancy then fainted. He took the key to open the door and call for help, then thought better of it. The animal he had with him was a trained mongoose that he used as part of his act.

Watson wanted know why Mrs Barclay had used the name David. In the Old Testament's Book of Samuel, Holmes points out that King David sent Uriah to his death at the hands of the enemy so that he could marry his wife Bathsheba.

The Resident Patient

'The Resident Patient' was first published in *Strand Magazine* in August 1893 with seven illustrations by Sidney Paget.

After taking an evening stroll, Holmes and Watson return to find a GP's brougham outside 221B. The GP's name is Dr Percy Trevelyan. He had been set up in practice in Brook Street by a man named Blessington, who has a weak heart and lives above the surgery as a resident patient. Some weeks before, Blessington had been seized by a mortal dread, but it passed.

Then, two days ago, Trevelyan received a letter announcing that a Russian nobleman wanted to consult him on catalepsy, as Trevelyan is an expert on the condition. When the nobleman turned up he was accompanied by a young man who introduced himself as the patient's son. During the consultation, the older man suffered a seizure. Trevelyan went to get some amyl nitrate, but when he returned they had gone.

That evening, they reappeared. Trevelyan completed his consultation and after they left Blessington burst in, panicked. Someone, he said, had been in his room. Nothing had been touched, but Blessington was so upset that Trevelyan had come to fetch Holmes.

They return to Brook Street and find Blessington brandishing a pistol at the top of the stairs. He claims to be defending his property – he does not believe in banks and keeps all his money in a cashbox. As Holmes and Watson walk home, Holmes remarks that it is a very interesting case and that he expects to hear more from Brook Street in the morning.

At 7.30 a.m., the brougham appears outside 221B again, carrying a note that says: 'For God's sake come at once. P.T.' Blessington has been found hanged.

Holmes finds cigar butts in Blessington's room and concludes they were from more than one man. He believe's that Blessington was murdered. He then takes away a photograph of Blessington, saying that he will be able to explain everything that afternoon. In the meantime, he suggests that the police arrest Trevelyan's page, who has gone missing.

Three men were involved, says Holmes – the Russian count, his young companion and a third, unidentified man. When they had arrived the previous evening, they had found the door locked and had broken in using a piece of wire, leaving visible scratches. On entering the room, they gagged Blessington and held some sort of trial. Then they hanged him.

After breakfast, Holmes goes out, saying he will back by three. The inspector and the doctor are there to meet him. The inspector says they have captured the page.

'Excellent,' says Holmes, 'and I have got the men.' At least, he knows who they are.

Blessington and the three men who killed him are the Worthingdon bank gang. In 1875, along with a fifth gang member named Cartwright, they had murdered a caretaker and stolen £7,000. Blessington, aka Sutton, had turned informer. Cartwright had been hanged. The others had been sentenced to fifteen years but had recently been released. They had tracked down Blessington and killed him.

They escaped, but Scotland Yard thought they had drowned on an ill-fated steamer off the coast of Portugal. Proceedings against the page broke down due to lack of evidence.

The Greek Interpreter

'The Greek Interpreter' was first published in *Strand Magazine* in September 1893 with eight illustrations by Sidney Paget.

The story begins with Holmes, talking for the first time about his family. He takes Watson to meet his elder brother Mycroft at the Diogenes Club in Pall Mall.

Mycroft introduces Holmes to a Greek interpreter named Melas, who two days earlier had been asked by a fashionably dressed young man named Harold Latimer to come to Kensington to translate for him. He agreed, but their carriage set off in the wrong direction. When Melas mentioned this,

Latimer pulled out a bludgeon. He then pulled up the windows, which had been obscured by paper.

After two hours, the carriage stopped and Melas was taken into a house where he met Latimer's accomplice: a pale, emaciated man wearing a loose dressing gown was brought in. He had sticking plaster across his face and a large pad taped over his mouth. Melas was to ask him questions in Greek and write his replies on a slate.

The first question was: 'Is he prepared to sign the papers?'

'Never,' was the man's reply but, when pressed, he said: 'Only if I see her married in my presence by a Greek priest whom I know.'

Melas was instructed to threaten the man. As the interview continued, Melas added supplementary questions of his own and discovered that the captive's name was Kratides. He was from Athens. A stranger in London, he had been held for three weeks and was being starved.

Then a black-haired woman burst in. Kratides managed to pull the plaster from his face, cried 'Sophy' and rushed to her arms. They were separated and dragged from the room. Melas was given five sovereigns and warned to say nothing. Then the carriage dropped him on Wandsworth Common. From there, he walked to Clapham Junction, and caught the last train to Victoria.

Mycroft has put an advertisement in the newspaper, soliciting information about Kratides and Sophy. Holmes suggests wiring the head of the Athens' police and fires off a number of telegrams.

Watson thinks that Sophy had been abducted by Latimer and that Kratides is her brother. He had come from Greece and was then seized by Latimer and his accomplice, who were trying to force him to signed over the girl's fortune.

Mycroft's ad is answered by a J. Davenport, from Lower Brixton. Davenport says that the Sophy they are seeking lives at The Myrtles, Beckenham. Mycroft wants to go to Brixton to find out more but Sherlock says the brother's life is more

important than the sister's story and they should head for
Beckenham with Inspector Gregson. Watson suggests they take
Melas to translate. But when they reach Pall Mall, Melas has left
with a gentleman in a carriage.

They reach Beckenham just in time to rescue Melas and
Kratides from a room full of noxious smoke. The villains have
flown with the girl. A month later, a newspaper cutting arrives
from Budapest, where two Englishmen were found stabbed to
death. The Hungarian police thought they had quarrelled and
had stabbed each other. Holmes thinks that Sophy had taken
her revenge.

The Naval Treaty
'The Naval Treaty' was first published in *Strand Magazine* in
two parts, first in October 1893 with eight illustrations by
Sidney Paget, and then in November 1893 with seven illustra-
tions by Paget. The story, yet again, takes place shortly after
Watson's marriage.

Watson receives a letter from old school friend Percy Phelps
who has been ill and begs Watson to bring Holmes to see him at
Briarbrae in Woking. They oblige and at Briarbrae they meet
Joseph Harrison, the brother of Phelps's fiancée, Annie.

Phelps had obtained a job at the Foreign Office via his uncle,
Lord Holdhurst, a minister there. Holdhurst entrusted Phelps
with making a copy of a secret naval treaty between Britain and
Italy, which the French or Russians would pay immense sums
to get their hands on.

He was eager to get on with the job as he hoped to catch the
eleven-o'clock train back to Woking with his future brother-in-
law, who had been in town. He felt drowsy and wanted a cup of
coffee. So he rang down to the commissionaire, whose wife
came up and took his order. When the coffee did not appear,
Phelps went down to the main entrance where he found the
commissionaire asleep. Then the bell connected to his office
rang. He ran back up to find the treaty had disappeared.

The thief, he realized, must have used a side door, but a

policeman at the corner of the street had seen no one pass except an old woman – the commissionaire's wife. It was a rainy night but there were no wet or muddy footprints in the office.

Scotland Yard were called in. The commissionaire's wife was suspected, but no sign of the treaty could be found in her home or on her person.

Realizing the consequences of the loss, Phelps came down with brain fever. He was given Harrison's room, where he was tended by Annie during the day and a nurse by night.

Back in London, Holmes interviews Lord Holdhurst, who is puzzled that nearly ten weeks after the treaty went missing, it had not found its way to either the French or Russian embassy. Holmes posits that the thief had a sudden illness.

'An attack of brain fever?' suggests Holdhurst.

Returning to Woking the following day, Holmes and Watson find Phelps recovered. The previous night, he had slept without the nurse in the room. Someone had broken in and had fled when he awoke.

Holmes then stations Annie in the sickroom and announces that he and Watson are taking Phelps to London. However, Holmes only accompanies them to the station, then stays in Woking.

In the morning, Holmes turns up at Baker Street and serves Phelps the naval treaty with his breakfast. The previous night Holmes had returned to Briarbrae and caught Harrison breaking into the sick room. He had opened a small hatch in the floor, and pulled out the treaty. After a struggle, Harrison fled. Scotland Yard were on his trail.

Holmes explained that on the night the treaty went missing, Harrison had come to collect Phelps from his office. Entering through the side door, he found the office empty, so he rang the bell. Then he spotted the treaty on the desk, grabbed it and made off the way he had come. He had not been seen by the policeman and had left no marks on the floor because he had come by cab.

Back at Briarbrae he had hidden the treaty under the floor,

but because Phelps had taken over his room, he could not recover it.

The Final Problem

'The Final Problem' was first published in *Strand Magazine* in December 1893 with nine illustrations by Sidney Paget.

Watson begins the tale with the words: 'It is with a heavy heart that I take up my pen to write these the last words in which I shall ever record the singular gifts by which my friend Mr Sherlock Holmes was distinguished.' However, one imagines that Conan Doyle's heart was not heavy at all. Although he intended this as his last Holmes story, it introduced Holmes' most notorious adversary.

Watson goes on to say that he had intended to stop his reports after 'The Naval Treaty' but letters from Colonel James Moriarty defending the memory of his brother has forced his hand. Previously, Holmes's death had only been reported in the *Journal de Genève* on 6 May 1891, followed by a Reuter's dispatch published in the English papers the following day. Now, for the first time, Watson intends to tell the whole story.

Since Watson's marriage, he and Holmes had grown apart. In 1890, he had only accompanied Holmes on three investigations. Holmes has been in France, but on 24 April 1891, he walked into Watson's consulting room and asked Watson to come to the Continent for a week. He was in pursuit of Professor Moriarty, who he dubbed 'the Napoleon of crime' and the only antagonist he had found to be his intellectual equal.

That morning, Moriarty had visited Holmes at Baker Street to warn him off. Holmes refused to drop his investigation. Later that day, Holmes was almost run down in the street. Then bricks fell from a roof, narrowly missing him. After spending the day at his brother's rooms in Pall Mall, he was attacked by a man with a bludgeon.

Holmes gives Watson detailed instructions of how to shake off any tail. After dashing through the Lowther Arcade in the Strand, he will find a brougham that will take him to Victoria station, where Holmes has booked seats on the Continental Express. Holmes turns up disguised as an aged Italian priest and, as the train pulls out, he spots Moriarty on the platform. In the morning paper there is a report of a fire at their rooms in Baker Street.

Fearing that Moriarty will catch them by the time they reach the continental packet, they get off at Canterbury and make their way to Newhaven. Holmes believes that Moriarty will follow their luggage to Paris, while they make their way unmolested to Switzerland.

Having given Moriarty the slip, Holmes and Watson have a pleasant holiday. Holmes is in reflective mood and says that he has not lived in vain – 'The air of London is the sweeter for my presence. In over a thousand cases I am not aware that I have ever used my powers upon the wrong side.' He is still confident that he will crown his career by the capture or extinction of the most dangerous and capable criminal in Europe.

On 3 May, they stay in the village of Meiringen and visit the Reichenbach Falls. A Swiss lad arrives with a letter from their hotel, asking Watson to return and attend to a woman dying of consumption. Leaving Holmes at the falls, Watson looked back to see a black-garbed figure. At the hotel, Watson discovers that there is no sick woman and that the letter must have been written by an Englishman who had recently arrived.

Watson heads back to the falls to find Holmes's walking stick leaning against the rock. Holmes himself has disappeared. Trained in Holmes's methods, Watson examines the footmarks in the damp soil. Two sets of prints lead to the edge of the falls; none returns. Then he spots Holmes's cigarette case. In it he finds a note from Holmes saying that he is about to meet Moriarty for a 'final discussion'. It is clear that Holmes intends to sacrifice his own life to rid society of his arch-enemy. Watson concludes that the two men have plunged over the falls, locked in each other's arms – 'Any attempt at recovering the bodies was absolutely hopeless . . .'

Chapter 7

The Hound of the Baskervilles and *The Valley of Fear*

Conan Doyle had abandoned writing novels about Sherlock Holmes after *The Sign of the Four* because he thought busy readers wanted short stories they could read in a single sitting. However, his story about a giant hound that terrorized the inhabitants of Dartmoor was clearly going to be a long one. Although Sherlock Holmes had been dead for eight years, Conan Doyle resuscitated him for *The Hound of the Baskervilles* because he needed a strong central character. The events in the book clearly predate Holmes's apparent death at the hands of Professor Moriarty.

The Hound of the Baskervilles

The Hound of the Baskervilles first appeared in *Strand Magazine* and ran in monthly episodes from August 1901 to April 1902, accompanied by sixty illustrations by Sidney Paget. It was first published as a book by George Newnes Ltd on 25 March 1902 with a print run of 25,000. The first American edition of 50,000 copies was published by McClure, Phillips & Co. on 15 April 1902.

The book carried a dedication that read:

MY DEAR ROBINSON: It was your account of a west country legend which first suggested the idea of this little

tale to my mind. For this, and for the help which you gave
me in its evolution, all thanks.

Yours most truly,

A. CONAN DOYLE

The story begins with another chapter headed 'Mr Sherlock
Holmes', where the great detective shows off his observational
powers. A walking stick has been left by a visitor to Baker Street
the night before. Holmes asks Watson what he can deduce from
it, then trumps him in every detail.

The owner of the stick, one James Mortimer, a surgeon,
arrives shortly afterwards with an eighteenth-century manuscript that had been entrusted to his care by Sir Charles
Baskerville, who had died suddenly three months before. It told
of the legend of the 'Hound of the Baskervilles'.

During the other 'Great Rebellion' – the English Civil Wars
– the then lord of Baskerville Manor, Hugo Baskerville, had
abducted a local girl and locked her in his bedroom, intending
to ravish her. But while he was drinking with three friends, she
escaped. Hugo chased after her with a pack of hounds. The girl
fell dead of fear and fatigue. But when his companions caught
up with him, they found Hugo dead too. Standing over his body,
plucking at its throat, was a huge hellhound. When it turned its
blazing eyes and dripping jaws towards them, they shrieked and
fled. One died that night from what he had seen; the other two
remained broken men for the rest of their days. Tales of the
hound have plagued the family ever since, says Mortimer.

Now Sir Charles Baskerville has been found dead in mysterious circumstances. Near his body were the footprints of a gigantic
hound. His nephew and heir, Henry Baskerville, is returning
from Canada to take over Baskerville Hall and Mortimer fears for
his safety. The only other relative that Mortimer has been able to
trace is his younger brother Rodger, the black sheep of the family.
He is said to be the image of Hugo, but is thought to have died of
yellow fever in Central America in 1876.

When Henry Baskerville arrives in London, Holmes and

Watson find he is being trailed by a mysterious, bearded stranger. A note, using letters cut from *The Times*, arrives at his hotel, warning him to stay away from the moors. One of Henry Baskerville's boots is stolen, then another; the first new, the second old. Holmes then announces that he is too busy accompany Henry Baskerville to Devon and sends Dr Watson to be his eyes and ears, insisting that he report back regularly.

When Watson arrives in Devon with Baskerville and Mortimer, they find prison wardens watching the station and the roads for an escaped convict named Selden. At Baskerville Hall, Watson meets the housekeeper, Mrs Barrymore, and her husband, the butler. He has a black beard; hence he is a suspect.

While walking on the moor Watson meets Baskerville's neighbour Jack Stapleton, a naturalist who shows him Grimpen Mire, a huge bog where one false step means 'death to man or beast'. Only the day before he had seen a pony sucked down to its death there. He also points out the ruins of stone huts where prehistoric men lived. Stapleton then makes off after a butterfly.

Soon after, Watson bumps into Stapleton's beautiful and fascinating sister Beryl and notes that the siblings do not look alike. She mistakes him for Sir Henry and warns him to go back to London. When her brother returns, she changes the subject. In conversation, it transpires that Stapleton had once run a school.

Later Sir Henry meets Miss Stapleton and shows a romantic interest. Her brother reacts jealously, then apologizes and invites Sir Henry to dine that Friday.

Watson meets another neighbour, Mr Frankland, a harmless eccentric whose primary pastime is initiating lawsuits. That night Watson sees the butler walk into an empty room with a candle which he holds up to a window that overlooks the moor. Watson tells Sir Henry about this and the two of them surprise Barrymore the following night. He refuses to answer questions, despite the threat of the sack, saying the secret is not his to tell. Mrs Barrymore then reveals that the escaped convict Selden is her brother. Her husband has been signalling with the candle to tell Selden that food and clothing have been left for him.

Sir Henry and Watson go out to try to catch the convict. He gets away but they see another man standing on top of a tor. He also escapes.

When Barrymore discovers that Sir Henry and Watson have been trying to catch Seldon, he gets them to agree to do nothing until he can arrange passage for Seldon to South America. In return, he reveals that on the night he had died, Sir Charles had gone outside to meet a woman. A letter addressed in a woman's hand had come from nearby Coombe Tracey that morning. Later Mrs Barrymore found fragments of the burnt letter in the grate. It was signed with the initials L.L.

Next day, Mortimer tells Watson that the initials could stand for Laura Lyons, Frankland's daughter, who lives in Coombe Tracey. When Watson goes to talk to her, she admits that she wrote to Sir Charles, a well-know philanthropist, asking him to meet her in the hope that he would help finance her divorce, but she did not keep the appointment as she had received help elsewhere.

Barrymore confirms Watson's suspicion that another man is hiding on the moor. Watson is determined to find him. He meets Frankland as he goes out to search. Frankland tells him he has just won two lawsuits and invites Watson in to help him celebrate. Frankland also unwittingly confirms that there is a second man on the moor, and using his roofing telescope to show him the young boy who is supplying him. Watson than follows the boy and finds in one of the prehistoric stone dwellings bedding, utensils and other detritus, showing that someone is living there. Watson waits, revolver at the ready.

The man living there turns out to be Holmes. Following up on Watson's reports that have been forwarded to him, he has discovered that Stapleton is actually married to the woman pretending to be his sister and that he has proposed marriage to Laura Lyons to gain her cooperation. Stapleton, Holmes surmises, is also the man who, disguised with a false beard, followed Sir Henry in London. Their conversation is brought to an end by a terrible scream.

They run towards the sound and find a body. At first they think it is Sir Henry. Then they realize that it is Selden dressed in the baronet's old tweeds provided by the Barrymores. Selden has been chased off a cliff, presumably by the hound. Then Stapleton appears. He can hardly conceal his disappointment and he lets slip that he was expecting Sir Henry.

Back at Baskerville Hall, Holmes examines the family portraits that show Hugo Baskerville's striking likeness to Stapleton. The following day, Holmes and Watson visit Laura Lyons and Holmes reveals that Stapleton is a married man. Mrs Lyons then admits that it was Stapleton who had dictated the letter that would lure Sir Charles to his death. He had later persuaded her not to meet him, saying that he would pay for her divorce himself.

They go to the railway station to meet Inspector Lestrade, whom Holmes had summoned by telegram. That night, Watson, Holmes and Lestrade lie in wait outside the Stapleton's house, where Sir Henry is dining. The fog rolls in. When Sir Henry leaves the house and sets off across the moor, Stapleton lets loose a giant hound which attacks Sir Henry; Holmes empties his revolver into it. The dog is half bloodhound, half mastiff. Phosphorus has been painted around its mouth and eyes.

In the house, they find Beryl Stapleton bound and unconscious. Revived, she tells them of Stapleton's hideout – an island deep in the Grimpen Mire. Mrs Stapleton leads them out there the following day. They find an abandoned tin mine where Stapleton kept the hound and Sir Henry's old boot which had been used to give it his scent. But there are no further signs of the villain and they conclude that he had lost his way in the night and drowned in the bog.

That November, back in Baker Street, Holmes reveals that Stapleton was the son of the wayward Rodger Baskerville who had married a Costa Rican beauty and, after embezzling public money, fled to England where he and his wife started a school in Yorkshire. After an outbreak of consumption, the school failed. Discovering that he was third in line to the Baskerville estate, they moved to Devon, and he supported them with a series of armed robberies. Learning of the legend of the Hound of the Baskervilles, he bought a large dog and hatched his plan. Beryl Stapleton was supposed to ensnare Sir Charles, but she proved obdurate, so Stapleton employed Laura Lyons instead. When Sir Charles was confronted by the beast painted with phosphorus, he fled, eventually dying of fright.

Stapleton travelled to London, where he hoped to kill the newly arrived Sir Henry. When he learned that Sherlock Holmes was on the case, he returned to Dartmoor. The note that had been delivered to Sir Henry's hotel smelt faintly of women's perfume. Beryl Stapleton was the only woman who lived near Baskerville Hall, so Holmes went down to the West Country to keep an eye on the Stapletons with a messenger boy for support. Although matters were complicated by Selden, Holmes had cracked the case by the time Watson found him. But he did not have enough evidence to put before a jury.

On the night the hound attacked Sir Henry, Stapleton's wife had refused to have any further part in the plot, but her abusive husband beat her and tied her up to prevent her from sounding a warning.

The Valley of Fear

The Valley of Fear was first published in the *Strand Magazine* from September 1914 to May 1915 with thirty-one illustrations by Frank Wiles. The first book edition was published by G.H. Doran Co. in New York on 27 February 1915, though the series had not finished in the *Strand*. The first British book edition was published by Smith, Elder & Co. on 3 June 1915. They printed 6,000 copies. By then it was clear that Holmes was indestructible. Nevertheless, the action is again set before the events at the Reichenbach Falls as Professor Moriarty features and no effort was ever made to resurrect him.

Like *At Study in Scarlet*, this story comes in two parts. Part One is called 'The Tragedy of Birlstone':

Sherlock Holmes receives a letter from an informant known by the pseudonym Fred Porlock. He is an associate of Professor Moriarty, 'the controlling mind of the underworld'. The letter is written in code. A second letter from Porlock tells Holmes that Moriarty suspects him so he is unable to send the key.

Holmes deduces that the key to the code is a book, the previous year's almanac, which he uses, and he discovers that John Douglas of Birlstone House is in danger.

Inspector Alec MacDonald of Scotland Yard arrives and is astonished when he sees the deciphered message on the table: Mr Douglas had died at Birlstone Manor House the previous night and MacDonald had come to ask Holmes to go to Birlstone with him.

Holmes and Watson travel down to Birlstone in Sussex with MacDonald. Birlstone House is an old manor with a moat and a drawbridge that John Douglas had restored using the money he had made in the California gold rush.

At the time of the murder, Cecil Barker, an Englishman who had met Douglas in America, was staying in the house as a guest of Douglas and his wife. Baker raised the alarm at 11.45 p.m. when he rang the bell of the small local police station. He raced back to the seventeenth-century house. He was followed by Sergeant Wilson of the Sussex Constabulary, who arrived there a little after twelve. The dead man was found in the study, lying on his back next to a sawn-off shotgun that had blown his head to bits.

Barker said he had been upstairs when he heard a muffled shot. He came rushing down to find Douglas dead. Mrs Douglas came downstairs after him but Mrs Allen, the housekeeper, took her away. Then Ames, the butler, turned up. As the drawbridge was up at the time, Sergeant Wilson concluded that Douglas must have shot himself. Then Barker pointed out a smudge of blood and a boot mark on the windowsill and suggested that the killer had climbed out of the window and waded across the moat. As the drawbridge was raised at six, the killer must have been hiding in the house from then until Douglas had entered the room. Indeed, there were marks of muddy boots in the corner.

Beside the body, the sergeant found a card with the letters V.V. and the number 341 on it. On his arm was a brand – a brown triangle inside a circle. Ames then pointed out that his master's wedding ring was missing but the ring with a gold nugget and a twisted snake that he wore above it was still in place. At three in the morning, Sussex Chief Detective White Mason turned up and contacted Scotland Yard who, in turn, enlisted Holmes.

Holmes noticed that the gun was made by the Pennsylvania Small Arms Company. White Mason ruled out suicide as no man would take off his wedding ring, trample mud into the carpet and smear blood on the windowsill before killing himself. MacDonald agreed.

On the other hand, a murderer had picked the noisiest weapon he could find and after the sound he would have had less than a minute to remove the wedding ring from the dead man's finger and flee. If the murder had been committed by an insider, he would then have to trample mud in the corner and smear blood on the windowsill. Holmes agreed this was impossible. If it had been committed by an outsider, he must have entered the house before six and hidden behind the curtains until after eleven. When Douglas entered the room, he must have brandished the gun, forced Douglas to take off his wedding ring, shot him, dropped the gun and the card, then made his escape through the window. Holmes found this scenario interesting but unconvincing.

He then noticed a small plaster on the neck of the corpse, though Ames said Mr Douglas rarely cut himself shaving. However, he had been restless and excited the day before – perhaps expecting the attack.

MacDonald and White Mason believed that the card, like the brand tattoo, showed that a secret society was at work. When the card was mentioned in the newspapers it would tell other members that vengeance had been taken.

But why the noisy weapons? Why the missing wedding ring? And why no arrest? Since dawn, every constable within forty miles had been on the lookout for a stranger.

Holmes noted that the muddy footprint on the windowsill did not match those in the mud-stained corner. Then Ames pointed out Mr Douglas's dumb-bell. There was only one. The other is missing. Barker then interrupts to say that a bicycle has been found hidden in the bushes.

Holmes discovered that Douglas seldom left the village but the day before the murder he had been shopping in Tunbridge Wells. The following day he had been irritable and had not gone to bed; and that night, Mrs Allen and Ames had been alerted by a violent ringing of the bell. They had reached the bottom of the stairs as Mrs Douglas came down. Barker rushed from the study and begged her to go back, telling her that Jack was dead. After some persuasion she returned upstairs. Ames and Barker said they went back into the study and looked out of the window but could see nothing. They then lowered the drawbridge so that Barker could fetch the police.

Barker said that Douglas had suddenly sold up and left California. He had been a widower at the time. His wife had been of German extraction and had died a year before Barker had met him. Back in England Douglas had rented a quiet place, as if some danger were hanging over his head. He had also led a quiet life in California and, within a week of him leaving, half-a-dozen hard-looking men came asking for him.

Douglas's wife also thought something was hanging over her husband's head: he had often mentioned 'the valley of fear', but never explained what he meant. And once, in a fever, he'd mentioned 'Bodymaster McGinty'. She couldn't say why her husband had taken off his wedding ring.

Holmes asked Ames to bring him Barker's bedroom slippers. The soles were stained with blood and they matched the stain on the windowsill. There was no doubt in Holmes's mind. Barker had made the marks himself.

Watson was in the garden when he heard Mrs Douglas

laughing. She was with Barker, who seems to have said something that amused her. As Watson approached, they resume solemn expressions.

Holmes concluded that Mrs Douglas and Barker were lying. For the assassin to have done all that he had to do before the corpse was discovered, the murder had to have taken place earlier. Neither Ames, who was in the pantry at the other end of the house, nor Mrs Allen, who was a little deaf, heard the gunshots. However, Mrs Allen said she had heard what she took to be a door slamming half-an-hour earlier. That, Holmes believed, was the real time of the murder. But what had Mrs Douglas and Barker been doing in the intervening half-hour? And why was she laughing in the garden with Barker just a few hours later?

MacDonald and White Mason had taken the bicycle to Tunbridge Wells where it was identified as belonging to an American called Hargrave, who had arrived from London with a small valise. He had left his hotel the previous morning wearing a yellow cycling coat and leaving a cycle map of the county on the bedroom table. He had not returned. Those who had seen him said he had a face that was fierce and forbidding. Otherwise, Holmes noted, their descriptions would have matched Douglas himself. The sawn-off shotgun could have fitted inside the valise. It was clear that Hargrave was their man. But where was he now? Holmes promised to solve the case that night with the use of Dr Watson's umbrella. The clue, he said, was the missing dumb-bell.

The following morning Holmes mocked the police's efforts to locate the missing cyclist and told MacDonald and White Mason to stop wasting their time. When asked if he was hiding anything from them, Holmes produced an historic tract and starts reading about the Civil War when Charles I had hidden in Birlstone Manor for several days. Holmes then said he has found the missing dumb-bell.

He then asked MacDonald and White Mason to take the day off, but to return at dusk without fail. In the meantime,

MacDonald is to send a note to Barker, informing him that the police were going to drain the moat.

That evening Holmes, Watson, MacDonald and White Mason gathered by the moat and saw the study window open. A man's head and shoulders appear. He reached into the water and begins to haul something in. Then they rushed into the house to find Barker in the study. Under the writing table, Holmes found a sodden bundle which had been weighted with the missing dumb-bell. The night before Holmes had found the bundle with the crook of Watson's umbrella, then returned it to the moat. He opened the bundle to reveal a pair of American boots and a complete outfit of clothing, including the yellow cycling coat Hargrave had been wearing. It had a long pocket that a sawn-off shotgun would fit into and a label of an outfitter in Vermissa, USA, a coal-mining district. Holmes contended that V.V. stood for Vermissa Valley – the valley of fear.

Despite having been caught with this evidence, Barker refuses to talk. Then Mrs Douglas spoke up, but Holmes said that Mr Douglas should tell his own story.

Mr Douglas then emerged from the wall. He had been hiding in the very place where King Charles had been concealed some two hundred and fifty years before. Holmes explained that when he had found the bundle of clothing he concluded that the dead body was that of the cyclist and what he had to do was find John Douglas. It was clear that his wife and friend were covering up for him until he could make his escape.

There were men, said Douglas, who would give their last dollar to know that he was dead. They had chased him from Chicago to California, then out of America. Three days before he had been in Tunbridge Wells when he had seen his worst enemy. He had returned home on his guard, but when the draw-bridge was up he felt safe and he dressed for bed. When he had gone into study, his enemy was waiting. They fought. The man pulled out his sawn-off shotgun. In the struggle it went off, killing him. The dead man's name was Ted Baldwin.

Barker and Mrs Douglas had come running. He sent his wife

away. Then he came up with a brilliant idea. Baldwin had the same brand on his arm as he did. His hair, height and build matched, but his face was gone. They stripped him of his clothes, tied them in a bundle and dropped it in the moat, weighted with a dumb-bell. Then they dressed him in Douglas's night clothes and put the card in place. They tried to put Douglas's rings on his finger, but his wedding ring would not come off. Then they faked the evidence to make it look as if the assassin had escaped through the window.

Part two is called 'The Scowrers' and is set back in 1875. A man named John McMurdo is on a train to Vermissa Valley. He gets into conversation with a fellow passenger named Scanlan. It transpires that they are both members of the Eminent Order of Freeman. McMurdo is from Lodge 29 in Chicago; Scanlan is from Lodge 341 in Vermissa, whose Bodymaster is Black Jack McGinty. When McMurdo gets to Vermissa, he pretends not to have heard of McGinty. He is told, *sotto voce*, that McGinty has been in the newspapers due to 'the affairs of the Scowrers'. McMurdo says he has read about the Scowrers in Chicago – 'A gang of murderers, are they not?' he says. He is told to be quiet. Men have been beaten to death for less.

He finds lodgings, where he falls for Ettie Shafter, the daughter of his German landlord, who warns him off, saying that he has a rival in Teddy Baldwin, boss of the Scowrers – that is, of the Eminent Order of Freeman. McMurdo says that he is one himself. Shafter says that he wants nothing to do with them and tells McMurdo to leave. Before he moves out, he declares his love to Ettie, who begs him to take her away. He says he can't leave. Baldwin turns up and he and McMurdo fall out. For his own protection, McMurdo goes to the Union House Hotel, the saloon owned by McGinty, to make friends with the Bodymaster.

McGinty pulls a gun, but McMurdo introduces himself as a counterfeiter and a murderer, and reveals that he has a gun in his pocket and has had McGinty covered all the time. McGinty is impressed. Ted Baldwin turns up to complain about

McMurdo. McGinty rules that it is up to the girl to choose between them.

McMurdo is initiated into Lodge 341, and is branded with their mark. Then he is sent to stand guard while Baldwin and others beat up the editor of the local newspaper. But McMurdo steps in to prevent them killing him, pulling a gun and saying that the Bodymaster had not sanctioned murder. The other members of the Lodge begin to suspect McMurdo when he is seen talking with Brother Morris, who warns him about becoming too involved in the murderous goings-on in 'the valley of fear, the valley of death'. But his disciplinary hearing with McGinty is brought to an end when Captain Marvin, formerly of the Chicago Police, now of the Mine Constabulary, bursts in and arrests McMurdo for assault on the editor. Baldwin is already in jail, but the magistrate cannot hold them as the witnesses against them refuse to come forward.

Ettie then finds McMurdo writing a letter. When he will not show it to her she accuses him of writing to another woman – his wife, perhaps. He denies it. She believes him and begs him to flee the valley of fear with her to Philadelphia or New York, or even England or Germany. McMurdo promises that, within a year, they will.

Baldwin improves his position in the lodge by killing a mine owner who had sacked two members of the brotherhood. Then McGinty orders McMurdo to match this by killing Chester Wilcox, chief foreman of the Iron Dike Company, who has seen off two assassination attempts already. McMurdo is to blow up Wilcox's house with his wife and three children inside. He asks for two days to make plans. Then, at night, he puts a bag of blasting powder against the door of the Wilcox house and lights the fuse. The house is destroyed, but Wilcox and his family have already moved out and are in protective custody.

Although his first attempt failed, McMurdo promises the lodge that he will kill Wilcox, even if it takes a year, and receives a vote of confidence. A few weeks later, the papers report that Wilcox has been shot and McMurdo takes the credit.

McMurdo's stock rises and he is seen as McGinty's successor. Then news comes that Pinkerton's have sent an agent named Birdy Edwards to break up the Scowrers. McMurdo goes to Ettie and tells her to get ready to leave. A lodge meeting is called to discuss the intervention of Birdy Edwards.

'Does anyone know him by sight?' asks McGinty.

'Yes,' said McMurdo. 'I do.'

An action committee is formed and McMurdo tells McGinty, Baldwin and five others that Edwards is living under the alias Steve Wilson in nearby Hobson's Patch. McMurdo volunteers to lure him to a house in Vermissa where the others can kill him.

When McGinty and the others turn up at the house, he asks: 'Is Birdy Edwards here?'

'Yes, Birdy Edwards is here,' says McMurdo. 'I am Birdy Edwards.'

They are surrounded by police and arrested at gunpoint.

Early the following morning, Edwards and Ettie leave the valley of fear. Ten days later, they marry in Chicago. The Scowrers are tried and convicted. McGinty and eight others are hanged. But Baldwin escapes the hangman's noose and is imprisoned. He and others swear to avenge themselves on Edwards when they are released in ten years. After several attempts on his life, Edwards leaves Chicago for California, where Ettie dies. He meets Barker and they amass a fortune. When Baldwin and his men are released and track Edwards to California, he changes his name to John Douglas and heads for London, where he marries for a second time and settles in a quiet Sussex village.

At the quarter sessions, Douglas is acquitted of the murder of Ted Baldwin on the grounds of self-defence. But Holmes tells the Douglases that they are still in danger and must leave England immediately. Two months later, news comes that Douglas has been lost overboard from a ship taking the couple to South Africa. Holmes blames Moriarty – he must succeed where others fail. Holmes then says he can beat Moriarty, but he needs time.

Chapter 8

The Return of Sherlock Holmes

The Return of Sherlock Holmes was first published in the US in February 1905 by McClure, Phillips & Co., and illustrated by Charles R. Macauley. The first British edition was published in March 1905 by G. Newnes Ltd as part of the The Strand Library. It comprises thirteen stories published in the *Strand* in 1903 and 1904.

The Adventure of the Empty House

'The Adventure of the Empty House' was first published in *Collier's Weekly* in the US in September 1903 with seven illustrations by Frederic Dorr Steele, then in *Strand Magazine* in the UK in October 1903 with seven illustrations by Sidney Paget. Although *The Hound of the Baskervilles* had brought Holmes back to life the year before, Conan Doyle still had to rescue him from Reichenbach Falls.

In the spring of 1894, all London was talking about the death of the Honourable Ronald Adair. Many details came out at the time but now, nearly ten years later, Watson can tell the whole story. He would have done so sooner but he had only been released from his vow of silence on the third of the previous month.

On the evening of 30 March 1894, Adair had been playing whist at the Bagatelle club where, some weeks earlier, he and his partner Colonel Sebastian Moran had won £420 (£35,500 at today's prices). At 10 p.m. he returned to his home in Park

Lane. When his mother and sister return later at 11.20, they found the door to the sitting room on the second floor locked. When the door was forced, Adair is found dead. He has been shot in the head with a revolver bullet. There was money on the table and he appeared to have been calculating his losses or winnings at cards.

The window was open, but at the bottom of a twenty-foot (six-metre) drop was a flower bed. This was undisturbed. No one could have got close enough to have shot Adair with a revolver. And no shot was heard. Adair had no known enemy and nothing appeared to have been taken.

Despite the apparent death of Sherlock Holmes, Watson has lost interest in crime and decides to visit Park Lane. In the crowd outside Adair's house he bumps into an elderly, deformed man. Then when he returns to his home in Kensington, the man turns up, introducing himself as the local bookseller. He distracts Watson for a second and throws off his disguise. Watson turns back to find Holmes standing before him.

He explains that he has some knowledge of '*baristu*' – which he says is 'the Japanese system of wrestling' – and, while grappling with Moriarty, managed to throw him over the falls. But Moriarty was not the only one who wanted rid of him, so he decided to fake his own death.

In 'The Final Bow', which Holmes had read, it said that the rock wall beside the path was sheer. It was not. Holmes had scaled it. He then escaped from one of Moriarty's accomplices and made his way to Florence. With money sent by Mycroft, he had travelled widely, only to return to London to investigate the 'Park Lane Mystery'. Mycroft had kept his rooms at 221B Baker Street and Holmes had returned to Mrs Hudson's establishment. He and Watson have much to discuss, but first they have to tackle 'the notable adventure of the empty house'.

That night Holmes and Watson, revolver in pocket, set out in a hansom. It is just like old times. But instead of heading for Baker Street, Holmes stops the cab at the corner of Cavendish Square. From there, they take the back alleys to Blandford

Street. Entering an empty house, they find themselves in a darkened room opposite their old quarters. On the blind, Watson could see a perfect silhouette of Holmes, provided by a wax bust which is moved, regularly, by Mrs Hudson for a more lifelike effect.

His rooms are being watched by accomplices of Moriarty, who Holmes spotted on his return that morning. The man Holmes escaped from at Reichenbach Falls is still out to kill him. When they heard someone enter the house, Holmes and Watson waited in silence while the intruder sets up a strange gun. There was a loud 'whiz' and a tinkle of glass. Then Holmes springs on the gunman. Watson hits him on the head with the butt of his pistol, Holmes blows a whistle and Lestrade comes running.

Their prisoner is Colonel Sebastian Moran, who Holmes had not seen since the Reichenbach Falls. Holmes explains that Adair had discovered that Moran had been cheating and threatened to ruin him. The strange weapon is a custom-made airgun that could fire a revolver bullet accurately over a long distance.

The Adventure of the Norwood Builder

'The Adventure of the Norwood Builder' was first published in *Collier's Weekly* in October 1903 with seven illustrations by Frederic Dorr Steele, then in *Strand* in November 1903 with seven illustrations by Sidney Paget.

Watson has sold his practice and returned to live in Baker Street. One morning a young man named John Hector McFarlane arrives in a great agitation. He expects to be arrested for the murder of Mr Jonas Oldacre of Lower Norwood. Watson reads the details from the *Daily Telegraph*. Oldacre was a retired builder who lived in Deep Dene House, which had a small wood yard at the back of it. At twelve o'clock the previous night, the yard had caught fire. When Oldacre did not appear, it was found that his bed had not been slept in. His safe was open. Documents and traces of blood were found, along with a walking stick with blood on its handle.

The *Telegraph* also reported that Oldacre had had a late

visitor in his bedroom, a young solicitor named John Hector McFarlane. A murder warrant had been issued. The French windows of Oldacre's ground-floor bedroom had been found open and there were signs that a bulky object had been dragged across to the woodpile. Charred remains had been found among the ashes. The police believed that the victim was clubbed to death in his bedroom, his papers rifled and his dead body dragged across to the wood-stack where it had been burned.

McFarlane explains that he lives in Blackheath. He had late meeting with Oldacre and stayed at a hotel in Norwood. He knew nothing of the murder until he read about it in paper on the train. Lestrade arrives and arrests McFarlane, but Holmes begs for half-an-hour to hear his side of the story.

McFarlane explains that he knew little of Oldacre, who had been a friend of his parents years before but who had walked into McFarlane's office in the City with some notes and asked for them to be drawn up as a will, which was when McFarlane learned that he would be Oldacre's sole beneficiary. The will was drawn up, signed and witnessed. Oldacre asked McFarlane to come to Norwood for supper to see various leases, title deeds, mortgages and certificates but on the promise that he wouldn't tell his parents.

He reached Oldacre's house a 9.30 p.m. and was admitted by the housekeeper. After supper, Oldacre took him into the bedroom where the safe was and took out some papers, which they examined together. When they finished, between eleven and twelve, he left via the French windows to avoid disturbing the housekeeper. He could not find his walking stick, which had been left with his hat in the hall and which Oldacre said he would keep until he returned.

Lestrade asks Holmes whether he has any more questions.

'Not until I have been to Blackheath.'

'You mean to Norwood,' says Lestrade.

'Oh, yes, no doubt that is what I must have meant,' says Holmes with an enigmatic smile.

Holmes points out that the notes Oldacre's will was based on were written on a train and it was most unlikely that, if McFarlane had killed Oldacre and gone to such lengths to conceal his body, he would have left his walking stick behind. Holmes then heads for Blackheath, where he discovers that McFarlane's mother had once been engaged to Oldacre, but broke it off when she discovered that he was a vicious brute: before she married McFarlane's father, Oldacre defaced and mutilated her with a knife.

Holmes then headed to Norwood, where, in the charred remains in the wood yard, he finds some trouser buttons with the name of Oldacre's tailor on them. In Oldacre's bedroom, Holmes found the footmarks of the two men, no one else's. Among the papers, he finds nothing valuable, though there were references to a deed that is not present. This is the only ray of sunlight, for who would steal a thing if they were about to inherit it?

Finally, Holmes speaks to the housekeeper, Mrs Lexington. She confirms the details as far as he knows them, but he is convinced she is holding something back.

Holmes had noticed from Oldacre's bank book that he had been making large payments to a Mr Cornelius for the last year. But there is no indication who this is and Holmes despairs that the case will end with Lestrade hanging his client.

Nevertheless, Holmes regains confidence the next morning, after a note arrives from Lestrade that reads: 'Important fresh evidence to hand. McFarlane's guilt definitely established. Advise you to abandon case.' After all, Holmes points out, fresh evidence is a two-edged sword.

Holmes travels back to Norwood with Watson. Lestrade triumphantly takes them into the hall where there is blood on the wall, left, Lestrade says, when McFarlane went to get his hat. But Holmes notices that it is more than a blood stain: it is a thumbprint.

Somehow Holmes had anticipated this and has with him a wax impression of McFarlane's thumb. The two are identical. Lestrade is cock-a-hoop and Holmes concedes that this appears to be damning evidence, though it was not a natural action to press your thumb against the wall when you take your hat from a peg.

It transpires that Mrs Lexington had drawn a constable's attention to it, and Holmes knew that it had not been there when he had visited the day before. Interrupting Lestrade, who is writing his report, Holmes remarks that this is premature as there is an important witness that he has not seen. Lestrade asks Holmes to produce him.

To do so, straw had to be carried upstairs. Holmes asks Watson to set fire to it, and while they all shout 'fire!'. Suddenly a door opens in what appeared to be a solid wall. Out comes Oldacre. He had been swindling his creditors by making payments to the fictitious Mr Cornelius: himself under another name. He then intended to disappear but it struck him that he could frame McFarlane and revenge himself on his mother. The blood from a dead dog or a couple of rabbits was sprinkled around the crime scene which were then burned in the wood yard along with a pair of his old trousers to simulate a corpse. The damning thumbprint had come from an impression in wax McFarlane had made when they had been sealing documents.

There is one thing wrong here: Francis Galton, who introduced fingerprinting to Scotland Yard in 1901, wrote to Conan Doyle saying that 'wax and blood do not take kindly to one another, neither is it possible to get good impressions from a hard engraved material upon a hard uneven surface'.

The Adventure of the Dancing Men
'The Adventure of the Dancing Men' was first published in *Collier's Weekly* in December 1903 with six illustrations by Frederic Dorr Steele, then in *Strand* in December 1903 with seven illustrations by Sidney Paget.

A letter has arrived from a Mr Hilton Cubitt of Riding Thorpe Manor in Norfolk and depicts a series of stick men who appear to be dancing. In due course, Cubitt arrives at

Baker Street. He says these childish figures terrified his American wife Elsie when they appeared scrawled in chalk around their manor. They have been married for a year; however, she refuses to talk about the 'very disagreeable associations' she has had in her past life and when a letter arrives from the US she turns deathly white and throws it in the fire.

Holmes tells Cubitt to return to Norfolk and make exact copies of any further hieroglyphs that appear. A few days later, Cubitt returns with more dancing men. His wife is now sick with worry and suggests they take a trip, but Cubitt refuses to be driven out of his own home.

Growing gravely concerned by the accumulating messages, Holmes and Watson head for Norfolk but by the time they arrive, Cubitt and his wife have been shot. He is dead; she is critically wounded. Inspector Martin of the Norfolk Constabulary believes that Elsie shot her husband before turning the gun on herself.

When they arrive at Riding Thorpe Manor, the servants tell them that the window of the room where the couple were found was shut and fastened on the inside. The doors, too, were fastened on the inside. No one could have escaped.

While Cubitt had been his night clothes, his wife was fully dressed. There were powder burns on Mrs Cubitt, but none on her husband. Then Holmes discovers a third bullet hole.

When they were woken by the gunshots, the servants had smelled gunpowder upstairs and from this Holmes deduces that the window and inner door must have been open at the time of the incident. Then, in Elsie's handbag, Holmes finds twenty £50 notes.

In the flowerbed outside the window, Holmes finds the footmarks of two large masculine feet and a cartridge case. Next, he draws a series of dancing men on a piece of paper, which he sends to Mr Abe Slaney at nearby Elrige's Farm.

Holmes explains that he has broken the code: the dancing men represent letters. Knowing that E is the most common letter in the English language and taking an educated guess as to words that might appear, he can decipher the messages. One of them announces that Abe Slaney is here. As Abe is an American diminutive, Holmes cabled the New York Police Bureau, who replied, telling him that Slaney is the most dangerous crook in Chicago.

A second message says that he is 'at Elrige's'. A third tells Elsie to prepared to meet her God. Pretending to be Elsie, Holmes has used the same code to summon Slaney. When he arrives, they arrest him.

In Chicago, Slaney had been in a gang run by Elsie's father, who had invented the code. They had been engaged but she sought freedom from a life of crime and fled to England, where she married. Slaney had come after her. When she refused to go away with him, he threatened her. He came to the house at three in the morning when her husband was asleep. She tried to bribe him to go away but he tried to pull her out of the window. Then her husband arrived with a revolver and Elsie sank to the ground. In the ensuing gun battle, Slaney and Cubitt pulled the trigger at the same time. Slaney fled and heard the window slam behind him. A stray shot had cut through the sash.

Slaney was convicted at Norwich assizes; Mrs Cubitt made a full recovery.

The Adventure of the Solitary Cyclist

'The Adventure of the Solitary Cyclist' was first published in *Collier's Weekly* in December 1903 with five illustrations by Frederic Dorr Steele, then in the *Strand* in January 1904 with seven illustrations by Sidney Paget.

According to Watson's notebook, Miss Violet Smith visited Baker Street on 23 April 1895. Holmes spots immediately that she is a cyclist and a musician, and that she lives in the country. Four months ago, two men named Carruthers and Woodley arrived in Farnham, Surrey, where Violet lives with her mother. They claimed to be friends of Violet's uncle who had recently died in poverty in South Africa.

The older man, Carruthers, was agreeable, but Woodley was odious – not the sort of person her fiancé Cyril Morton would have wished her to know. Carruthers, a widower, offered Violet £100 a year to give his ten-year-old daughter music lessons at Chiltern Grange, some six miles from Farnham and where he lived with a elderly housekeeper named Mrs Dixon. Violet stayed there during the week and returned to Farnham at the weekends.

Everything went well at first, but then Woodley came to stay. He boasted of his wealth and said if she married him she would have the finest diamonds in London. One evening, he grabbed her and tried to kiss her. Carruthers burst in and knocked him down. She has not seen Woodley since.

Every Saturday she cycled from Chiltern Grange to catch the 12.22 home. On the way, there was a lonely stretch of road with Charlington Heath on one side and the woods around Charlington Hall on the other. Two weeks ago, she had been followed by a bearded man on a bicycle, but he had disappeared by the time she reached the station. Returning on Monday, she saw the same man on the same stretch of road. The following Saturday, he followed her again. When she slowed down, he slowed down. When she stopped, he stopped. So she pedalled quickly around a corner, stopped and waited, but he did not appear. Looking back round the corner, he was nowhere to be seen, though there were no side turnings for over a mile. Holmes concludes that he went into Charlington Hall.

Watson travels to Farnham but discovers little. Holmes then receives a letter from Violet saying that Carruthers has proposed to her. She has, of course, turned him down. Holmes then travels to Farnham, drops into a local pub and discovers that the resident of Charlington Hall is a former priest named Williamson and that Woodley also stays there.

Another letter from Violet informs Holmes that she is quitting her job because of the reappearance of Woodley. That Saturday, Holmes and Watson travel to see her. They see the dog-cart carrying Violet to the station in the distance but they have mistimed it. She will have passed Charlington Hall before they get there. And by the time the dog-cart reaches them, it is empty.

They grab the dog-cart, turn it around and head off back down the road. Coming the other way is the bearded cyclist. They demand to know where Violet is. He wants to know the same thing.

'They've got her, that hell-hound Woodley and the black-guard parson,' he cries and they set off to save her. On the way, they find the dog-cart's driver unconscious in a bush. They follow tracks into the grounds of the hall, where they find a wedding ceremony underway.

Woodley, the groom, tells Carruthers to take his off beard and introduces Violet as his wife.

'No, she's your widow,' says Carruthers, brandishing a revolver. He shoots Woodley.

Holmes and Watson disarm Carruthers and send for the police.

Carruthers explains that he loves Violet and had donned a disguise to follow her past the house where he knew Woodley was staying. He did not tell her of the danger because she would have left him.

Violet's uncle had not died in poverty in South Africa; he had been wealthy. Carruthers and Woodley had conspired to cheat her out of her inheritance through marriage. When she rejected Woodley, Carruthers proposed. Meanwhile Woodley had picked up the rogue priest and decided to abduct her and marry her by force.

The police arrive to arrest the conspirators. Holmes considers that Carruthers has made amends for his share in the plot and gives him his card in case he is needed to give evidence on Carruthers's behalf at his trial. Violet inherits her uncle's fortune and marries her true love.

The Adventure of the Priory School

'The Adventure of the Priory School' was first published in *Collier's Weekly* in January 1904 with six illustrations by Frederic Dorr Steele, then in *Strand Magazine* in February 1904 with nine illustrations by Sidney Paget.

Holmes receives a visit from Thorneycroft Huxtable, the headmaster of a prep school in northern England. One of his pupils, ten-year-old Lord Saltire, the only son of the Duke of Holdernesse, has been kidnapped. The duke has offered £5,000 to anyone who can tell him where his son is and another £1,000 if they can give the names of the men who have taken him. Although the boy missed his mother, who had gone to live in the south of France, he seemed happy enough at school. Heidegger, the German master, is also missing along with his bicycle, though he has left behind some of his clothes.

Holmes and Watson accompany Huxtable back to the school. As the boy would have been seen if he had left by the road, he must have gone across the moor, where his school cap is found. Holmes and Watson also find bicycle tracks, but they are not from Heidegger's bike and are soon obliterated by the tracks of cows.

Then they do find the tracks of Heidegger's bicycle, along with the bicycle – and Heidegger, beaten to death. As he is partially dressed, Holmes concludes that Heidegger had seen the boy leaving and had chased after him. As he did not catch him, the boy must have been on the other bike and must have left the school voluntarily because he was fully dressed. He also must have had an adult with him because he wouldn't have been strong enough himself to beat Heidegger's head in. But there were no footprints near Heidegger's corpse, only the tracks of cows – though they had seen no cattle.

On the other side of the moor, Holmes and Watson reach an inn and meet the landlord Reuben Hayes. Holmes offers him a sovereign for the use of a bicycle so that he can go to nearby Holdernesse Hall and take the duke news of his lost son. Hayes says that he has no wish to help the duke as he was his head coachman once and had been sacked. What's more, he does not have a bicycle. But for a sovereign he is willing to rent them two horses. Holmes notices that the horses have old shoes, held on with new nails.

On the road, they hide from an oncoming cyclist they recognize as the duke's secretary James Wilder. They follow him back to the inn, where they see a man in a trap make off in the direction of Chesterfield. It is not Wilder, as he is at the inn door. Another man arrives. Holmes then climbs on Watson's shoulders to peer through an upstairs window.

The following morning Holmes goes to Holdernesse Hall, asks the duke for £6,000 and reveals that his son is being held at the inn. When the duke asks who took him, Holmes replies: 'I accuse you.'

The duke offers him another £6,000 to keep quiet about the matter; however, there is the matter of the death of Heidegger. The duke insists that Wilder was not responsible; Reuben Hayes was. Holmes had already sent a telegram and has had Hayes arrested in Chesterfield. However, having organized the kidnapping, Wilder was responsible in law.

The duke then reveals that Wilder is his illegitimate son. He was jealous of Lord Saltire, who the duke sent off to school for his own safety. Wilder then fell in with Hayes. They sent a note to the boy, saying his mother was waiting on the moor. He was met by Wilder, who took him to the inn.

What had wrecked the scheme was Holmes's discovery of Heidegger's body. Wilder was distraught and made a full confession to the duke, but he also warned Hayes, who tried to escape.

Holmes then upbraids the duke for leaving his son at the inn while Hayes made his escape. Servants are then sent to fetch Lord Saltire. Hayes is certain to hang, while Lord Holdernesse sends Wilder to seek his fortune in Australia. Holmes is still puzzled by the cattle tracks on the moor, believing that Hayes had shod his horses with shoes that left the tracks of cows. The duke showed him just such shoes, explaining that the marauding barons of Holdernesse had used them in the Middle Ages to throw off pursuers.

The Adventure of Black Peter

'The Adventure of Black Peter' was first published in *Collier's Weekly* in February 1904 with six illustrations by Frederic Dorr Steele, then in *Strand Magazine* in March 1904 with seven illustrations by Sidney Paget.

In 1895, Holmes arrives at breakfast one day carrying a harpoon. He has been at the local butchers stabbing a pig's carcass with it because he thought it would have a bearing on the 'mystery of Woodman's Lee'. Inspector Stanley Hopkins turns up to discuss the case. It concerns the death of Peter Carey, the captain of a whaling ship who had retired to Woodman's Lee, near Forest Row in Sussex. The man was a violent drunkard and was known at sea as 'Black Peter'. He spent his time at home in a wooden outhouse he called the 'cabin' where no one else was allowed. However, two days before his death a witness had seen the silhouette of a figure on a cabin blind that was not the captain.

The following day, Carey had been in one of his blackest moods. At two the next morning, his daughter heard a yell, which was common when Carey had been drinking. At seven, the maid noticed that the cabin door was open. It was only at midday that anyone dared look in. Inspector Hopkins was called. He found the place buzzing with flies. It was decked out like a captain's cabin with a picture of his old whaler, *Sea Unicorn* and a shelf of log books. Carey was pinned on the wall by a harpoon pulled from a rack, quite dead.

There was a bottle of rum and two glasses on the table, along with a sealskin pouch containing strong seamen's tobacco with the initial's P.C. on it. But no pipe was found. On the floor lay an old notebook with the initials J.H.N. on it. The second page had C.P.R. followed by several pages of numbers. Then came the names of several places in Latin America, again with figures after them. Holmes suggests that C.P.R. stands for Canadian Pacific Railway. The notebook had been found on top of a bloodstain near the door, indicating that it had been dropped after murder. A knife, still in its sheath, lay at the dead man's feet. Intrigued, Holmes agrees to visit the scene of the crime.

When they arrive at the cabin, Hopkins notices that someone had tried to force the lock and was sure that marks on it had not been there the day before. Holmes concludes that whomever had tried to break in would try again. That night they wait in the bushes at the back of the hut. At half past two they hear some-one enter. A match is struck. Through the window they see a young man examining one of the logs and, when he turns to leave, Hopkins nabs him.

The intruder's name in John Hopley Neligan. He is the son of a partner in a failed West Country bank. It was said that his father stole all the securities and fled. In fact, his son insists he was intending to sell them and pay off his creditors. He left a list with John's mother and headed for Norway in a small yacht. Both his father and the yacht disappeared. Years later they heard that the securities were being traded on the London market. The original seller had been Peter Carey. He had been at sea at the same time his father had vanished.

Neligan came to Sussex to see Carey, only to find that he had been killed. He returned to look for clues about the fate of his father in Carey's logs. However, he cannot account for the note-book bearing his initials found at the crime scene, saying it had been lost. Hopkins arrests him.

Holmes returns to Baker Street and sends two telegrams: One is to a Shipping Agent on the Radcliff Highway in the East End asking him to send three men at ten the following morning, signed 'Basil'; the other invites Hopkins for breakfast at 9.30 a.m. He then proceeds to pick holes in his case. In the notebook, there were ticks against some of the securities, indi-cating that those were the ones traced on the London market. The majority had no tick. Where were they? What's more, it was physically impossible for a slight young man to thrust a harpoon through a body. Holmes had tried it with a pig's carcass. There was also the unidentified man whose silhouette had been seen on the blind, and the one who had drunk rum with Carey.

'But where is this man?' asks Hopkins.

'I rather fancy that he is on the stairs,' says Holmes and tells Watson to put his revolver where he can reach it.

Mrs Hudson announces that three men have arrived, asking for Captain Basil. Holmes tells her to send them in one at a time. He asks the first his name, then gives him a half-sovereign and sends him to wait in the next room. The second is despatched the same way. The third says his name is Patrick Cairns. He is a harpooner. Holmes asks him to sign a piece of paper, then handcuffs him. Even so, they have to struggle to restrain him.

Cairns claims that Carey pulled a knife and that he killed him in self-defence. Holmes explains that the rum, the strength of the assailant, the skilled use of the harpoon and the seal-skin tobacco pouch all pointed to the killer being a sailor. The pouch did not belong to Peter Carey as no pipe was found, so he was looking for someone else with the initials 'P.C.'.

Telegrams to the *Sea Unicorn*'s home port, Dundee, yield names of the crew in 1883. The harpooner was Patrick Cairns. Figuring that a man who would want to leave the country for some time would be looking for a ship in London's East End, Holmes invented an Arctic expedition under Captain Basil, which bore fruit.

The Adventure of Charles Augustus Milverton

'The Adventure of Charles Augustus Milverton' was first published in *Collier's Weekly* in March 1904 with six illustrations by Frederic Dorr Steele, then in *Strand Magazine* in April 1904 with seven illustrations by Sidney Paget.

Holmes has been hired by Lady Eva Blackwell to deal with the blackmailer Charles Augustus Milverton, who held compromising letters of hers. Milverton arrives at Baker Street and demands £7,000 (£560,000 at today's prices), saying that otherwise he will scupper Lady Eva's forthcoming wedding. Holmes offers £2,000, which is all Lady Eva can pay, but Milverton will not budge. Holmes and Watson attempt to detain him, but Milverton is armed.

For the next few days, Holmes leaves home disguised as a workman. Then he announces that he is to get married – to Milverton's housemaid, from whom he hopes to garner information. He is also planning to burgle Milverton's house that night. Watson insists on going along.

When they break into Milverton's study, Holmes opens the safe and retrieves a package. But as he closes the safe, Milverton comes in and Holmes and Watson dart behind a curtain. A woman in a veil turns up. She purports to be a maidservant selling letters that would compromise her mistress. Then she drops her veil, revealing herself to be one of his victims: her husband has died heartbroken thanks to Milverton. She pulls a gun and shoots him, then grinds her foot in his face.

Instinctively, Watson tries to spring out to stop her, but Holmes restrains him. Then Watson realizes 'that it was no affair of ours; that justice had overtaken a villain . . .' The woman runs away. Milverton's household is roused by the shots, but Holmes quickly returns to the safe and dumps the rest of the contents in the fire. Then they make their escape.

As they are scaling the garden wall, Watson feels a hand on his leg. He kicks at his pursuer to get free.

The following morning, Inspector Lestrade calls to ask for Holmes's help in investigating Milverton's murder.

'It is probable that the criminals were men of good position, whose sole object was to prevent social exposure,' says Lestrade.

'Criminals?' queries Holmes.

Two burglars had been seen escaping over the garden wall. One was 'a middle-sized, strongly built, man – square jaw, thick neck, moustache . . .'.

'It might be a description of Watson!' scoffs Holmes.

But Holmes refuses to help Lestrade, saying: 'My sympathies are with the criminals rather than the victim.'

Later, Holmes takes Watson to see a display of photographs of celebrities in a shop window. Among them is the picture of a woman in court dress. Holmes puts a finger to his lips as they turn away.

The Adventure of the Six Napoleons

'The Adventure of the Six Napoleons' was first published in *Collier's Weekly* in April 1904 with six illustrations by Frederic Dorr Steele, then in *Strand Magazine* in May 1904 with seven illustrations by Sidney Paget.

Inspector Lestrade has a case that involves a man who goes around smashing plaster busts of Napoleon. One was smashed in Morse Hudson's shop in Kennington Road. A similar bust, sold by Hudson to a Dr Barnicot, was also smashed after the doctor's house was burgled. Nothing was taken. A second bust in his surgery was smashed as well. Lestrade believes this is the work of a madman with an unreasoned hatred of Napoleon.

The following morning, a telegram comes from Lestrade, summoning Holmes to a house in Kensington. A burglar had broken in and stolen a plaster bust of Napoleon. On the doorstep, there was a dead man with his throat cut. In his pocket, he had a shilling map of London and the photograph of an ape-like man. The shattered bust of Napoleon was found a few hundred yards away at a spot where, Holmes points out, there is a street lamp.

Holmes goes to shop where the first bust was broken. The owner, Morse Hudson, recognizes the man in the picture as Beppo, an Italian immigrant who had quit his job in shop a few days earlier. Holmes next goes to the manufacturers, Gelder & Co., where he is told that the busts were part of a batch of six. The manager also recognizes Beppo's picture. He had once worked there but the year before had been imprisoned for a stabbing, though he was probably out of jail by now.

That evening, Lestrade brings news that the dead man has been identified as Pietro Venucci, a Mafioso. Lestrade believes that Venucci was sent to kill Beppo, but wound up dead himself.

According to the manufacturers, three busts had gone to Morse Hudson; the other three to Harding Brothers, where Holmes obtains the addresses of the purchasers of the last two busts – one in Chiswick, one in Reading. That night they stake out the house in Chiswick. Beppo arrives and breaks in. He emerges with a bust, then smashes it. While Lestrade arrests Beppo, Holmes examines the fragments.

As Beppo will not talk, Holmes buys the last bust from the owner in Reading, paying £10 for what he had paid fifteen shillings (75p). Holmes then smashes the bust and finds inside the black pearl of the Borgias. It had been stolen the previous year and suspicion had fallen on a maid named Lucretia Venucci – the dead man's sister.

The pearl had gone missing two days before Beppo was arrested. He had the pearl and, when the police came to arrest him at Gelder & Co.'s factory, he hid it by dropping it in the mould where six plaster casts of Napoleon were drying. When he was released, he tracked down the busts and smashed them one after another in an effort to find the pearl.

The Adventure of the Three Students

'The Adventure of the Three Students' was first published in *Strand Magazine* in June 1904 with seven illustrations by Sidney Paget, then in *Collier's Weekly* in September 1904 with nine illustrations by Frederic Dorr Steele.

In 1895, Holmes and Watson spent some weeks in one of England's great university towns where Hilton Soames, a tutor at St Luke's College, solicits Holmes's help. Soames left the proofs of examination papers on his desk while he took tea in a friend's room. When he returned, he found a key in his door. His servant Bannister had carelessly left it there. Inside he found the proofs had been disturbed. Asked about this, Bannister nearly fainted and had to be helped to a chair while Soames searched the room. On the table by the window Soames spotted some pencil shavings and a broken lead, and concluded that someone had been copying the paper in a hurry and had broken the tip of their pencil. The leather top of his writing table had a cut in it and on it he found a small pyramid of black clay speckled with sawdust.

Soames's sitting room had a latticed window, but Holmes had to stand on tiptoe to see in. Behind a curtain in Soames's bedroom, Holmes finds another small pyramid of putty-like clay, exactly like the one Soames had found on the table in the study. Plainly, the culprit hid there when Soames had returned unexpectedly.

The students sitting the exam, which is for a valuable scholarship, live above the tutor's rooms. Daulat Ras, an Indian student who had visited the tutor's room since the proofs arrived, is on the second floor. Above him is Miles McLaren, who is bright but lazy and unprincipled. Below on the first floor is Gilchrist, who is hard-working and athletic but also the son of the notorious Sir Jabez Gilchrist, who ruined himself gambling.

Holmes interviews Bannister, then looks in on the three students. In Gilchrist's room, he breaks the tip of his pencil, borrows another from the student, then asks for a knife to sharpen his own. The same thing at happened in Daulat Ras's room. But McLaren will not open the door as the exam is on the following day and he refuses to be disturbed. Holmes then asks Soames how tall McLaren is. Soames can't say exactly, but he is taller than Daulat Ras and shorter than Gilchrist. With that, Holmes bids Soames goodnight, leaving Soames unsure whether to cancel the exam. Holmes tells him to do nothing yet. He will explain everything in the morning. Holmes then makes off with the black clay and the pencil shavings. Visiting the four stationers in town, Holmes finds that none of them has a pencil in stock to match the shavings.

Skipping breakfast the next morning, Holmes and Watson head for St Luke's. Holmes says he has solved the mystery. Up at six that morning, he had covered five miles and now has three small pyramids of black clay. After telling Soames to allow the examination to proceed, he summons Bannister. Then he sends for Gilchrist and asks him to explain himself. Gilchrist looks reproachfully at Bannister, who says: 'No, no, Mr Gilchrist, sir, I never said a word.'

Gilchrist, the athlete, had returned from practice that morning. With his running spikes having given him extra height, he had seen the proofs on the table. Then he saw the key in the door. He took off his shoes and put them on the table while making a copy of the exam questions. When surprised, he fled into the bedroom, grabbing the running shoes, whose spikes ripped the leather topped desk. Black clay covered with sawdust from the long-jump pit had adhered to the spikes. It came off on the table and in the bedroom. Gilchrist then produces a letter that he had written the night before. He was not going to sit the exam. He had been offered a commission in the Rhodesian police and was leaving for South Africa at once.

'There is the man who set me in the right path,' said Gilchrist, pointing to Bannister.

Bannister had been butler to Gilchrist's father. He recognized the gloves Gilchrist had left on the chair. Pretending to faint he had sat on them until Soames had gone to fetch Holmes. Then Gilchrist, who was hiding in the bedroom, came out and confessed all. Bannister, who had known the boy since he was a child, persuaded him he could not profit from such a deed.

The Adventure of the Golden Pince-Nez

'The Adventure of the Golden Pince-Nez' was first published in *Strand Magazine* in July 1904 with eight illustrations by Sidney Paget, then in *Collier's Weekly* in October 1904 with six illustrations by Frederic Dorr Steele.

On a rainy night in November 1894, Inspector Hopkins turns up at Baker Street. He is investigating a murder that has no apparent motive. At Yoxley Old Place near Chatham the invalid Professor Coram lived with his housekeeper and a maid, both of good character. He had a secretary, Mr Willoughby Smith, and a gardener named Mortimer, a veteran of Crimea.

One morning, while the professor was still in bed, the maid heard Smith walk down the passageway to the study. Then she heard a scream and found Smith prostrate on the floor with blood pouring from his neck. A small sealing-wax knife lay beside him.

He opened his eyes for an instant and said: 'The professor – it was she.' Then he fell back dead. There were no discernable footprints and nothing appeared to have been taken. However, in his right hand there was a pair of golden pince-nez that he must have snatched from the face of his killer.

Holmes agrees to accompany Hopkins to Yoxley Old Place the following morning. Around the lock on the desk in the study, Holmes finds a fresh scratch that he thinks was made by the person surprised by Smith. They then grabbed the sealing-knife and stabbed him. However, after Smith cried out, the maid had come running down the corridor, blocking the killer's only exit.

Holmes interviews the professor, whose book-lined bedroom lies at the end of another corridor that leads from the study. He is propped up in bed, smoking, and offers Holmes a cigarette. Holmes asks what he makes of Smith's last words. The maid is a stupid country girl, says the professor. The dying man probably mumbled something incoherent. Smith's death was either an accident or suicide – both already ruled out by Hopkins. And the glasses? A love-token, perhaps, says the professor.

What is in the cupboard in the desk? asks Holmes. Family papers. Look for yourself, says the professor, handing him the key. Holmes looks at it for an instant and hands it back.

Holmes seeks out the housekeeper and remarks that the amount that the professor smokes must surely suppress his appetite. She says he is eating more heartily than ever.

Holmes later returns to talk to the professor, who asks whether Holmes has solved the case and passes him the box of cigarettes. Holmes drops it and while picking up the cigarettes takes the opportunity to examine the carpet. Then he says: 'Yes, I have solved it . . . A lady yesterday entered your study. She came with the intention of possessing herself of certain documents which were in your bureau. She had a key of her own. I have had an opportunity of examining yours, and I do not find that slight discolouration which the scratch made upon the varnish would have produced.'

She had stabbed Smith in an attempt to escape but lost her pince-nez in the struggle. Being short sighted, she had chosen the wrong exit and had run into the professor's room. She is now hiding behind a hinged bookcase and, at Holmes' words, emerges.

She explains that the professor is not an Englishman but a Russian – but she will not give his name. They had married years before in Russia. They were revolutionaries. But when a policeman was killed, the professor betrayed his comrades. Some were hanged. She was sent to Siberia. He escaped to England.

When she was released, she went to England to get the letters and diaries that would procure the release of another comrade now working in the salt mines. After stabbing the secretary she ran into the wrong room. Her husband threatened to give her up to the law, but if he did, she said she would tell the brotherhood where he was and that they would come and kill him. So he hid her.

She pulled out the documents she had taken and asked that they be delivered to the Russian Embassy. They would free her comrade. Then she swallowed a phial of poison and died. While Hopkins returns to headquarters, Holmes and Watson drive to the Russian Embassy.

The Adventure of the Missing Three-Quarter
'The Adventure of the Missing Three-Quarter' was first published in *Strand Magazine* in August 1904 with seven illustrations by Sidney Paget, then in *Collier's Weekly* in November 1904 with seven illustrations by Frederic Dorr Steele.

Holmes receives a telegram that reads: 'Please await me. Terrible misfortune. Right wing three-quarter missing, indispensable tomorrow. Overton.'

Soon after, Cyril Overton, rugby player at Trinity College, Cambridge, arrives at Baker Street. His star player Godfrey Staunton has disappeared and there is an important match against Oxford the next day. Late the previous evening, a bearded man had come to the team's London hotel with a note for Staunton, whom he left with.

Overton wired Cambridge, but no one had seen him there.

He then wired Staunton's nearest relative Lord Mount-James, whose fortune Staunton was due to inherit.

At the hotel, Holmes questions the porter. At six o'clock he had delivered a telegram to Staunton and waited while he wrote a reply. On the blotter in Staunton's room, Holmes finds the words: 'Stand by us for God's sake.'

At the telegraph office, Holmes tricks the clerk into showing him the telegram's counterfoil. Then Holmes and Watson head for Kings Cross. The telegram was addressed to Dr Leslie Armstrong, a Cambridge academic who shows no surprise at the news of Staunton's disappearance and confirms that Staunton is very healthy. So why has Staunton paid him thirteen guineas? asks Holmes brandishing the bill that he has taken from Staunton's desk. Furious, Armstrong refuses to answer any more questions.

Holmes and Watson lodge at an inn just over the road from Armstrong's house, so they can keep an eye him. Armstrong goes out in his brougham and returns after three hours. He makes this journey daily, Holmes learns, and the following day tries to follow on a bicycle but Armstrong gives him the slip.

On the advice of Overton, Holmes borrows a mongrel named Pompey, half beagle, half foxhound. The following morning Watson is horrified to see Holmes with a syringe. But rather than injecting cocaine, he has used it to spray aniseed over the rear wheel of Armstrong's brougham. Pompey follows the trail to a cottage where they find Staunton, grieving over his young wife, who has just died of consumption. Their marriage had been kept secret as Lord Mount-James would have disapproved and disowned him. The bearded stranger who came to fetch Staunton was the girl's father.

The Adventure of the Abbey Grange
'The Adventure of the Abbey Grange' was first published in *Strand Magazine* in September 1904 with eight illustrations by Sidney Paget, then in *Collier's Weekly* in December 1904 with six illustrations by Frederic Dorr Steele.

One frosty morning in 1897, Watson awakes to find Holmes with a candle and stooping over his bed. As soon as he is dressed, they take a cab to Charing Cross. Inspector Hopkins has cabled from Abbey Grange in Marsham, Kent, asking for their assistance.

Sir Eustace Brackenstall has been found dead, hit on the head apparently with a poker. Lady Brackenstall, his wife, is reclining on the couch when they enter. Holmes immediately notices two vivid red marks on her arms, which she hastily covers. Prompted by Hopkins, she tells her story.

She had been married for about a year, but her husband was a drunkard. The previous evening he had gone to bed at about half past ten. The servants had also retired, while she remained downstairs reading a book. She checked the house before she turned in and felt a breeze from the French windows in the dining room. When she pulled back the curtain, she found herself face to face with three men. They hit her and she fell to the ground, unconscious. When she came to, she was tied to a chair with the bell-pull. Aroused by the noise, her husband appeared in his night shirt, brandishing a cudgel. The gang leader picked up the poker from the grate and struck him. He fell and did not move again.

She then fainted. When she revived, the men had collected the silver from the sideboard and were drinking a bottle of wine they had opened. When they left they closed the window behind them. Her screams woke the servants, who called the police.

Holmes questions Lady Brackenstall's maid, who had come with her mistress from South Australia and had been with her all her life. She says she had seen three men in the garden earlier. Inspector Hopkins has already volunteered that, from their description, he thought they were the Randall family, who had done a job in Sydenham a fortnight earlier.

Holmes is puzzled by the bell-pull used to tie up Lady Brackenstall. When they pulled it down, the bell would have rung in the kitchen. The wine bottle they had drunk from was still two-thirds full. Why would such men leave wine undrunk?

Though three glasses had traces of wine, only one contained the 'beeswing' that forms after a wine has been kept for a long time. He reasons that there had only been two drinkers, who poured their dregs into the third glass, and although there was a cork-screw on the table, the cork had been drawn using a smaller screw found on a pocket knife.

Holmes climbs onto the mantelpiece to examine the remaining piece of the bell-pull. Although the piece used to tie up Lady Brackenstall had been frayed to make it look like as if had been pulled down, the remaining section showed signs that it had been cut. Whoever had done it must have been at least three inches taller than Holmes. He also finds blood in the seat of the chair, blood which must have been there before Lady Brackenstall sat down.

Holmes talks with the maid again. She tells him that her mistress had been cruelly mistreated by her husband. Holmes notes that, in the frozen pond in the garden, there is a hole in the ice where a swan is swimming. He leaves a note for Hopkins. Then Holmes and Watson head to the offices of the Adelaide – Southampton line in Pall Mall, where Holmes quickly identifies the ship that Lady Brackenstall, under her maiden name Mary Fraser, had travelled to England on in 1895. The ship is now on the other end of the Suez Canal and the crew is the same as it was in 1895, with the exception of the first officer, Jack Crocker.

Hopkins comes to Baker Street to report that he has found the stolen silver in the garden pond as Holmes's note had said he would. However, the Randalls had been arrested in New York.

After Hopkins leaves, Captain Crocker turns up, summoned by telegram. Holmes asks him to give a true account of what happened at Abbey Grange. Otherwise he will blow a police whistle out of the window.

Crocker said that he fell in love with Mary Fraser during the voyage. But he was a penniless sailor and Mary went on to marry Lord Brackenstall. After being promoted, he was waiting with his family in Sydenham until he was assigned to a ship. He bumped into Lady Brackenstall's maid, who told him of her husband's cruelty. He went to Abbey Grange that night and Mary let him in. Her husband came downstairs and he struck Mary, knocking her out. The two men fought. Crocker grabbed the poker and struck Lord Brackenstall, killing him.

He opened the wine and poured a little between Mary's lips to revive her. He drank some too. They had read about the Randalls in the paper and, together with Mary's maid, they concocted the story of the burglary, tied up Mary and dropped the silverware in the pond.

Holmes promises to keep quiet for twenty-four hours, giving Crocker time to disappear, but Crocker refuses to leave Mary to face the law alone. Holmes was only testing him and he empanels Watson as a one-man jury that then finds Crocker not guilty.

The Adventure of the Second Stain

'The Adventure of the Second Stain' was first published in *Strand Magazine* in December 1904 with eight illustrations by Sidney Paget, then in *Collier's Weekly* in January 1905 with six illustrations by Frederic Dorr Steele.

The incident was first mentioned by Watson in 'The Naval Treaty' back in 1893, but it would not be made public at the time because it involved many of the first families of the kingdom (sic). He had to wait until the new century before the story could safely be told. Now that time had come.

Lord Bellinger, the prime minister, and Trelawney Hope, the secretary of state for European Affairs, had gone to Holmes about a sensitive document stolen from Hope's dispatch box, while it was in his home in Whitehall Terrace. The stolen document was a rather injudicious letter from a foreign potentate and its loss could mean war.

According to the morning paper, Eduardo Lucas, a spy known to Holmes, had been stabbed to death in his home in Godolphin Street, near Whitehall, the previous night.

Lady Hilda Trelawney Hope, the European secretary's wife,

arrives at Baker Street and she asks Holmes about the stolen document. He can only reveal that there will be dire consequences if the document is not found. She begs Holmes to tell her husband nothing of her visit.

A newspaper report from Paris connects Madame Henri Fournaye to Lucas's death. Photographs demonstrate that Eduardo Lucas and Henri Fournaye are the same person and a woman matching her description was seen in London. She is thought to be insane.

Inspector Lestrade invites Holmes to the murder scene to show him something interesting. Lucas's blood had soaked through the carpet but, curiously, there is no bloodstain on the floor underneath. However, there is a second stain under another part of the carpet. Holmes says the explanation is simple. The rug had been turned around.

While Lestrade goes off to upbraid the constable who is supposed to be guarding the crime scene, Holmes pulls back the carpet and finds a small compartment hidden in the floor underneath. It is empty. Lestrade returns with the constable, who tells Holmes that there was an unauthorized visitor – a young woman. She apparently fainted at the sight of the blood and the constable went out to get some brandy to revive her. When he returned, she had gone.

Holmes goes to Whitehall Terrace and confronts Lady Hilda. He knows of her visit to Lucas's and she hands over the letter, which Holmes returns to her husband's dispatch-box. She explains that Eduardo Lucas had got hold of a compromising letter she had written before she was married. In exchange he demanded a certain document he knew would be in her husband's possession. When she delivered it and got her own letter back, there was a sound at the door and footsteps in the passage. Lucas quickly hid the document under the carpet. A woman came in screaming in French and in a jealous rage pulled a knife. Lady Hilda fled, only learning the next day of the murder. When she realized how important the document was to her husband, she tricked her way back into Lucas's house and recovered it.

Hope then arrives home with the prime minister. Holmes says he has nothing definite to report, but feels they are out of danger. The document never left the house. In fact, it is still in the dispatch box. Protesting, Hope looks and finds it. He calls Holmes a wizard, a sorcerer and goes to tell his wife the good news. The prime minister says quizzically: 'There is more in this than meets the eye.'

'We also have our diplomatic secrets,' says Holmes.

Chapter 9

His Last Bow

This collection was first published in October 1917 by John Murray with a print run of 10,684 copies. The first American edition was also published that month by the G.H. Doran Co. in New York. It contains eight stories published largely between 1908 and 1913, plus one from 1917 and 'The Adventure of the Cardboard Box', which was originally published in *Strand* in 1893 but omitted from earlier collections in the UK at the request of the author.

In his preface Watson says: 'The friends of Mr Sherlock Holmes will be glad to learn that he is still alive and well, though somewhat crippled by occasional attacks of rheumatism. He has, for many years, lived in a small farm upon the downs five miles from Eastbourne, where his time is divided between philosophy and agriculture. During this period of rest he has refused the most princely offers to take up various cases, having determined that his retirement was a permanent one. The approach of the German war caused him, however, to lay his remarkable combination of intellectual and practical activity at the disposal of the government, with historical results which are recounted in "His Last Bow". Several previous experiences which have lain long in my portfolio have been added to *His Last Bow* so as to complete the volume.'

The Adventure of Wisteria Lodge

'The Adventure of Wisteria Lodge' was first published in *Collier's Weekly* in August 1908 with six illustrations by Frederic Dorr Steele, then in two parts in *Strand Magazine* in September and October 1908 under the collective title 'A Reminiscence of Mr Sherlock Holmes' with ten illustrations by Arthur Twidle. It is in two parts: 'The Singular Experience of Mr John Scott Eccles' and 'The Tiger of San Pedro'.

Holmes is visited by John Scott Eccles, who wants to discuss something 'grotesque', but before he has a chance to tell his tale, Inspector Gregson arrives with Inspector Baynes of the Surrey Constabulary. They want him to make a statement about the murder of Aloysius Garcia of Wisteria Lodge, near Esher.

Eccles is shocked to hear of Garcia's death. He had spent last night at Wisteria Lodge, but when he woke in the morning, he found himself alone in an empty house. He last saw Garcia at one o'clock in the morning when he had come to Eccles's room.

Eccles had seen Garcia receive a note, which is produced by Inspector Baynes. In a woman's handwriting, it reads: 'Our own colours, green and white. Green open, white shut. Main stair, first corridor, seventh right, green baize. Godspeed. D.'

Garcia's body had been found about a mile from his home. He had been beaten to death. Baynes deduced that Garcia's body had been lying out in the open since one o'clock. Holmes believes that Eccles has been set up by Garcia as an alibi in a crime that has clearly gone wrong. From the note, Holmes deduces that the murderer lives near Wisteria Lodge, and in a big house.

Part two, 'The Tiger of San Pedro', sees Holmes and Watson visit Wisteria Lodge with Inspector Baynes. The constable guarding the house says he has seen the devil himself looking in at the window. Holmes finds footprints, indicating that the intruder must be a giant. In the kitchen, they find something resembling a mummified baby, a white cock savagely dismembered, a pail of blood and a platter heaped with charred bones. Holmes suspects voodoo.

Five days after the murder, Holmes reads in the newspaper

that Baynes has arrested the ugly giant that gave the constable such a start. But Holmes is convinced that he is not the murderer.

Holmes has been spending time reconnoitring the local country houses and finds one of interest. The master, a man named Henderson, has obviously spent time in the tropics. He is rich, violent and afraid. He has a black manservant and his two girls have an English governess named Burnet. She, Holmes believes, is the source of Garcia's note.

Then Holmes hears that the Hendersons have fled by train, but Miss Burnet though drugged with opium has escaped. 'Henderson', it transpires, is Don Juan Murillo, the Tiger of San Pedro – a recently overthrown Central American dictator. Miss Burnet is the widow of the former San Pedro ambassador to London whom Murrillo had executed. She and Garcia had been involved in a plot to assassinate the despot. In the note, the green and white are the colours of San Pedro. What followed were directions to Murrillo's bedroom. The 'D' was Miss Burnet – her married name was Durando. Garcia then invited Eccles to Wisteria Lodge to provide an alibi but Murrillo's secretary had seen Miss Burnet write the note and intercept Garcia on his way and had him killed.

Although they give the police the slip in London, Murillo and his secretary resurface under new aliases in Madrid, where they were both murdered. Their killers are never caught.

The Adventure of the Cardboard Box

'The Adventure of the Cardboard Box' was first published in *Strand Magazine* in January 1893 with eight illustrations by Sidney Paget. The story was not included in the first English edition of *The Memoirs of Sherlock Holmes*, though it was in the first American edition published by Harper in 1894.

One sweltering August, Miss Susan Cushing, a fifty-year-old spinster living in Croydon, receives a parcel containing two severed human ears packed in coarse salt. Lestrade suspects a prank by medical students but when Holmes examines the parcel, he is convinced they are dealing with a serious crime. He notes that the ears are not a pair and had been hacked off roughly. A medical student would have made a neater incision and preserved them in spirit, not salt. The address had been roughly written, Croydon misspelt and the knots used to tie the parcel suggested that a seaman was responsible. The package came from Belfast and was addressed to 'Miss S. Cushing'.

Questioning Miss Cushing, Holmes discovers that she had two sisters: Mary, who had married a sailor named Jim Browner with a taste for the drink. He fell out with Mary's sisters, but Sarah had a temper and, to get her revenge, she encouraged Mary to take a lover. Browner found his wife and her beau boating off New Brighton. Shrouded by sea haze, he killed them and cut off their ears. He disposed of their bodies by tying them to the boat and stoving in the planks. At his next port of call, Belfast, he posted the ears to Miss S. Cushing, meaning Sarah, who had lived briefly with her sister Susan in Croydon before they, too, fell out.

When his ship docks in London, Browner confesses everything. Tormented with guilt, he welcomes the hangman.

The Adventure of the Red Circle

'The Adventure of the Red Circle' was first published in *Strand Magazine* in March and April 1911 with three illustrations by H.M. Brock and one by Joseph Simpson, then in an American edition of the *Strand Magazine* in April and May 1911 with the same illustrations.

Mrs Warren, a Bloomsbury landlady, goes to Baker Street with some concerns about her lodger, a bearded foreigner. He said he would pay double the standard rent provided he was not disturbed. He went out the first night and came back after the household had retired. After that, he had stayed in his room. His meals were left outside, along with a copy of the *Daily Gazette*.

The landlady brought with her two burnt matches and a cigarette end he had left on his tray that morning. Holmes deduces that the cigarette had not been smoked by a bearded man. Whoever had returned at the dead of night and had not been seen since was clean shaven. Holmes also surmises that the lodger is receiving messages via the agony column of the *Daily Gazette*. He has these on file. Two days after Mrs Warren's lodger had arrived, he finds: 'Will find some sure means of communication. Meanwhile, this column. G.' Yesterday, there was: 'The path is clearing. If I find chance signal message remember code agreed – one A, two B, and so on. You will hear soon. G.' And today's column carries: 'High red house with white stone facings. Third floor. Second window left. After dusk. G.'

Mrs Warren leaves, but then returns complaining that her husband had been kidnapped that morning and taken to Hampstead Heath, where he was dumped. Holmes deduces that his captors mistook him for her lodger and dumped him after realizing their mistake.

Outside Mrs Warren's house in Bloomsbury, Holmes notes that the lodger's window commands a good view down the street to a house matching the one mentioned in the agony column. Inside, Holmes and Watson hide in a boxroom to catch a glimpse of the lodger collecting lunch. The person who appears is a woman.

That evening, Holmes and Watson see a flashing light. It is a signal: one flash is 'a'; twenty, 't'. The code spells out '*attenta*', which Holmes recognizes as Italian for 'beware'. (This would not work as there is no 'j' or 'k' in Italian; 't' would be the eighteenth letter of the alphabet.) Then the word '*pericolo*' – 'danger' – is broken off halfway through.

Holmes and Watson race down the street, where they bump into Inspector Gregson, who is with Leverton from Pinkerton's American Agency. They are lying in wait for Giuseppe Gorgiano.

'What! Gorgiano of the Red Circle?' says Holmes.

He is a vicious killer and Leverton has followed him to London from New York. In the room where Holmes and Watson saw the signal light they find Gorgiano dead.

Holmes then signals '*vieni*' – 'come' – and Mrs Warren's female lodger arrives. She is delighted to see Gorgiano dead and asks where Gennero, her husband, is. Her name is Emilia Lucca. She explains that as a youth her husband had been initiated by Gorgiano to a Neapolitan gang called the Red Circle. They married and moved first to New York then to London, but there was no escaping the Red Circle or Gorgiano. Now Gennero has killed him. What Gregson cannot understand is how Holmes got involved in the case.

The Adventure of the Bruce-Partington Plans

'The Adventure of the Bruce-Partington Plans' was first published in *Strand Magazine* in December 1908 with six illustrations by Arthur Twidle, then in *Collier's Weekly* in December 1908 with five illustrations by Frederic Dorr Steele.

In the third week of November 1895 it is unusually foggy in London. Holmes receives a telegram from his brother Mycroft, telling him to come at once. A government employee named Cadogan West has been found dead on the Underground. A clerk at Woolwich Arsenal, he was last seen by his fiancée, Miss Violent Westbury, at 7.30 p.m. the previous evening, when he left abruptly. His body was found on the track just outside Aldgate Station and it appears that he had fallen from the train, but there is no ticket in his pocket. However, he had been carrying seven pages of the top-secret plans of the Bruce-Partington submarine. Three are still missing.

Holmes quickly deduces that West had been killed elsewhere and his body deposited on the roof of the train. At the bend at Aldgate, it had fallen off.

Holmes goes to see Sir James Walter, the expert in charge of the project and official guardian of the plans. But Sir James has just died. His brother Colonel Valentine Walter says that loss of the plans was responsible for his death.

West's fiancée says he had something on his mind for the last week or so and feared foreign spies getting their hands on the plans. On the night in question, they had been walking past his office when he dashed off without a word.

At West's office, the senior clerk Sidney Johnson says anyone trying to steal the plans would have needed three keys – for the building, the office and the safe. Only he and Sir James had the keys. No duplicates were found on Cadogan West's body.

At Woolwich station, the ticket clerk remembers seeing West on Monday night. He looked nervous and shaky, and took a train to London Bridge.

Using his government connections, Mycroft supplies the name of a spy, Hugo Oberstein, who had left town that Monday. Holmes discovers that Oberstein's house backs on to a place near Gloucester Road Station where the Underground line is above ground. A nearby junction means that trains often stop there. Holmes and Watson break in and find a bloodstain on a windowsill overlooking the track.

In a cash box, they find calculations concerning water pressure and enigmatic cuttings from the agony column of the *Daily Telegraph*, posted by 'Pierrot', which hint at some transaction. Holmes posts another message, under the name 'Pierrot', suggesting another meeting.

That night, Colonel Walter shows up at Oberstein's house to find Holmes, Watson, Lestrade and Mycroft waiting. He confesses to the theft of the plans. His motive – money. He had taken impressions of his brother's keys and with the duplicates had broken in to the office but West saw him and followed him to the rendezvous with Oberstein. When West intervened, Oberstein killed him and kept three originals that were too complicated to copy. He put the other seven in West's pocket to throw the police off the scent and placed the body on the roof of a halted Underground train.

At Holmes's behest Colonel Walter writes a letter to Oberstein, who is in Paris, asking for £500 for another vital document. Oberstein takes the bait and returns to London where he is arrested. The missing pages of the Bruce-Partington plans are recovered from his trunk. He is sentenced to fifteen years. Colonel Walter dies in prison, and Holmes receives and emerald tie pin from 'a certain gracious lady'.

'I fancy that I could guess at that lady's august name,' says Watson.

The Adventure of the Dying Detective

'The Adventure of the Dying Detective' was first published in *Collier's Weekly* in November 1913 with three illustrations by Frederic Dorr Steele, then in *Strand Magazine* in December 1913 with four illustrations by Sidney Paget's brother, Walter.

Two years after Watson has moved out to live with his wife, he is called back to Baker Street to tend to Holmes, who is apparently dying of a rare Asian disease contracted while he was solving a case in Rotherhithe. Holmes shows all the signs of fever, but he won't let Watson touch him.

Watson begs Holmes to let him summon eminent physicians and experts on tropical medicine, but Holmes leaps from the bed and locks the door. Among the usual litter of pipes, tobacco pouches, syringes, penknives, revolver cartridges and other debris, Watson spots a little black-and-white ivory box with a sliding lid. Holmes orders him to put it down. The rest of the time he raves deliriously.

At six o'clock, Holmes tells Watson to turn the gaslight on, but only half way. He then tells him to fetch Mr Culverton Smith of 13 Lower Burke Street – an expert in the disease that ails him. But he warns Watson that Culverton Smith does not like him because Holmes once accused him of killing his nephew. He tells Watson to return to Baker Street separately. Outside, Watson bumps into Inspector Morton of Scotland Yard.

Culverton Smith agrees to go to see Sherlock Holmes when Watson tells him he is dying. Watson excuses himself and returns to Baker Street, getting there before Smith arrives. Holmes tells Watson to hide behind the screen next to the bed.

Believing they are alone, Culverton Smith tells Holmes that he is dying of the same disease that Smith had used to murder his nephew. Smith had sent the little ivory box, which contains a sharp spring infected with the virulent strain. He pockets it, removing the evidence of his crime, and says he will stay and watch Holmes die.

Holmes asks him to turn the gas up full. This is a signal. Holmes then makes a miraculous recovery, Inspector Morton rushes in and arrests Culverton Smith for his nephew's murder and for the attempted murder of Sherlock Holmes. Watson was a witness to his confession. Holmes had feigned illness by starving himself for three days and applying a little Vaseline, belladonna, rouge and beeswax.

The Disappearance of Lady Frances Carfax
'The Disappearance of Lady Frances Carfax' was first published in *Strand Magazine* in December 1911 with five illustrations by Alec Ball, and in the *American Magazine* that same month with five illustrations by Frederic Dorr Steele.

Holmes sends Watson to Lausanne to investigate the disappearance of Lady Frances Carfax. She is not wealthy but does possess valuable jewellery which she carries with her. She had been staying at the Hôtel National, but left no forwarding address. Her bank has received two cheques: one paid her hotel bill; the other was made out to her maid and cashed in Montpelier.

In Switzerland Watson discovers that Lady Frances had left suddenly after being approached by a tall, bearded man. According to Cook's, she went on to Baden, where she stayed at the Englischer Hof and met Dr Shlessinger, a missionary, and his wife. Lady Frances left for London with them three weeks ago. Watson is told that the bearded Englishman is also on her trail and when Watson wires the news to Holmes, he cables back asking for a description of Shlessinger's left ear. Watson thinks Holmes is kidding and heads to Montpelier where he finds the maid. She had left Lady Frances's employ to marry and the cheque had been a wedding present. She, too, believes that the bearded man was the reason her mistress left Lausanne and, while they are talking, she sees him in the street. Watson confronts him and in the ensuing fight is rescued by a French workman, who turns out to be Holmes in disguise.

Holmes has discovered that the bearded man is the Honourable Philip Green, an old suitor of Lady Frances's. As a younger man, he was not rich. But he has since made his fortune in South Africa and still hopes to win her heart. Holmes recommends that he go back to London, where he will be contacted if the need arises.

Back at Baker Street Holmes receives a telegram from the Englischer Hof in Baden telling him that Dr Shlessinger's left ear is 'jagged or torn'. This confirms Holmes's suspicion that Shlessinger is in fact Henry Peters, a vicious crook from Adelaide. He believes that Lady Frances is in London, possibly dead or confined in some way.

Then a pendant matching one owned by Lady Frances is pawned by a man answering Shlessinger's description. Holmes stations Philip Green in the pawnshop. After two days, the woman posing as Shlessinger's wife turns up to pawn a matching pendant. Green follows her, first to an undertaker's, where he overhears her discussing an 'out of the ordinary' order, then to an address in Brixton. He watches the house and sees two men deliver a coffin.

Holmes sends Green to get a warrant. Meanwhile, Holmes and Watson go to the undertaker's, where they discover that there is to be a funeral at eight o'clock the next morning. They head to Brixton and force their way into the house. Inside they find the coffin, which contains the corpse of an old woman, not Lady Frances. The police arrive and tell Holmes and Watson that they must leave.

Back at Baker Street Holmes cannot sleep, turning over the case in his mind. In the morning inspiration strikes. Holmes and Watson rush to Brixton and unscrew the coffin lid and find Lady Frances inside, chloroformed. Watson revives her. Peters and his accomplice have fled. Overnight, Holmes had realized that the coffin was too big for the old lady they had seen in it. It was 'out of the ordinary' because it had been made big enough to fit two.

The Adventure of the Devil's Foot
'The Adventure of the Devil's Foot' was first published in the UK edition of *Strand Magazine* in December 1910 with seven

illustrations by Gilbert Halliday, and in the US edition of *Strand Magazine* in January and February 1911 with eight illustrations by Gilbert Halliday. An extra illustration was required for its publication in two parts.

In the spring of 1897, Holmes and Watson take a holiday in Poldhu. They get to know the local vicar Mr Roundhay and his lodger Mortimer Tregennis. One evening, Tregennis goes to visit his siblings in a nearby village to play whist. He returns the following morning and finds them still at the table where he had left them. His two brothers have gone insane and his sister, Brenda, is dead with a look of terror on her face.

Subsequently, Holmes examines the scene and is surprised to find they had lit a fire on a spring evening. Tregennis explains that the night had been cold and damp.

Dr Leon Sterndale, a famous hunter and explorer, turns up. A cousin of the Tregennises, he had missed his ship back to Africa and returned to Poldhu where he heard of the tragedy.

The following morning, Mortimer Tregennis is found dead with the same look of terror on his face. When Holmes and Watson visit Mortimer's room, they find the air foul and stuffy, even though the window had been opened. A lamp is burning on the table. Holmes scrapes some powder from the smoke guard and puts this on another lamp. It gives off noxious, hallucinogenic fumes. Watson is seized with terror but has the presence of mind to grab Holmes and drag him from the room.

It is clear to Holmes that Mortimer Tregennis had used the poison on his brothers and sister, but who had killed Mortimer? Clearly, it is Dr Sterndale. He confesses that he had been in love with Brenda for years, but could not marry her as the law at that time prevented him from divorcing his wife, even though she had abandoned him years before.

Sterndale pulls from his pocket a paper packet marked *Radix pedis diaboli* – 'Devil's-foot root' – that he had brought from Africa as a curiosity. He had once explained to Mortimer its effects. When he heard what had happened he realized that

Mortimer had stolen some and thrown it on the fire as he left the cottage, thinking Sterndale already at sea.

Tregennis had robbed Sterndale of the only person he ever loved, so he took the law into his own hands and killed him. Holmes's sympathies lie with Sterndale, and he tells him to go back to Africa and finish his work there.

His Last Bow

'His Last Bow' was first published in *Strand Magazine* in September 1917 with three illustrations by A. Gilbert, and in *Collier's Weekly* that same month with five illustrations by Frederic Dorr Steele. It is one of two Holmes stories written in third person and not, apparently, penned by Dr Watson.

On the eve of the the First World War, Von Bork, a German agent, is preparing to leave England. Bidding him farewell is the German ambassador Baron Von Herling. They mock their British hosts, saying England is not ready for war. Von Bork shows the baron the results of his four-year espionage campaign: he has a series of files that cover every aspect of Britain's defences. The only thing missing is the Admiralty's latest naval signals, but an Irish-American agent codenamed Altamont has wired to say that he will deliver that night without fail.

Von Bork offers the baron a glass of Tokay, Altamont's favourite wine, but he cannot delay and makes off in his hundred-horsepower Benz. Von Bork's wife and household have already left for the Netherlands, leaving only the elderly housekeeper, Martha, in the house. He begins packing the contents of his safe when a small car driven by an elderly chauffeur turns up. The passenger leaps out, waving a small brown-paper parcel. It contains the signals – 'Every last one of them, semaphore, lamp code, Marconi . . .', he says.

The visitor is a tall, gaunt man of sixty. His eyes alight on the safe and scoffs that any Yankee crook could open it with a can-opener. Von Bork boasts that the metal was resistant to any tool and has a double lock. Four years earlier, he had chosen for the combination the word 'August' and the numbers '1914'.

'Few of us even then could have guessed the date,' he boasts.

In the ensuing conversation, it transpires that all Von Bork's other agents have been arrested.

'I've heard that with you German politicians when an agent has done his work you are not sorry to see him put away,' says Altamont.

This annoys Von Bork. He insists on seeing the contents of the package before he hands over any money. Inside Von Bork finds a copy of the *Practical Handbook of Bee Culture*. At the same moment, he feels a grip of steel on the back of his neck and a chloroformed sponge on his face.

Holmes and Watson share a glass of Tokay while Holmes packs up Von Bork's files. Martha is also a British agent who switched off a light as a signal to Holmes that the coast was clear. Holmes had been on the case for two years, travelling to Chicago, Buffalo and Ireland to learn to play the part of a bitter Irish-American.

When Von Bork comes round, he cries: 'There is only one man . . .'

'Exactly,' says Holmes.

Chapter 10

The Case-Book of Sherlock Holmes

The Case-Book of Sherlock Holmes was published by John Murray in June 1927 with a print run of 15,150. The first American edition was published on the same day by the G. H. Doran Co. The collection contains twelve stories published between 1921 and 1927. However, unlike the other collection, *The Case-Book* Stories are not printed in the same order as they were when published in various magazines.

This time, Conan Doyle writes the preface and apologizes that 'Holmes may become like one of those popular tenors who, having outlived their time, are still tempted to make repeated farewell bows to their indulgent audiences'. He then gives a brief rundown of his publishing history and says that he 'had fully determined at the conclusion of *The Memoirs* to bring Holmes to an end'. He also rues that Holmes 'may perhaps have stood a little in the way of the recognition of my more serious literary work'. Then, thanking his readers for their constancy, he bids a final farewell to Sherlock Holmes.

The Adventure of the Illustrious Client
'The Adventure of the Illustrious Client' was first published in *Collier's Weekly* in November 1924 with four illustrations by John Richard Flanagan, then in *Strand Magazine* in February and March 1925 with eight illustrations by Howard K. Elcock.

The story begins on 3 September 1902, when Holmes and

Watson are at a Turkish bath in Northumberland Avenue. Holmes has received a message from Sir James Damery at the Carlton Club asking whether he could be consulted that afternoon on a very delicate and important matter.

Damery arrives at Baker Street and explains that he is there on behalf of an unnamed client who is concerned about General de Merville's innocent young daughter, Violet, who has fallen madly in love with the dashing Austrian Baron Adelbert Gruner. Holmes is equally concerned as he is convinced that the baron killed his first wife and was only saved from the gallows by the suspicious death of a witness.

Violet is strong-willed and will not hear a word against her fiancé, who has told her about his chequered past, but in such a way as to make himself out to be an innocent martyr. She intends to marry the baron the following month despite the wishes of her father.

Holmes visits Baron Adelbert Gruner, who is amused to see the great detective 'trying to play a hand with no cards in it'. He boasts that he has used post-hypnotic suggestion on Violet. As Holmes is leaving, the baron reminds him of the fate of Le Brun, a French agent who was crippled for life after making inquiries into the baron's affairs.

Shinwell Johnson, a criminal-turned-informer, introduces Holmes to Kitty Winter, the baron's former mistress who is bent on revenge. She tells Holmes that the baron 'collects' women and records details of his conquests in a leather-bound book, which he keeps in the bureau in his inner study. In the outer study, the baron keeps a collection of priceless porcelain. He is a connoisseur.

Holmes and Kitty go to see Violet – to no avail.

Watson sees a news vendor carrying a placard saying: 'Murderous attack on Sherlock Holmes.' The story says he was beaten with sticks and is seriously injured. Watson rushes to Baker Street, where he find Holmes battered but recovering. He tells Watson to exaggerate the tale of his injuries. For six days, the newspapers report that Holmes is at death's door. Then, without explanation, Holmes tells Watson to spend the next twenty-four hours studying Chinese pottery.

The following day, Holmes gives Watson a fake business card and a specimen set of Ming china to sell to the baron, who is not taken in. As the negotiation falters, he hears a noise from his inner study. Dashing in, he finds the French window open and Holmes, still swathed in bandages, fleeing into the garden. Gruner chases after him but Kitty is there and throws sulphuric acid in his face, leaving him hideously disfigured.

Holmes has the leather-bound book. Sir James takes it to show Violet and she breaks off the engagement. Due to extenuating circumstances, Kitty is given a minimal sentence. Burglary charges against Holmes are dropped, thanks to his illustrious client.

The Adventure of the Blanched Soldier

'The Adventure of the Blanched Soldier' was first published in *Liberty* magazine in October 1926 with five illustrations by Frederic Dorr Steele, then in *Strand Magazine* in November 1926 with five illustrations by Howard K. Elcock. It is the first of two stories narrated in the first person by Holmes himself – at Watson's instigation, of course – as the 'good Watson had at that time deserted me for a wife,' Holmes remarks petulantly.

The story is set in January 1903 when James M. Dodd consults Holmes about his missing friend, Godfrey Emsworth. Dodd and Emsworth served together in the Boer War, which had ended eight months earlier. Emsworth was wounded. From hospital, Dodd receives a letter from him, but he has heard nothing since. He wrote to Colonel Emsworth, his friend's father, who said his son had gone on a trip around the world. Dodd did not believe that his old pal would simply drop him like that and wrote to Godfrey's mother, who invited him to stay at the family home, Tuxbury Old Park in the wilds of Bedfordshire.

The colonel was a less than gracious host and refused Dodd

any help in contacting his son. After dinner, Dodd retired to his bedroom on the ground floor. Ralph, the butler, brought some coals and talked warmly of Godfrey but Dodd noticed that Ralph was talking of him in the past tense and asked if Godfrey were dead.

'I wish to God he was!' Ralph replied, dashing from the room.

Dodd was pondering this when he saw Godfrey standing outside the window, his face bleached white as a ghost. He disappeared into the darkness and, in the distance, Dodd heard a door closing.

The following day, he looked around the garden and found a detached building. A small bearded man emerged, locking the door behind him. Dodd tried to peer through the windows but the curtains were closed. He returned after dark and looked through a crack in the shutter. He saw the bearded man – and with his back to the shutters another man who he swore was Godfrey. Then he felt the tap on his shoulder. It was Colonel Emsworth. White with rage, he arranged for Dodd to leave on the first available train.

Holmes agrees to go to Tuxbury Old Park with Dodd. Ralph answers the door, wearing leather gloves that give off a tarry smell. The colonel threatens to summon the police, but Holmes points out that involving the police would bring about the very thing that the colonel wants to avoid. Holmes writes one word in his notebook, which he shows to the colonel, who immediately gives way.

In the outbuilding, Godfrey tells his story. The night he was wounded in South Africa he found his way to a building, climbed into a bed and slept there. He awoke to find himself in a leper hospital. When he returned to England symptoms began to appear and his family hid him away.

Holmes has anticipated this and brought with him Sir James Saunders, a specialist from London. He determines that Godfrey does not have leprosy, but rather pseudo-leprosy, or ichthyosis, a condition that is treatable.

The Adventure of the Mazarin Stone

'The Adventure of the Mazarin Stone' was first published in *Strand Magazine* in October 1921 with three illustrations by A. Gilbert, then in *Hearst's International Magazine* in November 1921 with four illustrations by Frederic Dorr Steele.

Watson arrives at Baker Street to find Holmes in bed. Billy, the page, explains that Holmes has been disguising himself to follow someone. One day he is dressed as a workman looking for a job, the next an old woman. The case involves the missing Crown diamond worth £100,000. The prime minister and the home secretary had been to see Holmes, along with Lord Cantlemere, who seemed to have no time for the detective.

By the window but behind a curtain is a wax effigy of Holmes, just as in 'The Adventure of the Empty House'. Holmes emerges from his bedroom and explains that he is expecting an attempt on his life that evening by Count Negretto Sylvius. He tells Watson to write down the murderer's name and address. The count is also the thief who has stolen the Crown diamond, a great yellow Mazarin stone. Holmes had been following him when the count collected an airgun, which he thinks is trained on him from the window over the road.

Billy reappears with Count Negretto's card and in the street below Holmes can see Sam Merton, the Count's dimwitted henchman. Holmes writes a note for Watson to give to Youghal of the CID and ushers him out the back way, telling him to return with the police. By that time, he should have found out where the stone is.

Negretto enters the house, sees the effigy and, thinking it is Holmes, he is about to stave its head in with his cane when Holmes intervenes, saying: 'Count! Don't break it.'

Negretto complains that Holmes's agents are following him. Holmes is flattered and explains it was he himself who had been doing the shadowing. He wants to know where the Mazarin stone is. When the count protests, Holmes says that he and his henchman could go to jail for twenty years but will go free if he hands over the stone.

Billy is sent to fetch Sam Merton. When he comes up, Holmes says he will go into his bedroom to play the Hoffman Barcarole while the count and Merton talk over his offer.

Hearing the violin, they talk freely. Sylvius reveals that he is carrying the stone in a secret pocket and takes it out to show Merton, who is Holmes in disguise. He grabs the diamond and points a revolver to the Count's head. The violin music they were hearing is coming from a gramophone.

When Cantlemere arrives, Holmes asks how they should proceed against receivers of stolen goods. Cantlemere says they should arrest them. Holmes then pretends to find the Mazarin stone in Cantlemere's coat pocket. He is not amused, but is forced to admit Holmes's abilities.

The Adventure of the Three Gables

'The Adventure of the Three Gables' was first published in *Liberty* in September 1926 with six illustrations by Frederic Dorr Steele, then in *Strand Magazine* in October 1926 with four illustrations by Howard K. Elcock.

Holmes is visited by Steve Dixie, a ruffian, who warns him to keep away from Harrow at the behest of his boss Barney Stockdale. As a result, Holmes decides to take on the Harrow Weald case. It concerns Mary Maberley, who has a house called Three Gables there. She is an elderly woman whose gifted son Douglas had died recently in Rome.

Soon after, a man offered to buy her house and all its contents for a great deal more than she had paid for it. He produced an agreement that would prevent her removing anything from the house, including her personal possessions. So she called the deal off.

As she is telling the story, Holmes grabs her maid Susan, who had been eavesdropping. He quickly deduces that Susan knew of Mrs Maberley's letter summoning Holmes and told Barney Stockdale, who Susan says is working for a rich woman whose name she refuses to reveal. She then quits her job.

Whatever Stockdale's mistress wants, Holmes realizes, must have come into the house recently. He notices some trunks containing Douglas's belongings that have just returned from Italy. This, Holmes says, is a case for Langdale Pike, a man who makes his living selling gossip to the scandal sheets, and he returns to London.

A note comes recalling Holmes and Watson to Three Gables. Burglars have stolen a manuscript from Douglas's belongings.

Holmes and Watson go to see the celebrated beauty Isadora Klein, a wealthy woman who is used to getting what she wants. One of her former lovers was Douglas Maberley. She is about to marry the Duke of Lomond, who is young enough to be her son.

At first Isadora Klein refuses to see Holmes, but he writes 'Shall it be the police, then?' on a sheet from his notebook and passes the message to her via a footman. She tells Holmes that Douglas Maberley wanted to marry her, but she could not marry a penniless commoner. When she ended their affair, Douglas wrote a thinly veiled account of it as a novel. Its publication would have caused a scandal, scuppering her marriage. She hired Barney Stockdale and his confederates to secure the manuscript. They tried by legal means at first, then resorted to burglary. Once she had the manuscript, she burnt it.

Holmes then gets Isadora Klein to write a cheque for £5,000 so Mrs Maberley can take a first-class trip around the world.

The Adventure of the Sussex Vampire

'The Adventure of the Sussex Vampire' was first published in *Strand Magazine* in January 1924 with four illustrations by Howard K. Elcock, and in *Hearst's International Magazine* in the same month with four illustrations by W.T. Benda.

Holmes is contacted by Robert Ferguson, who believes his Peruvian wife is a vampire: the nurse had caught her sucking the blood of their baby son. Ferguson also has an fifteen-year-old son named Jack from his first marriage, who suffered an accident as a child. His stepmother beats him, though otherwise she is a devoted and loving wife. When Ferguson himself found his wife with blood from the baby's neck upon her lips, she locked herself in her room and would see only her Peruvian maid, Dolores.

Holmes and Watson travel down to the Fergusons' house, where Holmes is intrigued by a collection of weapons Mrs Ferguson had brought with her from South America. He also notices that this dog is suffering from some sort of paralysis that the vet is unable to diagnose. Dolores says that her mistress is ill, and Dr Watson offers to examine her. He finds her flushed and agitated, and in delirium, she says: 'A fiend! A fiend! Oh, what shall I do with this devil?'

Watson reassures her that her husband loves her. She says that she loves him too, and that she is sacrificing herself rather than break her husband's heart. She demands to see her baby, but Ferguson refuses to put the child in further danger.

Holmes notes that Jack is excessively devoted to his father. He then examines the wound on the baby's neck and it becomes is clear that he has solved the case. But he will only tell his conclusions in the presence of his wife, whom Ferguson says won't seen him. Holmes says she will and sends her a note.

They move to her bedroom, where Holmes reveals that the culprit is Jack. He is jealous of his young half-brother and has been shooting him with poisoned darts from his stepmother's weapons collection. When she had been caught with blood on her lips she had been sucking the poison out. She beat Jack only to try to stop him doing it again but could not tell her husband of Jack's misdeeds as it would break his heart. Holmes recommends a year at sea for young Jack.

The Adventure of the Three Garridebs

'The Adventure of the Three Garridebs' was first published in *Collier's Weekly* in October 1924 with three illustrations by John Richard Flanagan, then in *Strand Magazine* in January 1925 with five illustrations by Howard K. Elcock.

The story is set in June 1902 when, unlike Conan Doyle, Holmes turned down a knighthood.

Holmes receives a letter from a Nathan Garrideb of 136

(or 156 in some editions) Little Ryder Street, asking for help tracing another man with the same surname. John Garrideb, a lawyer from Kansas, then pays a visit. He is annoyed that Nathan has involved a detective but, even so, he tells Holmes that he was a beneficiary of Kansas millionaire Alexander Hamilton Garrideb's $15 million estate, provided he find two more Garridebs to share it with. Having failed to do so in the US, he came to England but so far he has found only Nathan.

Holmes concludes this is a tissue of lies.

Holmes and Watson visit Nathan Garrideb and find an elderly eccentric who rarely leaves the room that he has turned into a makeshift museum. John Garrideb arrives, saying he has found a third Garrideb and produces a newspaper with an advertisement purportedly placed by a Howard Garrideb, a maker of agricultural machinery. He has made an appointment for Nathan to see him at his office in Birmingham the following day. Holmes notes that there are various Americanisms in the advertisement, making it plain that John Garrideb had placed the advertisement himself.

Holmes goes to see Inspector Lestrade at Scotland Yard, where photographic records identify John Garrideb as James Winter, alias Morecroft, alias 'Killer' Evans, who was imprisoned for shooting Rodger Prescott, a forger from Chicago, but was spared the gallows when Prescott was shown to have been the aggressor. Prescott, Holmes believes, was the previous occupant of Nathan Garrideb's room.

When Nathan goes to Birmingham, Holmes and Watson conceal themselves in his apartment. John Garrideb turns up and jimmies open a trapdoor revealing a small cellar. Holmes and Watson approach with guns drawn. Garrideb pulls his own gun and shoots Watson in the thigh. Holmes then hits Garrideb on the head and knocks him out.

In the cellar, they find a printing press and stacks of counterfeit banknotes left there by Prescott. Winter is returned to prison. His hopes dashed of having the money to become the

Hans Sloane of the Edwardian age, Nathan Garrideb disappears into nursing home in Brixton.

The Problem of Thor Bridge

'The Problem of Thor Bridge' was first published in *Strand Magazine* in February and March 1922 with seven illustrations by A. Gilbert, and in *Hearst's International Magazine* in the same month with three illustrations by G. Patrick Nelson.

Mining magnate Neil Gibson, 'the Gold King' and former US senator for a western state now living in Hampshire, approaches Holmes to investigate the murder of his middle-aged wife, Maria, and clear the name of his children's attractive young governess, Grace Dunbar, who has been jailed for the crime.

Maria Gibson was found on Thor Bridge in the grounds of the senator's house with a bullet in her brain and a note from the governess in her hand. A recently discharged revolver with one empty chamber was found in Miss Dunbar's wardrobe.

Gibson had met his wife in Brazil, but soon after they married he realized they had nothing in common. He became attracted to Miss Dunbar. Although he could not marry her, he tried to please her by turning to philanthropy. Nevertheless, his wife was fiercely jealous.

The contention was that Miss Dunbar coolly planned to kill her employer's wife, then carelessly tossed the murder weapon into her wardrobe. But the gun was one of a pair and the other could not be found.

At Thor Bridge, Holmes notices a strange chip on the balustrade. From that, he deduces that Mrs Gibson had decided to kill herself and frame Miss Dunbar. She arranged a meeting on the bridge with an exchange of notes. After an altercation, Miss Dunbar fled. Mrs Gibson had already fired one of the pair of pistols and left it in Miss Dunbar's wardrobe. She tied the other to a rock suspended over the side of the bridge, then put the gun to her head and shot herself. The rock pulled the gun from her hand. The gun then hit the balustrade, chipping it, then disappeared into the water below.

Tellingly, Gibson's situation reflected Conan Doyle's, who had long been encumbered with a wife he no longer loved while passionately enthralled by a younger woman.

The Adventure of the Creeping Man

'The Adventure of the Creeping Man' was first published in *Strand Magazine* in March 1923 with five illustrations by Howard K. Elcock, and in *Hearst's International Magazine* the same month with six illustrations by Frederic Dorr Steele.

In September 1903, Watson receives a note that read: 'Come at once if convenient – if inconvenient come all the same. S.H.' He arrives at Baker Street to find Holmes pondering why Professor Presbury's dog wants to bite him.

Presbury's secretary Trevor Bennett comes to consult Holmes. Bennett is engaged to the professor's only daughter, Edith. Meanwhile her sixty-one-year-old father has himself become engaged to a colleague's daughter. They are concerned that the professor's behaviour is becoming erratic: he disappeared for a fortnight without telling anyone and they only discovered later that he was in Prague.

Normally Bennett opened all the professor's letters as part of his secretarial duties but now he has been told not to open letters with a cross under the stamp. When a mysterious box arrived Presbury became angry when Bennett touched it.

The professor's wolfhound, Roy, has attacked him three times at intervals of nine days. One night, Bennett opened his bedroom door to see the professor creeping along the hall on all fours and when Bennett spoke to him, the professor swore at him and hurried off down the stairs. He did not return until after dawn.

Edith Presbury is the next person to arrive at Baker Street. She says that one night Roy's frenzied barking woke her, and she saw her father's face pressed against the window of her bedroom which is on the second floor.

The following day, Holmes and Watson travel to Camford to see the professor. The interview becomes quite heated. Holmes predicts a crisis the following Tuesday.

Meanwhile, Bennett has discovered that the name of the professor's mysterious correspondent is Dorak. Holmes's 'general utility man' Mercer tracks Dorak, a Bohemian, down to a general store in the Commercial Road.

The following Tuesday, Holmes and Watson return to Camford and stake out the professor's house. Holmes has noticed that the professor's knuckles are thick and horny and, when he appears in his dressing gown he is standing erect, but leaning forward with his arms dangling. He then starts climbing the ivy that covers the house while the wolfhound barks. He torments the dog, but Roy gets loose and attacks the professor. They manage to get the dog off and tend the professor's wounds.

Holmes then examines the professor's little wooden box, which contained a drug supplied by Dorak, and with it is a letter from an Austrian named Lowenstein. Holmes has read in the newspapers that Lowenstein has developed a rejuvenating cure. The letter explains that Presbury has been injecting himself with serum from a langur, an Asian monkey, which has clearly had an effect on his behaviour.

The Adventure of the Lion's Mane
'The Adventure of the Lion's Mane' was first published in *Liberty* in November 1926 with seven illustrations by Frederic Dorr Steele, then in *Strand Magazine* in December 1926 with three illustrations by Howard K. Elcock.

It is the second of two stories narrated in the first person by Holmes. This time Watson is nowhere to be seen. It is now July 1907 and Holmes has retired to the Sussex coast.

On the day after a storm, Holmes is walking along the clifftop, where he meets his friend Harold Stackhurst, the headmaster of a nearby preparatory school, who is going down to the beach for a swim. Suddenly the science master, Fitzroy McPherson, also appears on the clifftop, wearing only an overcoat and trousers. He lets out a cry and collapses, shrieking the words 'the lion's mane' before he dies. There are red welts all over his back as if he had been scourged.

Moments later, the mathematics teacher Ian Murdoch shows up. Murdoch and McPherson had once been enemies, but Stackhurst maintains they are now the best of friends. Holmes goes down to the lagoon the local men have been using as the bathing pool and finds McPherson's towel there. It is dry.

A note indicating that McPherson has a meeting with 'Maudie' is found in his pocket. This turns out Maud Bellamy, a local girl. Holmes and Stackhurst go to visit her and find Murdoch coming out of her house. Maud's family disapprove of her relationship with McPherson and Maud admits Murdoch had once been an 'admirer'. Then McPherson's dog, once a bone of contention between Murdoch and McPherson, is found dead at the edge of the bathing pool. It, too, died in agony.

Inspector Bardle of the Sussex Constabulary visits Holmes to ask if there is enough evidence to arrest Ian Murdoch. Holmes is sure there is not. Bardle is about to leave when Murdoch arrives followed by Stackhurst. Murdoch is in agony. He has the same marks on his body as McPherson. But copious amounts of brandy keep him alive.

Returning to the bathing pond, Holmes reveals the killer. It is a Lion's Mane jellyfish that has a lethal poison in its long tentacles. They drop a rock on it and kill it. Murdoch explains that he had been acting as a go-between between McPherson and Maud.

The Adventure of the Veiled Lodger
'The Adventure of the Veiled Lodger' was first published in *Liberty* in January 1927 with four illustrations by Frederic Dorr Steele, then in *Strand Magazine* in February 1927 with three illustrations by Frank Wiles.

One afternoon in late 1896, Watson is summoned by Holmes. He arrives to find Holmes with Mrs Merrilow, a landlady from South Brixton who has an unusual lodger named Mrs Ronder. In seven years, she has never shown her face. Mrs Merrilow once saw it accidentally and it was hideously mutilated.

Last night Mrs Ronder cried out 'Murder!' and 'You cruel beast! You monster!'

In the morning Mrs Merrilow went to Mrs Ronder to see if she could help. She refused the assistance of the clergy or the police, but she said she wanted to tell the truth to someone before she died and told Mrs Merrilow to fetch 'this detective man what we read about'. If Holmes won't come, Mrs Ronder says she should mention the name Abbas Parva.

Holmes knew the case. It had perplexed him at the time and he was sure the corone's verdict was wrong. Years before, Ronder had been one of the greatest showmen of the age. One night his wild-beast show had halted at Abbas Parva, a small village in Berkshire. The camp was awoken by a woman's screams. They found Ronder outside the open lion's cage with his head crushed and claw marks across his scalp. His wife was also badly mauled. In her agony she had cried out: 'Coward! Coward!'

She recovered and when an inquest was finally convened, the coroner returned a verdict of death by misadventure. But a young policeman named Edmunds was suspicious and consulted Holmes. They could not understand why Mrs Ronder had been calling her dead husband a coward. What could he have done?

Holmes and Watson go to Brixton to see Mrs Ronder, who wears a veil. She shows them a photograph of Leonardo, the strong man with the show. Her husband was a beast, she says, murderous when drunk and cruel to the animals. Leonardo was the one man he was afraid of and Mrs Ronder took him as her lover.

They decided to kill her husband and Leonardo made a club with five nails in it. That night, he used it to stove Ronder's head in, leaving marks that looked like claws. Mrs Ronder then released the lion so it looked as if it had got out and killed her husband. Instead, it turned on her. The coward was Leonardo, who ran away. But even then she could not deliver him to the gallows. Last month she learnt that he had drowned while bathing near Margate.

Fearing that Mrs Ronder is contemplating suicide, Holmes reminds her that her life is worthwhile as she is an example of patient suffering in an impatient world. She responds by lifting her veil. The sight is terrible.

Two days later, a bottle of prussic acid arrives in the post from Mrs Ronder; she had been tempted to use it, but has taken Holmes's advice.

The Adventure of Shoscombe Old Place

'The Adventure of Shoscombe Old Place' was first published in *Liberty* in March 1927 with seven illustrations by Frederic Dorr Steele, then in *Strand Magazine* in April 1927 with five illustrations by Frank Wiles.

John Mason, the head trainer at Shoscombe Old Place, a racing stable in Berkshire, comes to see Holmes. He thinks his master, Sir Robert Norberton, has gone mad. Shoscombe is owned by Sir Robert's sister, Lady Beatrice Falder, but it will revert to her late husband's brother when she dies. Meanwhile Noberton has racked up huge debts, but he will be saved if his horse, Shoscombe Prince, wins the Derby.

Sir Robert does not sleep and has become wild-eyed. His sister has lost interest in the horses and does not stop at the stables any more. Noberton has given her pet spaniel to a local innkeeper and she has taken to drink. Mason has seen her visit an old crypt at night. He met a stranger there, who ran away when challenged. Then Mason produces a human bone found in the household furnace.

Holmes and Watson go to Berkshire posing as anglers. They borrow Lady Beatrice's dog from the innkeeper and take it for a walk, releasing it when Lady Beatrice's carriage comes by. At first, the dog dashes forward, but then starts snapping at her dress. Although only Lady Beatrice and her maid are in the carriage, they hear a male voice yell: 'Drive on!'

Mason takes them to the crypt. A heap of bones that were there earlier is now gone. After Mason leaves, Holmes begins opening coffins. Noberton catches him in the act. He is furious but, instead of shrinking away, Holmes tears off the lid of another casket to reveal a fresh body inside it.

Sir Robert invites them back to the house, where he explains everything. A week ago, Lady Beatrice had died. Sir Robert was compelled to keep this secret or his creditors would have swooped before had a chance to win the Derby and pay off all his debts. They hid her body in a coffin in the crypt, burning the bones of the previous occupant. The husband of Lady Beatrice's maid was an actor and took the old lady's place. The spaniel knew that he was not her mistress, so Sir Robert had to give the dog away.

Holmes refers the matter to the police, but the authorities take a lenient view of his attempt to delay the registration of the death of his sister. Shoscombe Prince then wins the Derby and Sir Robert pays off his creditors.

The Adventure of the Retired Colourman

'The Adventure of the Retired Colourman' was first published in *Liberty* in December 1926 with four illustrations by Frederic Dorr Steele, then in *Strand Magazine* in January 1927 with five illustrations by Frank Wiles.

Scotland Yard send Josiah Amberley retired art-supply dealer – or colourman – from Lewisham, to see Holmes. Amberley says his wife, twenty years his junior, had run off with a neighbour, Dr Ray Ernest, and took with her much of his life's savings. Amberley wants Holmes to track them down.

Holmes is busy so sends Watson, who is directed to the address by a man of a military bearing loitering nearby. Amberley is busy painting his house. On the night his wife left, they were going to the theatre but at the last moment she had complained of a headache and Amberley had to go alone. He produces her unused theatre ticket and Watson notes the seat number.

Amberley shows Watson the strong room, built like a bank vault, where he kept his savings. He claims his wife had a duplicate key and had taken £7,000 worth of cash and securities.

On the way back to Baker Street, Watson again sees the man

with a military bearing. Holmes recognizes the man from Watson's description.

Holmes sends Watson and Amberley on a fool's errand to a little village in Essex while he goes to Lewisham to investigate. When they return to Baker Street Watson and Amberley are directed to meet Holmes in Lewisham, where they find him with the man with military bearing. Holmes introduces him as Barker. They both have the same question for Amberley: 'What did you do with the bodies?'

Holmes springs on Amberley just in time to stop him from taking a poison pill. They take him to the police station. Holmes returns with Inspector MacKinnon and constables are called in to search the premises for bodies. Holmes suggests they look for a disused well.

He explains that the first clue was the smell of paint. To Holmes's mind it had been obvious that Amberley was trying to cover up one smell with another. Then he noted that the strong room was hermetically sealed. He had already been to the Haymarket Theatre and had discovered that neither of the seats Amberley had booked had been occupied that night.

While Watson and Amberley were in Essex, Holmes broke into Amberley's house. He found a gas pipe leading into the strong room with a tap outside. Amberley had lured his wife and Dr Ernest into the strong room and gassed them.

While breaking in, Holmes had been caught by Baker, who had been employed by Dr Ernest's family to investigate the case. They decided to join forces.

Holmes had spotted another clue. Just above the skirting board in the strong room he found the words 'We we . . .' written in indelible pencil. He surmises Dr Ernest had been writing 'We were murdered' but had lost consciousness before he could finish.

Holmes said Amberley hired him out of 'pure swank', believing that no one would ever find him out. Holmes believes that Amberley will likely end up at Broadmoor rather than on the scaffold. A few days later the *North Surrey Observer* carries the news that the bodies have been found in a disused well under a dog kennel. All the credit goes to Inspector MacKinnon. Holmes is not mentioned.

Chapter 11

The Life of a Mastermind

Although Watson knew Holmes for many years – from around 1882 when they had first met until at least 1914, when they are last seen in action together – he learns remarkably little about him. In 'The Greek Interpreter', nearly six years after Watson had first introduced Holmes to the reading public, he says: 'During my long and intimate acquaintance with Mr Sherlock Holmes I had never heard him refer to his relations, and hardly ever to his own early life.' Watson had come to believe that Holmes was an orphan with no living relatives. Then, to Watson's great surprise, Holmes begins to talk about his brother.

This is the first time Holmes mentions Mycroft, who lives in Pall Mall, less than two miles from Baker Street, but they are not estranged. Holmes takes Watson to the Diogenes Club to introduce them. The only other mention Holmes makes of his background is that his ancestors had been country squires 'who appear to have led much the same life as is natural to their class' and then says no more about them. However, he does know that his grandmother was the sister of the French artist Vernet – presumably Horace Vernet, born in 1789, the youngest of a family of well-known painters and best known for his sporting subjects and vast battle panoramas. Holmes certainly attributes his ability as a detective to hereditary factors: 'Art in the blood is liable to take the strangest forms,' he says.

Later, in 'The Adventure of the Norwood Builder', Watson mentions that Holmes has a distant relative, a Dr Verner, who bought Watson's Kensington practice, though it was Holmes who had actually put up the money.

There is no mention of Holmes's parents or his early schooling and his date of birth can only be guessed at. In 'The Last Bow', which is set in August 1914, he is described as a 'tall, gaunt man of sixty'. This would mean that he had been born in 1854.

In 'The *Gloria Scott*', Holmes is still at university when he becomes involved in his first case, which concerns the father of his only friend at college, Victor Trevor (See page 82) Trevor Senior had been cast adrift from the *Gloria Scott* when she blew up in November 1855. After that he had spent time in Australia, where he had made his fortune, before returning to England, where 'for more than twenty years we have led peaceful and useful lives'. If he had spent just five years in Australia earning enough to buy a country estate in Norfolk it would have been 1880 when Holmes, the student, met him and by then Holmes would have been twenty-six. As one can hardly imagine Holmes as a late developer, it must have been his family's financial circumstances that led to him beginning university so late in life. Certainly, he never seems to be a wealthy man, despite the large fees he commands. True, he had enough money to pay a high price for Dr Watson's Kensington practice, but early in his career he had to share rooms in Baker Street to get by. He spent only two years at university and there is never any mention of Holmes having a degree.

It is unclear which university he attended. However, the stories show a strong prejudice against Oxford. Both John Clay, the villain in 'The Red-Headed League', and Colonel Sebastian Moran, Moriarty's sidekick in 'The Adventure of the Empty House', were alumni. Cambridge gets a better show. Holmes is happy to take on Cyril Overton of Trinity College as a client in 'The Adventure of the Missing Three-Quarter' and Watson's school friend Percy Phelps in 'The Naval Treaty' is also a Cambridge man. In 'The Adventure of the Creeping Man', Holmes investigates the case of Professor Presbury in 'Camford', as if Oxford is too distasteful to mention.

In 'The Adventure of the Three Students' Holmes and Watson become involved in an investigation at 'St Luke's College' when they spend some weeks in 'one of our great university towns' while Holmes researches early English charters. Neither Oxford nor Cambridge has a St Luke's, but Watson occasionally alters names out of discretion.

In 'The Musgrave Ritual', Holmes says: 'When I first came up to London I had rooms in Montague Street, just round the corner from the British Museum, and there I waited, filling in my too abundant leisure time by studying all those branches of science which might make me more efficient.' This would have been handy for University College, London, my own alma mater. And if he had been to Oxford or Cambridge, surely he would have said that he 'went down' to London.

He had only one friend during his time at college and, indeed, Watson notes Holmes's 'disinclination to form new friendships'.

'I was never a very sociable fellow,' Holmes admits, 'always rather fond of moping in my rooms and working out my own little methods of thought, so that I never mixed much with the men of my year. Bar fencing and boxing I had few athletic tastes, and then my line of study was quite distinct from that of the other fellows, so that we had no points of contact at all. Trevor was the only man I knew, and that only through the accident of his bull terrier freezing on to my ankle one morning as I went down to chapel.'

Victor Trevor visited while he was laid up. Holmes discovered that Trevor was as friendless as he was and by the end of term they had become close friends, close enough for Trevor to invite Holmes to stay during the vacation. Despite his landed ancestry, Holmes has no family estates to return to. Which is as well. In 'The Resident Patient', Watson mentions that neither the country nor the sea presents the slightest attraction to Holmes, who 'loves to lie in the very centre of five million people'; he certainly spends little time away from the metropolis.

Holmes may not have been popular at college, but he was well known. While living at Montague Street, he says: 'Now and again cases came in my way, principally through the introduction of old fellow-students, for during my last years at the university there was a good deal of talk there about myself and my methods.'

Reginald Musgrave, who had been at the same college and was a 'slight acquaintance', sought him out at Montague Street. At university they had 'once or twice drifted into talk', but Holmes had seen nothing of him for four years. The dates work only if Holmes had last seen Musgrave in 1878, when Holmes first went to college. We know that Holmes was around in 1880, when he spent the vacation with Victor Trevor. But by 1882, at the latest, he had moved out of Montague Street into Baker Street.

By the time Watson returned from convalescence after the Second Afghan war, Holmes was looking for somewhere new to live. He was working in a chemical laboratory 'up the hospital' but he was not a medical student. Watson's friend Stamford says that Holmes is 'well up in anatomy, and he is a first-class chemist; but, as far as I know, he has never taken out any systematic medical classes. His studies are very desultory and eccentric, but he has amassed a lot of out-of-the-way knowledge which would astonish his professors.' He is also uncommunicative and, Watson says, 'a little too scientific for my tastes – it approaches to cold-bloodedness. I could imagine his giving a friend a little pinch of the latest vegetable alkaloid, not out of malevolence, you understand, but simply out of a spirit of inquiry in order to have an accurate idea of the effects. To do him justice, I think that he would take it himself with the same readiness. He appears to have a passion for definite and exact knowledge.'

When Stamford and Watson find him in the laboratory, Holmes instantly spots that Watson had been in Afghanistan and demonstrates the powers of observation and deduction that keep the good doctor enthralled. Holmes, he says, was over six feet tall, and lean, with sharp, piercing eyes and a thin, hawk-like nose. And his chin 'had the prominence and squareness which mark the man of determination'. He admits to getting 'in the dumps at times' and not opening his mouth for days.

Holmes is voluble because he has just found a reagent that is precipitated by haemoglobin. He demonstrates this by stabbing himself in the finger, diluting his own blood, then flinging white crystals into the brew. This would give an infallible test for blood stains and he reels off cases where such a test would have been vital. Holmes is happy to experiment on himself (and Watson) in 'The Adventure of the Devil's Foot'.

Holmes has his eye on a place in Baker Street that would suit both himself and Watson, provided Watson would not mind the strong smell of tobacco and having chemicals about.

He had already found the apartment 221B Baker Street that 'consisted of a couple of comfortable bedrooms and a single large airy sitting-room, cheerfully furnished, and illuminated by two broad windows'. The rent, which they split, is low. Watson moved in that evening; Holmes the following morning.

Watson tells us that Holmes was not a difficult man to live with. He was quiet, usually in bed by 10 p.m. and often up and out before Watson rose in the morning. He spent his time in the chemical laboratory, the dissection room or on long walks the lowest part of the city. These days he would be considered bipolar. Watson says: 'Nothing could exceed his energy when the working fit was upon him; but now and again a reaction would seize him, and for days on end he would lie upon the sofa in the sitting-room, hardly uttering a word or moving a muscle from morning to night.'

Holmes admits his failings in this area. In *A Study in Scarlet*, he says: 'I am the most incurably lazy devil that ever stood in shoe leather – that is, when the fit is on me, for I can be spry enough at times.'

In *The Hound of the Baskervilles*, Watson remarks that Holmes has a 'catlike love of personal cleanliness which is one of his chief characteristics'. Even when sleeping out on Dartmoor 'his chin should be as smooth and his linen as perfect as if he were in Baker Street', though it is not clear how he achieved this.

However, back home in 221B, 'his hands were invariably blotted with ink and stained with chemicals'. He also shared with Watson a weakness for Turkish baths.

He may have been clean, but he was also incredibly untidy. A bohemian, he kept 'his cigars in the coal-scuttle, his tobacco in the toe end of a Persian slipper, and his unanswered correspondence transfixed by a jack-knife into the very centre of his wooden mantelpiece'. He had a horror of destroying documents. Month by month they would accumulate until stacked in every corner of the room. Somehow he also crammed into 221B an extensive library and a filing system that included biographies of Hebrew rabbis, of a staff-commander who wrote a monograph on deep-sea fishes and opera singers, such as Irene Adler. When 'in one of his queer humours', he would practise with his pistol indoors and 'proceed to adorn the opposite wall with a patriotic V.R. done in bullet-pocks'.

Both Holmes and Watson smoked pipes, cigars and cigarettes. In *The Hound of the Baskervilles*, Watson complains of the poisonous atmosphere caused by Holmes's black clay pipe. On the other hand, in 'The Veiled Lodger', Holmes says: 'Mrs Merrilow does not object to tobacco, Watson, if you wish to indulge your filthy habits.' But then Holmes was frequently sarcastic; after all, he considered 'The Red-Headed League' famously to be 'a three-pipe problem', but for which he needed just fifty minutes to solve.

Holmes is fond of whisky and soda – provided, no doubt, by the 'gasogene' in 221B. Brandy is used for medicinal purposes at the slightest excuse. Chianti and Tokay are favourite wines and a half-drunk bottle provides a vital clue in 'The Adventure of Abbey Grange'.

Holmes is also fond of drugs. When Watson first moves into Baker Street he notices a dreamy, vacant expression in Holmes's eyes and would have suspected him of being addicted to the use of some narcotic 'had not the temperance and cleanliness of his whole life forbidden such a notion'. He quickly learns better. *The Sign of the Four* opens with Holmes removing his hypodermic syringe from its Morocco-leather case.

'Which is it today, morphine or cocaine?' asks Watson.

'It is cocaine,' replies Holmes, 'a seven-per-cent solution. Would you care to try it?'

Watson declines on the grounds that his constitution had not yet recovered from the Afghan campaign; in fact, he disapproves. Holmes explains that he takes cocaine when he has no brainwork to do – when there is nothing else to live for. He is delighted when Watson gives him his watch to see what he can deduce from it, as this prevents him from taking a second dose. Nevertheless, he alternates 'from week to week between cocaine and ambition'. In the end Watson becomes inured to his friend's peccadillo. In 'The Yellow Face', he says: 'Save for the occasional use of cocaine, he had no vices, and he only turned to the drug as a protest against the monotony of existence when cases were scanty and the papers uninteresting.'

Of course, cocaine, morphine, opium (Holmes is found in an opium den in 'The Man with the Twisted Lip', but only to investigate a case) and, apparently, firing a pistol indoors were not against the law in Victorian England. The use of the drugs was not banned in the United Kingdom until the Dangerous Drugs Act of 1920, which implemented the laws drawn up at the Hague Convention of 1912.

Perhaps what is most puzzling about Holmes – to the modern reader – is his sexuality. These days, it would be all to easy to assume that two men who lived together – on and off, at least – were gay. But there is not the slightest indication of that. Watson certainly has an eye for the women. Holmes is simply sexless. Watson tells him that he is an 'automaton – a calculating machine. There is something positively inhuman in you at times.'

But Holmes is not completely without emotion. When Watson is shot through the thigh in 'The Adventure of the Three Garridebs', he writes: 'It was worth a wound – it was worth many wounds – to know the depth of loyalty and love which lay behind that cold mask. The clear, hard eyes were dimmed for a moment, and the firm lips were shaking. For the one and only time I caught a glimpse of a great heart as well as of a great brain. All my years of humble but single-minded service culminated in that moment of revelation.'

Holmes comes from a time when men did not show their emotions, which was generally considered bad form, especially in a detective. In *The Sign of the Four*, Holmes explains: 'It is of the first importance not to allow your judgment to be biased by personal qualities. A client is to me a mere unit, a factor in a problem. The emotional qualities are antagonistic to clear reasoning.' He is quite unmoved by the fact that his client is the attractive Miss Morstan, who Watson immediately falls for.

'I assure you that the most winning woman I ever knew was hanged for poisoning three little children for their insurance-money,' says Holmes.

When Watson goes to see his beloved Mary and her mistress, Mrs Cecil Forrester, Holmes warns: 'I would not tell them too much. Women are never to be entirely trusted – not the best of them.'

Watson describes this more strongly as Holmes's 'aversion to women . . . He disliked and distrusted the sex.' However, he did have a peculiarly ingratiating way with them and won their confidence easily. Mrs Hudson put this down to his remarkable gentleness and courtesy, even though to Watson, Holmes confided: 'I am not a whole-souled admirer of womankind,' whose motives he found inscrutable.

'How can you build on such a quicksand?' he asks. 'Their most trivial action may mean volumes, or their most extraordinary conduct may depend upon a hairpin or a curling tongs.'

In fact, it is love he mistrusts. In *The Sign of the Four*, he says: 'Love is an emotional thing, and whatever is emotional is opposed to that true cold reason which I place above all things. I should never marry myself, lest I bias my judgment.' Later this became a matter of regret. At the end of 'The Adventure of the Devil's Foot', Holmes says wistfully: 'I have never loved, Watson, but if I did and if the woman I loved had met such an end, I might act as our lawless lion-hunter had done.'

Holmes does have an eye for pulchritude though. In 'The

Adventure of the Illustrious Client', he describes Violet de Merville as 'beautiful, but with an other-world beauty . . . I have seen faces in the pictures of the old masters of the Middle Ages. How a beastman could have laid his vile paws upon such a being of the beyond I cannot imagine. You may have noticed how extremes call to each other, the spiritual to the animal, the caveman to the angel. You never saw a worse case than this.'

In 'The Adventure of Copper Beeches' Watson is momentarily hopeful that the great detective might find romance with Violet Hunter, but Holmes, 'rather to my disappointment, manifested no further interest in her when once she had ceased to be the centre of one of his problems'. And in 'A Case of Identity', Holmes finds 'that maiden' Miss Mary Sutherland 'quite an interesting study . . . more interesting than her little problem,' he says, leaving her to believe that her 'fiancé' will return to her, so leaving out the possibility that any romance will come of it.

Only Irene Adler from 'A Scandal in Bohemia' seemed to have struck a blow to his heart. The thirty-year-old contralto from New Jersey had performed at La Scala before becoming the prima donna of the Imperial Opera of Warsaw. It was there the Crown Prince – later King – of Bohemia had met her and by then she had already become a 'well-known adventuress'. For Holmes, Watson says, she would always be '*the* woman'.

'I have seldom heard him mention her under any other name,' says Watson. 'In his eyes she eclipses and predominates the whole of her sex.'

But it was not that he felt anything akin to love for Miss Alder. As Watson says: 'He never spoke of the softer passions, save with a gibe and a sneer.' No, he admired her because she had bested him intellectually. She had been a worthy opponent, though we are never told what became of her photograph, which he kept. He mentions her and his failure in that case several times over the course of the Holmes stories.

In 'The Adventure of Charles Augustus Milverton', Holmes – while acknowledging that he was not the marrying type

– becomes engaged to Milverton's housemaid, only to throw her aside. He happily assured Watson, 'I have a hated rival, who will certainly cut me out the instant that my back is turned.'

Nevertheless, he is positively puritanical when it came to other men's treatment of women. He sneers at Neil Gibson's love for Grace Dunbar in 'The Problem of the Thor Bridge', though it turned out to have been quite chaste. But then, as he admits in 'The Adventure of the Lion's Mane': 'Women have seldom been an attraction to me, for my brain has always governed my heart.'

Even so – though by then in his fifties and retired – he felt a stirring for Maud Bellamy, saying: 'I could not look upon her perfect clear-cut face, with all the soft freshness of the downlands in her delicate colouring, without realizing that no young man would cross her path unscathed.'

In fact, he is besotted, for 'she possessed strong character as well as great beauty . . . Maud Bellamy will always remain in my memory as a most complete and remarkable woman.'

'Bring them to justice, Mr Holmes,' she says.

Throwing aside his usual insistence on the primacy of pure reason, he replied: 'Thank you. I value a woman's instinct in such matters.'

He even asked to have a word alone with her, but her father would not allow it.

Chapter 12

Beneath the Deerstalker

When Watson moves in to Baker Street he observes: 'Of contemporary literature, philosophy and politics he appeared to know next to nothing. Upon my quoting Thomas Carlyle,' who had died only in 1881, 'he inquired in the naivest way who he might be and what he had done.'

Indeed, Holmes expresses very few political views. However, in 'The Adventure of the Noble Bachelor', when he insists that Francis May Moulton and his wife stay for supper, he says: 'It is always a joy to meet an American, Mr Moulton, for I am one of those who believe that the folly of a monarch and the blundering of a minister in far-gone years will not prevent our children from being someday citizens of the same world-wide country under a flag which shall be a quartering of the Union Jack with the Stars and Stripes.'

Watson is also amazed that Holmes does not know that the Earth orbits the Sun. Not only is Holmes astonished by the fact, but he immediately tries to forget it, explaining that there was only so much room in the brain and knowledge of the Earth's orbit made no difference to him or to his work.

'His ignorance, was as remarkable as his knowledge,' says Watson, who then draws up an assessment, which he heads: 'Sherlock Holmes – His Limits':

1. Knowledge of Literature – Nil.
2. " " Philosophy – Nil.

3. ""   Astronomy – Nil.
4. ""   Politics – Feeble.
5. ""   Botany – Variable. Well up in belladonna, opium, and poisons generally. Knows nothing of practical gardening.
6. Knowledge of Geology – Practical, but limited. Tells at a glance different soils from each other. After walks has shown me splashes upon his trousers, and told me by their colour and consistence in what part of London he had received them.
7. Knowledge of Chemistry – Profound.
8. ""   Anatomy – Accurate, but unsystematic.
9. ""   Sensational Literature – Immense. He appears to know every detail of every horror perpetrated in the century.
10. Plays the violin well.
11. Is an expert singlestick player, boxer, and swordsman.
12. Has a good practical knowledge of British law.

This is hardly fair: Holmes quotes Goethe in German and a letter from Gustave Flaubert to George Sand in French. At the end of 'A Case of Identity', he compares the works of the fourteenth-century Persian poet Hafiz to Horace, who he quotes, in Latin, at the end of *A Study in Scarlet*. He also quotes Thoreau and mentions, in passing, the Franco-Prussian War. He knows the work of Poe and Gaboriau and, while on his way to Swindon in 'The Boscombe Valley Mystery', he reads his pocket edition of Petrarch and is happy to discuss George Meredith. Returning to life in 'The Adventure of the Empty House', he quotes Shakespeare. Then in 'A Case of Identity', he paraphrases Byron. In 'The Crooked Man', he cites the Old Testament. (He attended chapel while at university but there is no other reference to churchgoing.) Holmes even knows Carlyle, quoting the epithet 'genius is an infinite capacity for taking pains', which is generally attributed to him in *A Study in Scarlet*, then admitting as much in *The Sign of the Four* but finding him inferior to the German humorist Johann Richter.

When criticizing Watson's rendition of *A Study of Scarlet*, Holmes drops in a reference to the fifth proposition of Euclid which, surely, has even less to do with detection that Copernican Theory. In *The Sign of the Four*, Watson and Holmes discuss the miracle plays, mediaeval pottery, Stradivarius violins, the Buddhism of Ceylon and the warships of the future – 'handling each as though he had made a special study of it'. In *The Hound of the Baskervilles*, they discuss the comparative anatomy of Bushmen and Hottentots. Holmes admits knowledge of the old masters and recognizes a painting by Jean-Baptiste Greuze in Moriarty's study – but then there is an artist in the family. Even knowledge of the Lion's Mane jellyfish is locked away in his cranium somewhere. Of course, Holmes has a special interest in Stradivarius. In *A Study in Scarlet* he prattles away on the topic of Cremona fiddles and the differences between a Stradivarius and an Amati. In 'The Cardbox Box', Watson and Holmes dine together and Holmes talks about nothing but violins – 'narrating with great exultation how he had purchased his own Stradivarius, which was worth at least five hundred guineas, at a Jew broker's in Tottenham Court Road for fifty-five shillings [£224 at today's prices]. This led him to Paganini, and we sat for an hour over a bottle of claret while he told me anecdote after anecdote of that extraordinary man.'

Holmes is an accomplished violinist, able to play difficult pieces including, at Watson's request, Mendelssohn's *Lieder*. When Watson first meet Holmes, he notices the extraordinary delicacy of touch he exhibits with his scientific instruments but, while contemplative, he would close his eyes and carelessly scrape at the fiddle on his knee. Although this tries Watson's patience, Holmes ends with a quick succession of his companion's favourites. 'Scraping upon his violin, Watson remarks, is Holmes's favourite occupation – though conducting malodorous chemistry experiments in the sitting room in Baker Street must come a close second.' Watson says he has a remarkable gift for improvisation and in the stories he picks up his violin at least twelve times.

In 'The Red-Headed League' Holmes and Watson take the afternoon off to hear a recital by the Spanish violinist Pablo Sarasate at St James's Hall. Holmes says: 'I observe that there is a good deal of German music on the programme, which is rather more to my taste than Italian or French. It is introspective, and I want to introspect.'

At the end of 'The Adventure of the Red Circle', they hurry to Covent Garden in time to catch the second act of Wagner, and in 'The Adventure of the Retired Colourman', they go to the Albert Hall to hear a singer named Carina. There is speculation about who this might be, including that by '*carina*' – meaning 'little darling' in pidgin Italian – Holmes means Irene Adler who has, perhaps, returned to the stage.

Holmes is also a published author with monographs on the 140 types of pipe, cigar and cigarette ash; the tracing of footsteps with some remarks upon the uses of plaster of Paris as a preserver of impressions; secret writing – analysing 160 separate ciphers; the dating of eighteenth-century documents and polyphonic motets of the Renaissance composer Orlande de Lassus. In 'A Case of Identity' he is thinking of writing a monograph on the typewriter and its relation to crime; one on malingering in 'The Adventure of the Dying Detective'; and one on dogs in the work of the detective in the 'The Adventure of the Creeping Man'. He has also made learned studies of early English charters in 'The Adventure of the Three Students', sixteenth-century ecclesiastical accountancy in 'The Adventure of the Gold Pince-Nez' and the relations between ancient Cornish and Chaldean in 'The Adventure of the Devil's Foot'. When he retires, Holmes writes the snappily titled *Practical Handbook of Bee Culture, with Some Observations upon the Segregation of the Queen*, which he uses to get one over on his German enemy in 'His Last Bow'. He also uses the absence of Watson to write 'The Adventure of the Blanched Solider' and 'The Adventure of the Lion's Mane'.

But surely his greatest contribution to the science of detection is his ambitiously entitled article 'The Book of Life', which appears in an unnamed magazine in *A Study in Scarlet*. It attempts to show how much an observant man might learn by an accurate and systematic examination of everything that came in his way. The reasoning was close and intense, but Watson finds the deductions far fetched and exaggerated and a remarkable mixture of shrewdness and absurdity. Holmes claims that through a momentary expression, a twitch of a muscle or a glance of an eye, it is possible to fathom a man's innermost thoughts. Deceit, according to Holmes, was an impossibility to one trained to observe and analyse.

'His conclusions were as infallible as so many propositions of Euclid,' says Watson. 'So startling would his results appear to the uninitiated that until they learned the processes by which he had arrived at them they might well consider him as a necromancer.'

According to the article:

From a drop of water, a logician could infer the possibility of an Atlantic or a Niagara without having seen or heard of one or the other. So all life is a great chain, the nature of which is known whenever we are shown a single link of it. Like all other arts, the Science of Deduction and Analysis is one which can only be acquired by long and patient study, nor is life long enough to allow any mortal to attain the highest possible perfection in it. Before turning to those moral and mental aspects of the matter which present the greatest difficulties, let the inquirer begin by mastering more elementary problems. Let him, on meeting a fellow-mortal, learn at a glance to distinguish the history of the man, and the trade or profession to which he belongs. Puerile as such an exercise may seem, it sharpens the faculties of observation, and teaches one where to look and what to look for. By a man's finger-nails, by his coat-sleeve, by his boots, by his trouser-knees, by the callosities of his forefinger and thumb, by his expression, by his shirt-cuffs – by each of these things a man's calling is plainly revealed. That all united should fail to enlighten the competent inquirer in any case is almost inconceivable.

Watson condemns this as 'ineffable twaddle', saying 'I never read such rubbish in my life.' Holmes does not take offence; instead, he points out that he depends on the theories he has laid out in the piece for his 'bread and cheese' and later, in 'The Five Orange Pips', ascribes his method to the French zoologist and palaeontologist Georges Cuvier, who 'could correctly describe a whole animal by the contemplation of a single bone'. (Holmes's Aristotelian form of reasoning had recently been given a fillip by the American scientist Charles S. Peirce, writing in *Popular Science Monthly* in 1877 and 1878; however, Peirce fell from grace in 1883 when he was dismissed from John Hopkins University for engaging in an extramarital affair. Surely, Holmes would not have approved.) He is more modest about his method in 'The Boscombe Valley Mystery', saying: 'It is founded upon the observation of trifles.' Things that Watson overlooks or deductions he fails to make are 'elementary', a word Holmes uses eight times in the stories.

Normally, though, Holmes is not much of a writer; he rarely uses the phone. Indeed, there is no mention of a telephone in 221B Baker Street until 'The Adventure of the Retired Colourman', usually dated to 1899, and in *The Sign of the Four*, Athelney Jones has to go over the road to telephone the Yard. However, Holmes is no Luddite and is happy to embrace the new technology: in 'The Adventure of the Mazarin Stone', thought to be set in 1903, Holmes has a gramophone, which went on sale in London just five years before, and by 1914, he owns a car, though Watson does the driving.

Holmes is a man of action as well as formidable intellect. He regularly carries a pistol, which he fires in *The Sign of the Four* and *The Hound of the Baskervilles*, and which he uses as a cudgel in 'The Adventure of the Empty House' and 'The Adventure of the Three Garridebs'. He fenced at university and Watson says he is an expert swordsman, though we never see him in action, and that he is also adept at singlestick, a form of fencing using a wooden stick, usually as practice. He regularly carries a cane, which he uses to defend against the snake in 'The Adventure of the Speckled Band'. In 'The Final Problem', he is attacked by a ruffian with a bludgeon, but knocks him down and has him arrested. However, being a singlestick expert does not help him when two stick-wielding miscreants rain blows on him outside the Café Royal in 'The Adventure of the Illustrious Client'.

'I took most of them on my guard,' says Holmes. 'It was the second man that was too much for me.'

Though he is no horseman, Holmes brings a hunting crop into play in 'A Case of Identity', dashes the pistol from John Clay's hand with it in 'The Red-Headed League', and it becomes his 'favourite weapon' in 'The Adventure of the Six Napoleons'.

In 'The Adventure of the Empty House', Holmes explains that he thwarted Moriarty because he has some knowledge of '*baritsu*, or the Japanese system of wrestling'. This is thought to be a reference to '*bartitsu*', a version of *jujitsu* imported by Edward Barton-Wright in 1898. Unfortunately, Holmes could not have learnt this in time to push Moriarty over the Reichenbach Falls as 'The Final Problem' was published in 1893.

Overall, Holmes prefers the old-fashioned way. Using his fists. He had been a boxer at university. In *The Sign of the Four* he meets McMurdo, Thaddeus Sholto's bodyguard and an ex-prizefighter. He says: 'Don't you remember that amateur who fought three rounds with you at Alison's rooms on the night of your benefit four years back?'

'Not Mr Sherlock Holmes!' says McMurdo. 'God's truth! How could I have mistook you? If instead o' standin' there so quiet you had just stepped up and given me that cross-hit of yours under the jaw, I'd ha' known you without a question. Ah, you're one that has wasted your gifts, you have! You might have aimed high, if you had joined the fancy.'

But Holmes has stayed in training. In 'The Yellow Face', Watson says: 'Sherlock Holmes was a man who seldom took exercise for exercise's sake. Few men were capable of greater muscular effort, and he was undoubtedly one of the finest boxers of his weight that I have ever seen; but he looked upon aimless bodily exertion as a waste of energy, and he seldom bestirred himself save where there was some professional object to be served. Then he was absolutely untiring and indefatigable. That he should have kept himself in training under such circumstances is remarkable, but his diet was usually of the sparest.' Nevertheless, he is unable to stop two men – one at least who is past his prime – who wrestle him to the ground in 'The Reigate Puzzle'. However, he is not at all intimidated by Steve Dixie in 'The Adventure of the Three Gables'.

He is certainly audacious. There are numerous examples of Holmes and Watson breaking and entering, concealing evidence from the police and involving themselves in other criminal activities. And Holmes does not mind taking the law into his own hands. When Watson escapes with a slight flesh wound in 'The Adventure of the Three Garridebs', Holmes tells John Garrideb: 'If you had killed Watson, you would not have got out of this room alive.'

Holmes does not eat when he is on a case. In 'The Adventure of the Mazarin Stone', Mrs Hudson asks when he wants to dine. He replies: 'Seven-thirty, the day after tomorrow.' He is already pale and thin, and the page, Billy, fears for his health. In 'the Adventure of the Dying Detective', Holmes deliberately starves himself to look gaunt.

Holmes and Watson do regularly eat in restaurants: in 'The Adventure of Shoscombe Old Place', Holmes is positively lethargic until he has consumed a dish of freshly caught trout for his supper. On Dartmoor in *The Hound of the Baskervilles* he is stocked up with a half-full bottle of spirits, a loaf of bread, tinned tongue and two tins of peaches – not to mention the litter of tins he has already emptied whose contents have been cooked and eaten, judging by the utensils. There is no harm in eating well after a case is solved nor even before: to steady their nerves for the shoot-out on the river in *The Sign of the Four*, Holmes treats Watson and Inspector Jones to oysters, a brace of grouse and a choice of white wines, saying: 'Watson, you have never yet recognized my merits as a housekeeper.' And in preparation for the dénouement of 'The Adventure of the Noble Bachelor', the confectioner's man delivers an epicurean cold supper, comprising 'a couple of brace of cold woodcock, a pheasant, a *pâté de foie gras* pie with a group of ancient and cobwebby bottles'. Woodcock is on the menu again in Baker Street in 'The Adventure of the Blue Carbuncle'.

Holmes is, of course, the master of disguise. Often Watson does not even recognize him, but then the good doctor is often quite slow on the uptake. In *The Sign of the Four*, Watson and Athelney Jones wait for Holmes when an aged seafarer turns up with a pea-jacket buttoned up to the throat, a coloured scarf around his chin, and bushy white brows and long grey sidewhiskers. It is Holmes. Jones even remarks that he had a proper workhouse cough and weak legs that were worth £10 a week as an actor. In 'A Scandal in Bohemia', he is a drunken groom and a Nonconformist clergyman, and he is an aged Italian priest in 'The Final Problem'. In 'The Adventure of the Empty House', he is a wizened bookseller. In 'The Adventure of Charles Augustus Milverton', he becomes a plumber called Escott to woo the blackmailer's maid. In 'The Man with the Twisted Lip', he is the aged denizen in an opium den. He is a French workman in 'The Disappearance of Lady Carfax'. Then in 'The Adventure of the Mazarin Stone', he is a workman looking for a job and an old lady with a baggy parasol. There is some bravura acting by Holmes in 'The Reigate Puzzle' and 'The Adventure of the Dying Detective' and on both occasions he feigns illness, even fooling Dr Watson – admittedly not the sharpest lancet in the medical bag, but diagnosis is his field. And in 'The Last Bow', he fools the German spymaster Von Bork into thinking he is an Irish-American.

Watson says little of what clothes Holmes normally wears, apart from the 'long grey travelling-cloak and close-fitting cloth cap' in 'The Boscombe Valley Mystery' and the 'ear-flapped travelling-cap' in 'The Adventure of the Silver Blaze'. At home in Baker Street, he wears a mouse-coloured dressing-gown, which he pulls from his effigy in 'The Adventure of the Empty House', after throwing off the seedy frock coat he had been wearing as a disguise. To follow 'Mrs Sawyer' in *A Study in Scarlet*, Holmes quickly dons a cravat and an Ulster – a long, loose overcoat.

Holmes seems to have little, if any, inherited wealth and needs to share the rent even for the humble apartment in Baker Street, hardly the most fashionable part of town. In 'The Problem of Thor Bridge', Holmes tells Senator Gibson: 'My professional charges are upon a fixed scale. I do not vary them, save when I remit them altogether.' Nor does he need to boost his reputation; apart from Watson's reports of the most interesting cases, Holmes receives as much work as he can handle and Watson frequently refers to other cases he has not written up – many of which occur abroad. Holmes, over the course of his career, is in demand from Odessa to Ceylon (Sri Lanka). The fact that he has not subsided completely into cocaine addiction must mean that he had been kept busy. By 'The Final Problem', Holmes boasts that he has worked on over a thousand cases.

The impression is that he likes to work *pro bono*. In 'The Adventure of Black Peter', Watson notes that Holmes is so unworldly, or so capricious, that he 'frequently refused his help to the powerful and wealthy where the problem made no appeal to his sympathies, while he would devote weeks of most intense application to the affairs of some humble client whose case presented those strange and dramatic qualities which appealed to his imagination and challenged his ingenuity.'

He is not overawed by rank and title. He unmasks the king of Bohemia, when he is pretending to be Count Von Kramm in 'A Scandal of Bohemia'; he turns down a knighthood; refuses to kowtow to Lord St Simon in 'The Adventure of the Noble Bachelor' – pointing out that his last client was the king of Scandinavia – and refuses to be intimidated by the bluster of Neil Gibson, the Gold King, in 'The Problem of Thor Bridge' and the page-boy Billy says Holmes put the prime minister, home secretary and Lord Cantlemere at their ease when they visited Baker Street.

'My profession is its own reward,' Holmes tells Helen Stoner in 'The Adventure of the Speckled Band'. But he will, of course, need some cash, asking her 'to defray whatever expenses I may be put to, at the time which suits you best'. After preventing a major theft from the Suburban Bank in 'The Red-Headed League', Holmes tells the bank manager, Mr Merryweather: 'I have been at some small expense over this matter, which I shall expect the bank to refund, but beyond that I am amply repaid by having had an experience which is in many ways unique . . .' In 'The Adventure of the Beryl Coronet', Holmes recovers the three beryls at a cost of £1,000 apiece, but asks for a cheque for £4,000, presumable taking £1,000 (£82,000 at today's prices) for himself. The banker, Alexander Holder, thinks this good value for the service rendered. In 'A Scandal in Bohemia', Holmes takes £300 in gold and £700 in notes – but then he is dealing with a king. He is offered an emerald ring as a reward but takes a picture of Irene Adler instead. Later, in 'A Case of Identity', we learn that the king of Bohemia also gave him a gold snuff box and that the diamond ring on his finger is payment from the Dutch royal family. He also keeps a sovereign given to him by Irene in memory of being a witness at her wedding.

He has no money worries after 'The Final Problem', when he says: 'Between ourselves, the recent cases in which I have been of assistance to the royal family of Scandinavia, and to the French republic, have left me in such a position that I could continue to live in the quiet fashion which is most congenial to me, and to concentrate my attention upon my chemical researches.' Additionally, he has enough spare cash to buy Watson's practice for an inflated price in 'The Adventure of the Norwood Builder'.

Nevertheless, more baubles are on their way. He gets the *légion d'honneur* from the president of France, along with an autographed letter at the beginning of the 'The Adventure of the Gold Pince-Nez' and an emerald tie-pin from an lady whose august name Watson fancies he could guess, in 'The Adventure of the Bruce-Partington Plans'. But nothing gives him more pleasure that taking £6,000 (nearly half-a-million pounds at today's prices) from the Duke of Holdernesse in 'The Adventure of the Priory School'. Holmes folds up the cheque and places it in his notebook, saying: 'I am a poor man.' A poor man no longer. By 'The Dying Detective', Holmes is paying the long-suffering Mrs Hudson princely sums for the Baker Street apartment.

'I have no doubt that the house might have been purchased at the price which Holmes paid for his rooms during the years that I was with him,' says Watson.

Consequently, Holmes retires at a relatively young age. In July 1907 we meet him in 'The Adventure of the Lion's Mane' living alone with his housekeeper and his bees on an estate on the South Downs, overlooking the English Channel. By then, he is only fifty-three and still up to solving a mystery. We don't see Holmes again until August 1914, when he is a sprightly sixty. There is no record of his death. Perhaps he was still alive when Conan Doyle died in 1930, when he would have been seventy-six.

Chapter 13

Dr Watson

In 'The Adventure of the Veiled Lodger' Watson mentions that he had documented cases over seventeen of the twenty-three years Holmes has been in practice. Although Holmes disapproves of how Watson romanticizes his cases, he deliberately seconds Watson into those cases he chronicles: 'I am lost without my Boswell,' says Holmes.

We know quite a lot about John H. Watson MD (though his wife calls him 'James' in 'The Man with the Twisted Lip'). He took his degree as a Doctor of Medicine at the University of London in 1878. At the time, the University did not run its own medical courses. Only later is it mentioned that Watson was at Bart's – St Bartholomew's Hospital – so it is possible that he attended the medical college there. After obtaining his degree he went to the Royal Victoria Military Hospital at Netley in Hampshire, where he took a course for army surgeons. He was then attached to the Fifth Northumberland Fusiliers as assistant surgeon. His regiment was stationed in India at the time, but before he could join it the Second Anglo-Afghan War had broken out. By the time he reached Bombay they had advanced through the passes and were deep in enemy territory. He followed, with other officers, and managed to catch up with his regiment at Kandahar.

During the campaign he was seconded into the 66th (Berkshire) Regiment of Foot, who lost 286 men, with thirty-two wounded at the battle of Maiwand. Watson was struck on the shoulder by a Jezail bullet, which shattered the bone and grazed the subclavian artery. In *A Study in Scarlet*, Holmes notes that Watson's left arm had been injured as he holds it in a stiff and unnatural manner. However, in *The Sign of the Four* and elsewhere Watson says had been wounded in the leg. In 'The Noble Bachelor', for example, he mentions 'the Jezail bullet which I had brought back in one of my limbs'.

It could have been worse. He says he would have fallen into the hands of the murderous Ghazis had it not been for his orderly, Murray, who had thrown him across a packhorse to take him safely to the British lines.

Weak and in pain, Watson was removed to the base hospital in Peshawar in British India. He was recovering when he was struck down with enteric fever – typhoid. For months, he hovered on the brink of death, but eventually rallied. By then he was so weak and emaciated that he was put on the first ship home. A month later, he arrived in Portsmouth on the troopship *Orontes*. Watson says that his health had been 'irretrievably ruined', but that he was given nine months' leave to convalesce. The good doctor is a bad judge of his own condition, for we see him hale and hearty over thirty years later in 'The Last Bow'. Indeed, he is still chronicling Holmes's escapades forty-six years on in 1927 in 'The Adventure of Shoscombe Old Place'. Nevertheless, he did not return to the army.

Watson says that he had neither kith nor kin in England and in *The Sign of the Four*, we learn of an older brother, H. Watson, who drank himself to death. Holmes deduces this much from the watch Watson he had inherited. It had previously belonged to his father, another H. Watson.

His time his own, Watson had eleven shillings and sixpence (£52 at today's prices) a day to live on. Under the circumstances, he gravitated to London – 'that great cesspool into which all the loungers and idlers of the Empire are irresistibly drained'. He stayed in a private hotel in the Strand, but soon found he was running short of money. He considered leaving the capital and rusticating somewhere in the countryside, but decided instead to find somewhere cheaper to live.

In the bar of the Criterion he ran into an old friend named Stamford, who had been a dresser at Bart's. They lunched at the Holborn Restaurant, then Stamford took him to see Holmes and make the momentous introduction. Initially, Watson was puzzled, even dismissive, of Holmes's profession but soon he was impressed. Holmes took him into his confidence and allowed him to read a letter from Inspector Gregson of Scotland Yard. Holmes then asked Watson to accompany him to the scene of the crime – 3, Lauriston Gardens off the Brixton Road – in what would be their first case together. At the end, Watson is a little peeved that the newspaper gave Gregson and Lestrade the credit for solving the case, while Holmes was dismissed as an amateur who might learn from such instructors.

'Never mind,' says Watson. 'I have all the facts in my journal, and the public shall know them.'

But when he does put them before the reading public in *A Study in Scarlet*, Holmes remarks: 'Detection is, or ought to be, an exact science and should be treated in the same cold and unemotional manner. You have attempted to tinge it with romanticism, which produces much the same effect as if you worked a love-story or an elopement into the fifth proposition of Euclid.'

Nevertheless, in his next case, *The Sign of the Four*, Holmes again wants his help. Which is just as well, because when Mary Morstan arrives to consult Holmes, Watson is instantly smitten: 'Miss Morstan entered the room with a firm step and an outward composure of manner,' he says. 'She was a blonde young lady, small, dainty, well gloved, and dressed in the most perfect taste.'

He goes on to describe, in detail, what she is wearing, the regularity of her features, her complexion, her expression and her large blue eyes that are 'singularly spiritual and sympathetic'.

'In an experience of women which extends over many nations and three separate continents,' says Watson, 'I have never looked upon a face which gave a clearer promise of a refined and sensitive nature.' (The third continent Watson says he has visited, after Europe and Asia, is assumed to be Australia. Later in *The Sign of the Four* he mentions seeing the mine workings at

Ballarat.) Miss Morstan is the daughter of an officer in the 34th Bombay Infantry who disappeared in mysterious circumstances in 1878. He sent her home when she was a child. Her mother was dead and she had no relatives in England. She went to a boarding school in Edinburgh, leaving when she was seventeen to become a governess to Mrs Cecil Forrester who, as Holmes's client, had been much impressed by his kindness and skill.

When Watson learns that she may inherit a fortune, he is downcast, fearing that it might come between them. However, in the gloom of Pondicherry Lodge, Miss Morstan suddenly seizes his wrist.

After Bartholomew Sholto is found dead and the treasure gone, Watson escorts Miss Morstan home. In the cab, she breaks down. Later, she tells him she found him cold and distant on the journey, and he says that at the time 'she little guessed the struggle within my breast, or the effort of self-restraint which held me back. My sympathies and my love went out to her, even as my hand had in the garden.'

She was weak and helpless but he was too much of a gentleman to 'take her at a disadvantage to obtrude love upon her at such a time'. Worse, she was rich. If Holmes was successful in cracking the case, she would be an heiress, the richest in England; Watson would still be a disabled army surgeon on half-pay.

'Might she not look upon me as a mere vulgar fortune-seeker?' thinks Watson. 'I could not bear to risk that such a thought should cross her mind.'

The treasure would be an impassable barrier between them. But after he drops her off and drives away, he turns to steal one final glance.

Watson and Holmes then devote themselves to the case and, after a particularly long day, they return Baker Street. Holmes takes up his violin. 'Then I seemed to be floated peacefully away upon a soft sea of sound until I found myself in dreamland, with the sweet face of Mary Morstan looking down upon me,' says Watson.

With his old service-revolver in his hand, Watson joins

Holmes and Athelney Jones in the shoot-out with Jonathan Small and his Andaman Islander. During the chase, Watson reveals himself to be an inveterate hunter, saying: 'I have coursed many creatures in many countries during my checkered career, but never did sport give me such a wild thrill as this mad, flying man-hunt down the Thames.'

It is then Watson's task to deliver the treasure chest to Miss Morstan, who is waiting, 'seated by the open window, dressed in some sort of white diaphanous material, with a little touch of scarlet at the neck and waist,' he says. 'The soft light of a shaded lamp fell upon her as she leaned back in the basket chair, playing over her sweet grave face, and tinting with a dull, metallic sparkle the rich coils of her luxuriant hair. One white arm and hand drooped over the side of the chair, and her whole pose and figure spoke of an absorbing melancholy. At the sound of my footfall she sprang to her feet, however, and a bright flush of surprise and of pleasure coloured her pale cheeks.'

He congratulates her on her new-found wealth, as if delighted – though admits to himself he is over-acting. When she hears of the danger he was in, she nearly faints. Then Watson breaks open the box with a poker to find it empty.

'"Thank God!" I ejaculated from my very heart,' he writes.

'Why do you say that?' she asks.

'Because you are within my reach again,' he says, taking her hand. 'Because I love you, Mary, as truly as ever a man loved a woman. Because this treasure, these riches, sealed my lips. Now that they are gone I can tell you how I love you. That is why I said, "Thank God."'

'Then I say "Thank God", too,' she whispers as he draws her to his side.

It has to be said that she is not entirely penniless, nor without a dowry. She has already received six very large and lustrous pearls – the finest Watson has ever seen.

When Watson tells Holmes that Miss Morstan has consented to be his bride, Holmes lets out a groan.

'I feared as much,' he says. 'I really cannot congratulate you.'

Watson is a little hurt, but Holmes reassures him that she is one of the most charming young ladies he has ever met and might even have been useful in their line of work.

While Holmes jacks up on cocaine, Watson is content with 'ship's' – identified as either 'naval cocoa tobacco' or *Schippers Tabak Special*, a strong Dutch tobacco favoured by sailors. Later, in 'The Crooked Man' – just a month after Watson is married, Holmes remarks: 'You still smoke the Arcadia mixture of your bachelor days, then!' He can tell, of course, from the ash on Watson's clothing. They continue to share cigars and cigarettes, along with whisky, brandy, wine and the occasional glass of port. But Watson has one vice that he does not share with Holmes – gambling. In 'The Adventure of Shoscombe Old Place', Holmes asks Watson: 'You know something of racing?' And Watson replies: 'I ought to. I pay for it with about half my wound pension.' Which would be about £2 a week, or £163 at today's prices.

By 'A Scandal in Bohemia', Watson is already married and has moved out of Baker Street. He has seen little of Holmes and expresses his own complete happiness at having a home of his own. Nevertheless, he spends two nights at 221B during the prosecution of the case with no indication that he informed his wife. This may, or may not, be connected to the fact that, when he first sees Irene Adler, he notes her 'superb figure outlined against the lights of the hall'.

Watson does not make the same mistake again. During 'The Red-Headed League', he pops home before the dénoument. He does not mention where exactly he has set up home with Mary, but when he returns to Baker Street he goes 'across the Park' and along Oxford Street. This can only be Hyde Park, so we must assume he lives in Kensington, where we later discover he had a practice.

In 'The Boscombe Valley Mystery', his wife encourages him to take off to the wilds of Herefordshire. And in 'The Man with the Twisted Lip', after Watson's wife sends him to the opium den, he makes off for the night again without so much as a by your leave. He and Holmes stay with Mrs St Clair, who again Watson views with an appreciative eye. She was a small blonde woman, clad in a light *mousseline de soie* – a sheer silk-muslin – with fluffy pink chiffon around the neck and wrists. 'She stood with her figure outlined against the flood of light,' says Watson, 'one hand upon the door, one half-raised in her eagerness, her body slightly bent, her head and face protruded, with eager eyes and parted lips, a standing question.'

'The Adventure of the Engineer's Thumb' takes place in the summer of 1889 – 'not long after my marriage,' Watson says. By then he has a practice and lives not far from Paddington station. He mentions it again in 'The Stock-Broker's Clerk'. And again that same summer he heads off to Aldershot with Holmes in 'The Crooked Man'.

In his farewell letter in 'The Final Problem', Holmes says: 'Pray give my greetings to Mrs Watson . . .' During Holmes's absence, she seems to have died as, after his return in 'The Adventure of the Empty Room', Watson writes: 'In some manner he had learned of my own sad bereavement . . .' As he has no other living relative, this can only have been his wife.

Holmes says brusquely: 'Work is the best antidote to sorrow.'

In the next story, 'The Adventure of the Norwood Builder', Watson is back in Baker Street, and mentions that he has recently sold his 'small Kensington practice' to Dr Verner. Later, in 'The Adventure of the Illustrious Client', he is living in Queen Anne Street, just a short walk away.

He has lost none of his eye for the women though. In *The Hound of the Baskervilles*, he comments on Miss Stapleton's 'sensitive mouth . . . beautiful dark, eager eyes' and her 'perfect figure'. Later he says she is 'fascinating and beautiful . . . tropical and exotic'. Then he meets Laura Lyons and his first impression is 'one of extreme beauty. Her eyes and hair were of the same rich hazel colour, and her cheeks, though considerably freckled, were flushed with the exquisite bloom of the brunette, the dainty pink which lurks at the heart of the sulphur rose.' After that in *The Valley of Fear*, he finds Mrs Douglas 'a beautiful

woman, tall, dark, and slender'. He is much more of a passion-
ate ladies' man that emotionally retarded Holmes. Which is as
well, for Watson seems to have married again. 'The Adventure
of the Blanched Soldier', Holmes complains that in January
1903 Watson 'deserted me for a wife, the only selfish action
which I can recall in our association'. This is long after Holmes
has returned from the dead in the spring of 1894, which post-
dates the death of Mary Watson, née Morstan, and could explain
the move to Queen Anne Street.

When Watson returns from India, Stamford says he is 'thin as
a lath and brown as a nut'. Holmes notes that, while his face was
brown, it was not the usual colour of his skin as his wrists were
still fair. His face is also haggard from hardship and sickness.
However, in 'The Adventure of Charles Augustus Milverton',
Lestrade gives a description of Watson as a 'middle-sized,
strongly built man – square jaw, thick neck, moustache . . .'.
Holmes concurs. Later, in 'The Adventure of the Sussex Vampire',
we learn that Watson once played rugby for Blackheath.

Watson was well aware of his role vis-à-vis Holmes. In 'The
Adventure of the Creeping Man', he writes: 'The relations
between us in those latter days were peculiar. He was a man of
habits, narrow and concentrated habits, and I had become one
of them. As an institution I was like the violin, the shag tobacco,
the old black pipe, the index books, and others perhaps less
excusable. When it was a case of active work and a comrade was
needed upon whose nerve he could place some reliance, my role
was obvious. But apart from this I had uses. I was a whetstone
for his mind. I stimulated him. He liked to think aloud in my
presence. His remarks could hardly be said to be made to me –
many of them would have been as appropriately addressed to
his bedstead – but none the less, having formed the habit, it had
become in some way helpful that I should register and interject.
If I irritated him by a certain methodical slowness in my mental-
ity, that irritation served only to make his own flame-like
intuitions and impressions flash up the more vividly and swiftly.
Such was my humble role in our alliance.'

Though Holmes sends Watson off on his own to investigate crimes, he then chides him for his lack of observation, insight and imagination. But when there is danger in view, he wants Watson there beside him with his service-revolver. Above all, Watson is loyal. When Holmes decides to burgle Charles Milverton's house, it takes Watson a single paragraph to turn it over in his mind and decide that it is 'morally justifiable'. In 'The Adventure of Abbey Grange', Holmes appoints Watson a one-man jury in the sure knowledge that he will acquit a self-confessed murderer.

Although Watson can never match Holmes's powers of deduction, he learns to follow his reasoning *post factum*. When Holmes notes that John Hector McFarlane is a bachelor, a solicitor, a Freemason and an asthmatic in 'The Adventure of the Norwood Builder', Watson says: 'Familiar as I was with my friend's methods, it was not difficult for me to follow his deductions, and to observe the untidiness of attire, the sheaf of legal papers, the watch-charm, and the breathing which had prompted them. Our client, however, stared in amazement.'

Watson is annoyed that the police get all the credit for Holmes's work. That is why he writes up the cases and publishes them, thereby making Holmes famous. And when, in *The Valley of Fear*, he teases Holmes over his feigned modesty, Holmes accuses Watson of 'developing a certain unexpected vein of pawky humour . . . against which I must learn to guard myself'.

When Holmes comes out of retirement in 1914 in 'The Last Bow', Watson is there to drive the car for him. Watson never mentions the money he receives for publishing his accounts of the Holmes cases, but when he leaves Baker Street with his new wife he encourages Holmes to take up the pen himself. He does, and in 'The Adventure of the Blanched Soldier' Holmes takes the opportunity to praise his erstwhile colleague.

'Speaking of my old friend and biographer,' says Holmes, 'I would take this opportunity to remark that if I burden myself with a companion in my various little inquiries it is not done out of sentiment or caprice, but it is that Watson has some remarkable characteristics of his own to which in his modesty he has given small attention amid his exaggerated estimates of my own performances. A confederate who foresees your conclusions and course of action is always dangerous, but one to whom each development comes as a perpetual surprise, and to whom the future is always a closed book, is indeed an ideal helpmate.'

Previously Holmes chided Watson, saying he 'often had occasion to point out to him how superficial are his own accounts and to accuse him of pandering to popular taste instead of confining himself rigidly to facts and figures'. Now he realizes, at last, that when writing up his cases for the public it is necessary to do it in such a way as to interest the reader.

This is as well, as Watson admits in *The Sign of the Four*: 'I was annoyed at this criticism of a work which had been specially designed to please him. I confess, too, that I was irritated by the egotism which seemed to demand that every line of my pamphlet should be devoted to his own special doings. More than once during the years that I had lived with him in Baker Street I had observed that a small vanity underlay my companion's quiet and didactic manner.'

Throughout Watson's substantial writing career, Holmes remains scornful. In 'The Adventure of Wisteria Lodge', he even refers to his stories as 'those narratives with which you have afflicted a long-suffering public'. Yet Watson, himself, admits at the beginning of 'The Yellow Face' that he concentrates on Holmes's successes, rather than his failures and, he says in 'The Second Stain', that there are 'many hundreds of cases to which I have never alluded'.

Holmes may just be indulging in a little tit-for-tat here. After all, when they first meet, Watson is a disparaging of Holmes's erudition. Judging by their conversation, Watson is well read. In *A Study in Scarlet*, he sits up at night reading *(La Scènes de la)Vie de Bohème* by Henri Murger, (presumably in French, though it was published in English as *The Bohemians of the Latin Quarter* in 1887. In 1896, Puccini turned the book into the opera *La Bohème*, which was produced in Covent Garden that year).

Faithful to the end, Watson continues to make the occasional weekend visit to Holmes, who had retired to the Sussex Downs, and occasionally solicits special permission to write up a new case. In 'The Adventure of the Veiled Lodger', we learn that his note-taking over the years crams a 'long row of year-books which fill a shelf'. There are also dispatch-cases filled with documents, 'a perfect quarry for the student not only of crime but of the social and official scandals of the late Victorian era'. Watson claims that he has not exploited this material because 'the discretion and high sense of professional honour which have always distinguished my friend are still at work in the choice of these memoirs'. But Watson is anything but discreet. He reveals not just the foibles of his closest friends, but the secrets of victims and perpetrators, their families and their friends. Nevertheless, having lain dormant for over a hundred years, these papers would be a treasure trove for anyone picking up where Dr Watson left off. And Watson tells us where to find them. They are in a 'travel-worn and battered tin dispatch-box with my name, John H. Watson, MD, Late Indian Army, painted upon the lid . . . in the vaults of the bank of Cox & Co at Charing Cross', which Sherlockians have identified as the Charing Cross branch of Lloyd's TSB at 48–49, The Strand.

Chapter 14

Mycroft and Other Helpmates

Sherlock's older brother Mycroft is introduced in 'The Greek Interpreter'. He is seven years older than Sherlock and possesses the Holmesian intelligence to a greater degree, Sherlock says. But despite his superior powers of observation and deduction, Mycroft is no detective.

'If the art of the detective began and ended in reasoning from an armchair, my brother would be the greatest criminal agent that ever lived,' says Holmes. 'But he has no ambition and no energy.'

Mycroft concedes: 'Sherlock has all the energy of the family.'

Holmes has more scathing criticism of his elder brother: 'He will not even go out of his way to verify his own solutions, and would rather be considered wrong than take the trouble to prove himself right. Again and again I have taken a problem to him, and have received an explanation which has afterwards proved to be the correct one. And yet he was absolutely incapable of working out the practical points which must be gone into before a case could be laid before a judge or jury.'

This is strange, for we never see Sherlock put a case before a judge and jury.

To Mycroft the work of a detective is merely the hobby of a dilettante; in contrast, he uses his extraordinary faculty for figures to audit the books in some of the government departments. Later, in 'The Adventure of the Bruce-Partington Plans', Holmes tells Watson that not only does Mycroft work for the British government, but that 'occasionally he is the British government [and] draws four hundred and fifty pounds a year, remains a subordinate, has no ambitions of any kind, will receive neither honour nor title, but remains the most indispensable man in the country.'

His position, Holmes says, is unique: Mycroft made it for himself; there has never been anything like it before, and never will be again. 'He has the tidiest and most orderly brain, with the greatest capacity for storing facts, of any man living. The same great powers which I have turned to the detection of crime he has used for this particular business. The conclusions of every department are passed to him, and he is the central exchange, the clearinghouse, which makes out the balance. All other men are specialists, but his specialism is omniscience. We will suppose that a minister needs information as to a point which involves the Navy, India, Canada and the bimetallic question; he could get his separate advices from various departments upon each, but only Mycroft can focus them all, and say offhand how each factor would affect the other.'

Apparently, the government used him at first as a short-cut, a convenience, but he went on to make himself essential.

'In that great brain of his everything is pigeon-holed and can be handed out in an instant,' says Holmes. 'Again and again his word has decided the national policy. He lives in it. He thinks of nothing else save when, as an intellectual exercise, he unbends if I call upon him and ask him to advise me on one of my little problems.'

Sherlock adds that his brother brings him some of his most interesting cases.

Mycroft lives in lodgings in Pall Mall and, each morning, walks around the corner to Whitehall; in the evening, he walks back. He is a founder member of the Diogenes Club, which, according to Sherlock, is 'the queerest club in London and Mycroft one of the queerest men'. (The word queer, in all its declensions, is used seventy-six times in the Holmes stories in a non-sexual way; however, during Conan Doyle's lifetime it had begun to take on the later meaning that refers to homosexuality. In 1894 the Marquess of Queensbury, father of Oscar Wilde's partner in crimes, referred to the prime minister, Lord Rosebery, whom he thought was having an affair with his older son, as a 'snob queer'.)

Like other London clubs, the Diogenes is provided with comfortable chairs and the latest periodicals even though its members are 'the most unsociable and unclubable men in town'. They are not allowed to take the least notice of each other. Except in the Stranger's Room, no talking is permitted in any circumstances. Three offences brought to the attention of the managing committee result in expulsion. Holmes says that he finds the atmosphere soothing, though Watson only mentions him going there once.

The club is opposite Mycroft's rooms in Pall Mall. He is there every day from quarter to five to twenty to eight. At the beginning of 'The Greek Interpreter' it is six o'clock on a beautiful evening and Holmes suggests to Watson that they take a stroll there to meet him. Five minutes later they are heading for 'Regent's Circus' – it is not clear whether this is Oxford Circus or Piccadilly Circus. The *Baedeker* of the period refers to both 'Regent Circus, Oxford Street' and 'Regent Circus, Piccadilly'.

Oddly, they enter Pall Mall from the St James's end and stop at a door 'some little distance from the Carlton', which is at number 94. Holmes warns Watson not to speak, then leads the way into the hall. Through a glass panel, Watson glimpses a luxurious room where men are sitting about, reading the papers, each man in his own little nook. Holmes then shows Watson into a small room and comes back with someone Watson knew could only be his brother. 'Mycroft Holmes was a much larger and stouter man than Sherlock,' says Watson. 'His body was absolutely corpulent, but his face, though massive, had preserved something of the sharpness of expression which was so remarkable in that of his brother. His eyes, which were of a peculiarly light, watery gray, seemed to always retain that far-away, introspective look which I had only observed in Sherlock's when he was exerting his full powers.' When introduced to Watson, Mycroft extends 'a broad, fat hand like the flipper of a seal.'

Likewise, in 'The Adventure of the Bruce-Partington Plans', Mycroft is described as 'tall and portly . . .'. And 'Heavily built and massive,' says Watson, 'there was a suggestion of uncouth physical inertia in the figure, but above this unwieldy frame there was perched a head so masterful in its brow, so alert in its steel gray, deep-set eyes, so firm in its lips, and so subtle in its play of expression, that after the first glance one forgot the gross body and remembered only the dominant mind.'

He reads Watson's accounts of his brother's doings and takes an interest in his cases. He also matches Sherlock's party piece, deducing who and what people are and where they come from merely by looking at them. He takes snuff, which he keeps in a tortoise-shell box and brushes grains from his coat with a large red-silk handkerchief.

And as Mycroft has introduced the client, Mr Melas, in 'The Greek Interpreter', he gets to assist (or interfere) in the case by putting an ad in the paper and speaking to the Greek embassy. Mycroft then astounds Sherlock with unexpected energy, beating Holmes and Watson back to Baker Street by taking a cab.

In 'The Adventure of the Bruce-Partington Plans', Holmes is similarly shocked that brother Mycroft is coming round. Explaining his surprise, he says: 'It is as if you met a tram-car coming down a country lane. Mycroft has his rails and he runs on them. His Pall Mall lodgings, the Diogenes Club, Whitehall – that is his cycle. Once, and only once, he has been here. What upheaval can possibly have derailed him?'

It is 'high matters of state' that brought him – in this case the death of a clerk from Woolwich Arsenal and the loss of submarine plans. It was as if Jupiter, the chief Roman god, were descending.

'This must be serious, Watson,' says Holmes. 'A death which has caused my brother to alter his habits can be no ordinary one.'

Of course, Holmes figures out the link before Mycroft turns up.

'I extremely dislike altering my habits,' says Mycroft, who finds the matter most annoying as it takes him away from other matters of state, 'but the powers that be would take no denial. In the present state of Siam it is most awkward that I should be away from the office. But it is a real crisis. I have never seen the Prime Minister so upset. As to the Admiralty – it is buzzing like an overturned bee-hive.'

As Mycroft knows every detail of the submarine project and its security arrangements, Sherlock points out that Mycroft could easily solve the case himself.

'Possibly, Sherlock. But it is a question of getting details,' says Mycroft. 'Give me your details, and from an armchair I will return you an excellent expert opinion. But to run here and run there, to cross-question railway guards, and lie on my face with a lens to my eye – it is not my métier. No, you are the one man who can clear the matter up. If you have a fancy to see your name in the next honours list . . .'

Holmes smiles and shakes his head. Nevertheless, he takes the case.

'Use your powers!' exhorts Mycroft. 'Go to the scene of the crime! See the people concerned! Leave no stone unturned! In all your career you have never had so great a chance of serving your country.'

Again Holmes is grateful to Mycroft for bringing him a stimulating case and, to be fair, Mycroft does go along on the investigation and provides valuable information about foreign spies, though he refuses to climb the railings when breaking into Oberstein's house.

Mycroft gets out of his chair again in 'The Final Problem', where he plays the coachman who conveys Watson to Charing Cross when Holmes fears he might be followed. And he is left in charge of Holmes's property after his younger brother goes to the Reichenbach Falls.

Only Mycroft knows that Holmes is not really dead. Maycroft sends the money he needs to live abroad and travel and it is Mycroft who keeps up Holmes's apartment in Baker Street.

Mrs Hudson

Holmes and Watson are Victorian gentlemen and as such they cannot be expected to cook, make their own beds, dust, clean, tidy or deal with their own linen. Consequently, they need a housekeeper. So, in *The Sign of the Four*, Mrs Hudson makes her first appearance as Holmes's and Watson's 'landlady' – though there is an unnamed landlady in *A Study in Scarlet*. She worries about Holmes's health when he spends the whole night pacing up and down.

In 'A Scandal in Bohemia', their landlady is a Mrs Turner; husband is, of course, the villain in 'The Boscome Valley Mystery'. But after that, Mrs Hudson reappears. She does not mind in the least being woken at 7.15 a.m. in 'The Adventure of the Speckled Band' and, by the time Watson is up and dressed, has 'had the good sense to light the fire'. There is no mention of her husband, though the accused Mr Hudson is the baddie in 'The *Gloria Scott*'. And a Morse Hudson runs the shop that sold three of the busts in 'The Adventure of the Six Napoleons'.

In 'The Naval Treaty', she serves up a breakfast of tea, coffee, curried chicken and ham and eggs. 'Her cuisine is a little limited, but she has as good an idea of breakfast as a Scotchwoman,' says Holmes, without further explanation. And she is ever on hand to provide a hearty breakfast. Holmes even cables from Montpelier to ask her to 'make one of her best efforts for two hungry travellers at 7.30 tomorrow' in 'The Disappearance of Lady Frances Carfax'.

When Holmes returns from the dead in 'The Adventure of the Empty House', his reappearance 'threw Mrs Hudson into violent hysterics', though she must have suspected something during Holmes's absence, as brother Mycroft had 'preserved my rooms and my papers exactly as they had always been' – even though, in 'The Final Problem', Moriarty had set fire to 221B. 'No great harm was done,' says Holmes, flippantly. But it had been enough of a fire to make the morning papers. This, apparently, merely gives Mrs Hudson a chance to tidy up. When Watson returns to Baker Street, he says: 'As I entered I saw, it is true, an unwonted tidiness, but the old landmarks were all in their place. There were the chemical corner and the acid-stained, deal-topped table. There upon a shelf was the row of formidable scrap-books and books of reference which many of our fellow-citizens would have been so glad to burn. The diagrams, the violin-case, and the pipe-rack – even the Persian slipper which contained the tobacco . . .' There were also scientific charts on the wall and a coal scuttle that contained more pipes and tobacco. Despite all this paraphernalia Mrs Hudson beams to see the two old chums back in their rightful place.

It is then that we see Mrs Hudson do her most sterling service. When Colonel Moran is bent on shooting Holmes, Mrs Hudson risks her life by going on her hands and knees to move Holmes's effigy every quarter of an hour. She even follows where the bullet goes. After it passes through the bust and flattens itself on the wall, she picks it up off the carpet.

Mrs Hudson is ever courteous, showing guests in and out and handling telegrams. But she is downright servile in 'The Adventure of the Second Stain', where she delivers Lady Hilda Trewlaney's card on a salver. Nathan Garrideb gets his delivered on a plain old tray.

Watson gives the most complete description of their housekeeper in 'The Dying Detective': 'Mrs Hudson, the landlady of Sherlock Holmes, was a long-suffering woman. Not only was her first-floor flat invaded at all hours by throngs of singular and often undesirable characters but her remarkable lodger showed an eccentricity and irregularity in his life which must have sorely tried her patience. His incredible untidiness, his addiction to music at strange hours, his occasional revolver practice within doors, his weird and often malodorous scientific experiments, and the atmosphere of violence and danger which hung around him made him the very worst tenant in London.'

However, she is 'in the deepest awe of him and never dared to interfere with him, however outrageous his proceedings might seem. She was fond of him, too . . .' Watson says that she has a genuine regard for Holmes. That is why he listens earnestly to her story when she comes to his rooms in the second year of his married life to tell him of the sad conditions Holmes has been reduced to in the opening of 'The Adventure of the Dying Detective'.

'He's dying, Dr Watson,' she says. 'For three days he has been sinking, and I doubt if he will last the day. He would not let me get a doctor. This morning when I saw his bones sticking out of his face and his great bright eyes looking at me I could stand no more of it. "With your leave or without it, Mr Holmes, I am going for a doctor this very hour," said I. "Let it be Watson, then," said he. I wouldn't waste an hour in coming to him, sir, or you may not see him alive.'

When Watson goes to help she is waiting in the passage, trembling and weeping. She need not have been so concerned: Holmes is only play-acting. Indeed, rushing to the scene, Watson finds him 'more masterful than ever', though it was 'pitiful . . . to see his exhaustion'.

In retirement in 'The Adventure of the Lion's Mane', Holmes says he is living on the Sussex Downs with his old housekeeper, who is generally assumed to be Mrs Hudson. However, in 'His Last Bow', he employs another housekeeper, Martha, getting her a job with Von Bork so that he can ensnare the German spy. Perhaps Mrs Hudson is dead by then.

Household staff

Even in Mrs Hudson's small establishment in Baker Street there is room for a page boy, who appears in ten of the Holmes stories. In 'A Case of Identity', he appears in uniform – a 'boy in buttons entered to announce Miss Mary Sutherland'. An unnamed page-boy also shows up in 'The Adventure of the Noble Bachelor', 'The Yellow Face', 'The Greek Interpreter', 'The Naval Treaty', 'The Adventure of Wisteria Lodge' and 'The Adventure of Shoscombe Old Place'. Only in *The Valley of Fear*, 'The Adventure of the Mazarin Stone' and 'The Problem of Thor Bridge' is he identified by name as Billy.

He is, however, very much part of the family. At the

beginning of 'The Adventure of the Mazarin Stone', Watson has quite a long chat with him. It appears he has been with the household for quite some time – Watson says: 'You don't change . . .' And Billy knows Holmes's ways.

'He is very hard at it just now,' says Billy. 'I'm frightened for his health. He gets paler and thinner, and he eats nothing . . . You know his way when he is keen on a case.'

He tells Watson that Holmes is following someone. Yesterday he was out disguised as a workman looking for a job; today as an old woman.

'Fairly took me in, he did, and I ought to know his ways by now,' Billy says with a grin, pointing to a parasol that was part of Holmes's old woman's outfit.

Billy even fills Watson in on the details of the case. He draws aside the curtain to reveal the effigy of Holmes in the window, then spoils the whole illusion by taking the head off.

'I wouldn't dare touch it if the blind were not down,' says Billy. 'But when it's up you can see this from across the way.'

Watson says: 'We used something of the sort once before' – meaning in 'The Adventure of the Empty House'.

'Before my time,' says Billy, which leads us to believe that the page in the stories before Holmes's resurrection is a different boy who, perhaps, grew up or found other employment when Mrs Hudson was left to manage an empty house.

Holmes emerges from his bedroom and dismisses Billy.

'That boy is a problem,' he tells Watson. 'How far am I justified in allowing him to be in danger?'

Mrs Hudson also employs a live-in maid, whom Watson hears going to bed when he is waiting up for Holmes in *A Study in Scarlet*. In 'The Five Orange Pips', Watson waits for her to bring his coffee and in 'The Adventure of the Bruce-Partington Plans', she brings Holmes a telegram. Some have suggested that she is the Mrs Turner who appears in 'A Scandal in Bohemia'.

The Baker Street Irregulars

In *A Study in Scarlet*, Watson meets the 'Baker Street Irregulars', the 'half a dozen of the dirtiest and most ragged street Arabs that ever I clapped eyes on,' he says. Their landlady makes 'audible expressions of disgust' at the sight of them and, to mollify her, Holmes says that in future only their leader, the redoubtable Wiggins, should come up and report. Watson finds Wiggins 'unsavoury'.

Holmes introduces this scruffy bunch of urchins as 'the Baker Street division of the detective police force' and drills them as if they are soldiers. They are sent to find a cabman that Holmes believes is a killer. They are each given a shilling – twelve old pence, five new pence, or over £4 at today's prices. They are key to the case and while the police are floundering, they track down the cabman, who Wiggins brings up to 221B to be handcuffed by Holmes.

They appear again in *The Sign of the Four*, where they have a chapter named after them. Again they are paid a shilling, this time to search for the *Aurora* from Millbank downriver. A guinea goes to the boy who finds her. They also get three shillings and sixpence expenses but are again told off for invading the house mob-handed. In future, they are to report to Wiggins, who will carry any message on to Holmes. At least seven years have passed since *A Study in Scarlet* and Wiggins is still 'a disreputable little scarecrow'; however, he is taller and older than all the others with an 'air of lounging superiority'. He can read, though it is not explained where he addressed the cable. Holmes sends a telegram to summon him and his gang. Eventually, as they are having no luck, Holmes dons his sailor's outfit and joins them.

In 'The Crooked Man', Holmes employs a small street Arab named Simpson to help him track down Henry Wood in Aldershot, but all Simpson gets is a pat on the head. Then in *The Hound of the Baskervilles*, Watson sees a small urchin – a 'ragged uncouth figure' – running errands out on the moor, but he does not put two and two together. It is only when he finds Holmes living in one of the Neolithic huts that he discovers that he has brought 'Cartwright' – not one of the Baker

Street Irregulars but a local messenger – down with him to keep him supplied and in touch. Disguised as a country boy, Cartwright also provides 'an extra pair of eyes upon a very active pair of feet', more often than not spying on Watson. When Holmes goes off with Watson, he does send word to Cartwright so that he will not pine away 'at the door of my hut, as a dog does at his master's grave'.

Langdale Pike

In 'The Adventure of the Three Gables', Holmes consults Langdale Pike, a 'human book of reference upon all matters of social scandal'. This strange, languid creature spends his waking hours in the bow window of a gentleman's club – White's at 37–38 St James's Street, it is thought – and was 'the receiving-station as well as the transmitter for all the gossip of the metropolis'. This is 1926 and Holmes has strayed into the age of radio.

It is said Pike makes a four-figure income from his weekly contributions to the red-top papers that cater to the inquisitive public. According to Watson: 'If ever, far down in the turbid depths of London life, there was some strange swirl or eddy, it was marked with automatic exactness by this human dial upon the surface.' However, it seems that Holmes discreetly helps Langdale by feeding him stories, therefore receiving Langdale's help in return.

Mercer

In 'The Adventure of the Creeping Man', Holmes tells Watson that, since his time, he has employed a 'general utility man' named Mercer, 'who looks up routine business'. Mercer tracks down Dorak, the man supplying Professor Presbury with the Langur serum, to the large general store he keeps in the Commercial Road.

Shinwell Johnson

Watson apologizes that his first – and only – mention of Shinwell Johnson appears in 'The Adventure of the Illustrious Client'. This was because he seldom draws his cases from the latter phases of Holmes's career. But during the first years of the twentieth century Porky Shinwell becomes a valuable assistant. He made his name first as a dangerous villain who had served two terms at Parkhurst but he has repented and allies himself to Holmes, acting as his agent in the huge criminal underworld of London and obtaining information that often proves to be of vital importance. Had Johnson been a 'nark' of the police he would soon have been exposed, but as he deals with cases which never come directly into the courts, his activities are never realized by his companions. His reputation gives him entrée to every nightclub, doss house and gambling den in the town, and his quick observation and active brain made him an ideal information-gathering agent.

'Johnson is on the prowl,' says Holmes. 'He may pick up some garbage in the darker recesses of the underworld, for it is down there, amid the black roots of crime, that we must hunt for this man's secrets.'

According to Watson, Johnson is 'a huge, coarse, red-faced, scorbutic man, with a pair of vivid black eyes which were the only external sign of the very cunning mind within'. As luck would have it, he shares an address with Kitty Winter, the discarded mistress of Baron Gruner, and is dismissive of the baron's collection of priceless porcelain.

'No fence wants stuff of that sort that you can neither melt nor sell,' he says.

After Holmes is beaten up, he tells Johnson to get Kitty out of town as she is in danger. Watson arranges for Johnson to take her to a quiet suburb where she can lie low until the danger had passed. He does not do his job very well for she gives him the slip and finds her way to Gruner's house in Kingston, where she throws sulphuric acid in the baron's face.

Barker
Sent to Lewisham in 'The Adventure of the Retired Colourman', Watson runs into a tall, dark, heavily moustached, rather military-looking man, who gives him a curiously questioning glance

outside Amberley's house. At London Bridge he sees him again, this time wearing grey-tinted sunglasses and a Masonic tie-pin. Holmes recognizes the man whom he introduces to Watson as Barker, 'my hated rival on the Surrey shore'. But Barker later teams up with him to snare Amberley before he leaves Barker at the police station to handle the formalities.

However, Holmes says to Inspector MacKinnon: 'He has several good cases to his credit, has he not, Inspector?'

When MacKinnon concedes that Barker has 'interfered several times', Holmes says: 'His methods are irregular, no doubt, like my own. The irregulars are useful sometimes, you know.' But on the other hand he also says that, 'Barker, he has done nothing save what I told him.'

As a result, the inspector seems considerably relieved.

Chapter 15

Professor Moriarty and Other Villains

Professor Moriarty is an odd villain. No sooner does he turn up in 'The Final Problem', he is killed off. It appears that Conan Doyle created him as a character powerful enough to kill Holmes and when that was done Conan Doyle thought he would have no further use for him.

As there had been twenty-five Holmes stories by this point it is perhaps surprising that Watson knows nothing of Moriarty. He has not come up in conversation and Holmes does not expect Watson to have heard of him.

'You have probably never heard of Professor Moriarty?' says Holmes.

'Never,' says Watson

'Ay, there's the genius and the wonder of the thing!' cries Holmes. 'The man pervades London, and no one has heard of him. That's what puts him on a pinnacle in the records of crime.'

But Holmes is nothing if not ambitious: he feels that his career would have reached its summit – if he could beat Moriarty and free society of him, even though at this point he has already done well enough to retire.

'But I could not rest, Watson,' he says. 'I could not sit quiet in my chair, if I thought that such a man as Professor Moriarty were walking the streets of London unchallenged.'

According to Holmes, Moriarty is a man of good birth and education, with a great brain for mathematics. At twenty-one he wrote a treatise upon the binomial theorem that was well known across Europe and which led to a chair in mathematics at a small British university. He had, to all appearances, a most brilliant career ahead of him. However, Moriarty has bad blood and had inherited criminal tendencies – which grew all the more diabolical because of his enormous intellect. Dark rumours surrounded him and he was forced to resign his chair and move to London, where he became an 'army coach' – a private tutor to officers preparing for exams.

'So much is known to the world,' says Holmes, though apparently not to Watson. Holmes now reveals what his own researches have uncovered, and boasts that no one knows the higher criminal world of London as well as he does.

'For years past I have continually been conscious of some power behind the malefactor,' says Holmes, 'some deep organizing power which forever stands in the way of the law, and throws its shield over the wrong-doer.'

He has seen Moriarty's hand in cases of forgery, robbery and murder, and has deduced his presence in many other crimes for which he had not been personally consulted. For years, he has tried to draw aside the veil of secrecy that surrounds Moriarty's actions until he finally found a thread, and seizing it, finds that it leads eventually to the evil professor.

'He is the Napoleon of crime, Watson,' insists Holmes. 'He is the organizer of half that is evil and of nearly all that is undetected in this great city. He is a genius, a philosopher, an abstract thinker. He has a brain of the first order.'

Holmes compares him to a spider sitting motionless in the centre of a web, detecting the quiver of each strand. He does little himself. Instead, he orchestrates his numerous agents. If there is a crime to be done – a house to be burgled, a man to be killed – the word is passed to the professor and the matter is organized and carried out. If the agent happens to be caught, money is found for his bail or his defence. But the central power is never caught, or even suspected – by anyone apart from Holmes. Once Holmes realizes what is going on, devotes all his energy to exposing the organization and breaking it up. However, the professor is so cunning that he finds it impossible to gather evidence that would convict him in a court of law. After three months, he was forced to confess that he had at last met an antagonist who was an intellectual equal.

'My horror at his crimes was lost in my admiration at his skill,' says Holmes.

But then Moriarty made a mistake. Holmes seized the chance and lays a trap. In three days time, the professor and the principal members of his gang will be in the hands of the police.

'Then will come the greatest criminal trial of the century, the clearing up of over forty mysteries . . .'

He believes they will all hang, but there is still a chance they will escape. Moriarty is so wily that he knows what Holmes is up to.

'Never have I risen to such a height,' says Holmes, 'and never have I been so hard pressed by an opponent.'

On the morning Holmes implements the last steps, he is sitting in his room when the door opens to reveal Moriarty. Holmes, normally so sanguine, admits to being startled when confronted by his arch-enemy, but fortunately he has a gun concealed in his dressing-gown pocket. He describes the villain to Watson: 'He is extremely tall and thin, his forehead domes out in a white curve, and his two eyes are deeply sunken in his head. He is clean-shaven, pale, and ascetic-looking, retaining something of the professor in his features. His shoulders are rounded from much study, and his face protrudes forward and is forever slowly oscillating from side to side in a curiously reptilian fashion. He peered at me with great curiosity in his puckered eyes.'

Moriarty then remarks that Holmes has less 'frontal development' than he expected. At the time, phrenology was in vogue and it was assumed that brighter people had bigger brains.

Like Holmes, Moriarty carries a notebook. It is filled with the details of where Holmes has crossed him. He too enjoys meeting his equal.

'It has been an intellectual treat to me to see the way in which you have grappled with this affair,' says Moriarty, before expressing regret that, if Holmes will not abandon his 'persecution', he is going to have to kill him. But Holmes says he is willing to sacrifice his life to rid the world of Moriarty.

We then see that Moriarty is clever enough to organize several attempts on Holmes's life and tail Watson and Holmes to Victoria station. They give him the slip, leaving him behind on the platform while they escape on the Continental Express. Moriarty is not to be put off. He engages a 'special' – a private train – to pursue Holmes and Watson, who see him steaming through at high speed when they get off at Canterbury. Holmes has outsmarted him.

'There are limits, you see, to our friend's intelligence,' says Holmes. 'It would have been a *coup-de-maître*' – a masterstroke – had he deduced what I would deduce and acted accordingly.'

Nevertheless, Moriarty is clever enough to track them to the Reichenbach Falls, even though they had left their luggage in Paris. In 'The Final Problem', Holmes says he has provided the London police with everything they need to convict the rest of Moriarty's gang. However, in 'The Adventure of the Empty House' we discover that both Parker, the garrotter, and Colonel Sebastian Moran escape arrest.

At the beginning of 'The Adventure of the Norwood Builder', Holmes expresses regret over the death of 'the late lamented Professor Moriarty'. 'With that man in the field, one's morning paper presented infinite possibilities,' rues Holmes. 'Often it was only the smallest trace, Watson, the faintest indication, and yet it was enough to tell me that the great malignant brain was there, as the gentlest tremors of the edges of the web remind one of the foul spider which lurks in the centre. Petty thefts, wanton assaults, purposeless outrage – to the man who held the clue all could be worked into one connected whole. To the scientific student of the higher criminal world, no capital in Europe offered the advantages which London then possessed.'

In 'The Adventure of the Missing Three-Quarter', Holmes provokes the wrath of Dr Leslie Armstrong, then says: 'I have not seen a man who, if he turns his talents that way, was more calculated to fill the gap left by the illustrious Moriarty' – though the man is entirely innocent and is only trying to protect his friend Godfrey Staunton.

In 'The Last Bow', Von Bork says: 'If it takes me all my life I shall get level with you!'

'The old sweet song,' says Holmes. 'How often have I heard it in days gone by. It was a favourite ditty of the late lamented Professor Moriarty. Colonel Sebastian Moran has also been known to warble it. And yet I live and keep bees upon the South Downs.'

And in the 'The Adventure of the Illustrious Client', Holmes is enthusiastic about making the acquaintance of the villain he is about to be introduced to by a new client, an aristocratic member of the Carlton Club. Holmes says: 'If your man is more danger-ous than the late Professor Moriarty, or than the living Colonel Sebastian Moran, then he is indeed worth meeting.'

The Valley of Fear takes the reader back to a time before Holmes and Moriarty meet at the Reichenbach Falls. Nevertheless, Holmes mentions Professor Moriarty, and Watson says: 'The famous scientific criminal, as famous among crooks as . . .' before Holmes stops him. This is curious as in 'The Final Problem' Watson claims never to have heard of Moriarty.

Holmes continues: 'My blushes, Watson! I was about to say, as he is unknown to the public.' So, perhaps in 'The Final Problem', Watson is simply trying not to gainsay Holmes again.

Nevertheless, Holmes feels it necessary to praise Moriarty: he is 'the greatest schemer of all time, the organizer of every deviltry, the controlling brain of the underworld, a brain which might have made or marred the destiny of nations'. Holmes says that Moriarty is so far above general suspicion that Watson risks being sued for slander by calling him a criminal. He compares him to Jonathan Wild, the most notorious criminal of the eighteenth century, and draws Watson's attention to the fact that Moriarty is the celebrated author of *The Dynamics of an Asteroid* – 'a book which ascends to such rarefied heights of pure mathematics that it is said that there was no man in the scientific press capable of criticizing it'. Even so, Holmes observes that 'if I am spared by lesser men, our day will surely come' – perhaps with good reason as one of Moriarty's henchmen, Fred Porlock, is already in contact with him.

Inspector MacDonald tells Holmes that the CID think he has 'a wee bit of a bee in [his] bonnet over this professor.'

'I made some inquiries myself about the matter,' he says. 'He seems to be a very respectable, learned, and talented sort of man.'

Holmes says that at least MacDonald recognizes Moriarty's talent. MacDonald says that Moriarty explained eclipses to him, though the book he lent him was a bit above his head. Even so, MacDonald was from Aberdeen that Moriarty would 'have made a grand meenister with his thin face and gray hair and solemn-like way of talking. When he put his hand on my shoulder as we were parting, it was like a father's blessing before you go out into the cold, cruel world.'

Moriarty owns a painting by Jean-Baptiste Greuze which is worth more than £40,000, a high price to pay for someone on a salary of a mere £700 a year, Holmes points out. MacDonald is puzzled by Holmes's knowledge of the painting, as he claims never to have met Moriarty. Holmes admits that he has 'visited' the professor's study. The painting proves that Moriarty is a rich man, but the question remains: how has he acquired this wealth? He is unmarried and his younger brother is a station master in the west of England. He pays Colonel Sebastian Moran over eight times his own professorial salary and hides his wealth partly by writing cheques from six different bank accounts merely to pay his household bills. Holmes has no doubt that he has twenty bank accounts and that the bulk of his fortune is aboard in Deutsche Bank or Credit Lyonnais.

In 'The Final Problem', Watson becomes acquainted with a Colonel James Moriarty, who has written letters defending the memory of his late brother. And, curiously, in 'The Adventure of the Empty House', Holmes mentions Professor James Moriarty, again chiding Watson for not having heard of him – it seems strange that two brothers should have the same first name.

Moriarty rules over his criminal gang with a rod of iron. There is only one punishment in his code – death. At the beginning of *The Valley of Fear* Holmes assumes that Jack Douglas is dead – killed because he had, in some way, betrayed the chief. His punishment would have served as an example to others, unless it had been engineered by Moriarty 'in the ordinary course of business'. But Holmes's assumption is too prescient: Douglas is still alive at this point in the story, though not for long.

At the end of the book, when Holmes hears that Douglas has been lost overboard on his way to Cape Town, he knows who is to blame. 'I can tell a Moriarty when I see one,' says Holmes. 'This crime is from London, not from America. . . it is done by a man who cannot afford to fail, one whose whole unique position depends upon the fact that all he does must succeed. A great brain and a huge organization have been turned to the extinction of one man. It is crushing the nut with the triphammer – an absurd extravagance of energy – but the nut is very effectually crushed all the same.'

Nevertheless, Holmes asserts that Moriaty can be beaten, given time.

So who was the real Moriarty? In his book *The Napoleon of Crime*, author Ben Macintyre names the American thief and fraudster Adam Worth, who, in 1907, Sir Robert Anderson, former assistant commissioner at Scotland Yard, called 'the Napoleon of the criminal world'.

Colonel Sebastian Moran

According to Holmes's index of criminal biographies, Sebastian Moran was born in London in 1840, the son of Sir Augustus Moran, Companion of the Order of the Bath, once British Minister to Persia. He was educated at Eton College and the University of Oxford before embarking upon a military career. Formerly of the 1st Bangalore Pioneers, he served in the Jowaki Expedition of 1877–8 and in the Second Anglo-Afghan War, seeing action at the Battle of Charasiab on 6

October 1879, when he was mentioned in dispatches; at the Battle of Sherpur on 23 December 1879; and at the Battle of Kabul on 23 December 1879. A devoted sportsman and highly skilled shot, he was author of the books *Heavy Game of the Western Himalayas* in 1881 and *Three Months in the Jungle* in 1884. He lives in Conduit Street, Mayfair and is a member of The Anglo-Indian, the Tankerville, and the Bagatelle Card clubs. Holmes notes in the margin that he is the 'second most dangerous man in London'.

Watson is shocked because Moran has been an honourable soldier. Holmes adds that he had been the 'best heavy-game shot that our Eastern Empire has ever produced'.

Turning to Moran he says: 'I believe I am correct, Colonel, in saying that your bag of tigers still remains unrivalled?'

Moran says nothing, and simply glares at Holmes.

'With his savage eyes and bristling moustache he was wonderfully like a tiger himself,' observes Watson.

'Up to a certain point he did well,' says Holmes. 'He was always a man of iron nerve, and the story is still told in India how he crawled down a drain after a wounded man-eating tiger.'

But then Colonel Moran began to go wrong.

'Without any open scandal, he still made India too hot to hold him,' says Holmes. 'He retired, came to London, and again acquired an evil name.'

Moriarty paid him £6,000 to be his chief of the staff and used him on one or two very high-class jobs that no ordinary criminal could have undertaken. Holmes was sure that he had been responsible for the death of Mrs Stewart, of Lauder, in 1887, though nothing could be proved.

Moran owned a noiseless and powerful airgun made by a blind German mechanic named Von Herder to Moriarty's specifications. Holmes knows about the gun. Once when he had visited Watson's rooms, he had insisted that they close the shutters just in case. Moran had followed them to the Reichenbach Falls. After seeing Moriarty plunge to his death, he rolled rocks down on Holmes, but he escaped.

When Moriarty's gang is arrested, there is no incriminating evidence against Colonel Moran. Deprived of the money he had earned from Moriarty, Moran goes into cardsharping, winning £420 in one sitting with Ronald Adair. However, when Adair discovers that Moran had been cheating Moran kills him to avoid being exposed.

Moran then hears from Parker, the garrotter, that Holmes is back in London. This is when he attempts to shoot Holmes from the empty house over the road from 221B. But, as ever, Holmes was a step ahead and manages to thwart him. Once they have their man, Watson gives a detailed description: 'It was a tremendously virile and yet sinister face which was turned towards us. With the brow of a philosopher above and the jaw of a sensualist below, the man must have started with great capacities for good or for evil. But one could not look upon his cruel blue eyes, with their drooping, cynical lids, or upon the fierce, aggressive nose and the threatening, deep-lined brow, without reading Nature's plainest danger signals. He took no heed of any of us, but his eyes were fixed upon Holmes's face with an expression in which hatred and amazement were equally blended. "You fiend!" he kept on muttering. "You clever, clever fiend!"'

Moran is jailed, but is still alive when Holmes takes on 'The Adventure of the Illustrious Client' rather later in his career.

Jonathan Small

Born near Pershore in Worcestershire, Small was no credit to his chapel-going family. When he was eighteen, he 'got into a mess over a girl and could only get out of it again by taking the Queen's shilling'. He joins the Third (East Kent) Regiment of Foot and goes to India. But he does not do much soldiering because his leg is bitten off by a crocodile when he goes swimming in the Ganges.

He becomes an overseer for an indigo planter, but the area is overwhelmed in the Indian Mutiny and he seeks refuge in Agra. There, under threat of death, he is forced joins three Sikhs in the murder of a merchant and the theft of the treasure he was carrying. But they are all caught, arrested and cheated out of their share of the loot.

After escaping with the Andaman Islander Tonga, Small returns to England, where Tonga is displayed at fairs as 'the black cannibal', eating raw meat and performing a war dance for pennies. Small claims that it was Tonga who killed Bartholomew Sholto, not him. Tonga dies anyway. Small did throw the treasure overboard, but otherwise it would have been shared by Thaddeus Sholto and Miss Morstan, who were hardly its rightful owners. There was then the small matter of fleeing justice . . .

Vincent Spaulding aka John Clay

Jabez Wilson's assistant Vincent Spaulding gives himself away in Holmes' eyes by taking a job for half pay when he is smart enough to earn twice as much elsewhere. He also spends a great deal of time in the cellar and knows rather too much about The Red Headed League.

He is small, stoutly built, clean-shaven and over thirty. There is a white splash of acid upon his forehead and his ears are pierced, he says, by a gypsy who had done it for him when he was a lad. After meeting him, Holmes says: 'He is, in my judgment, the fourth smartest man in London, and for daring I am not sure that he has not a claim to be third. I have known something of him before.' But the dirt on the knees of his trouser gives him away.

He turns out to be John Clay – 'murderer, thief, smasher and forger'.

'He's a remarkable man,' says Inspector Jones. 'His grandfather was a royal duke, and he himself has been to Eton and Oxford. His brain is as cunning as his fingers, and though we meet signs of him at every turn, we never know where to find the man himself. He'll crack a crib in Scotland one week, and be raising money to build an orphanage in Cornwall the next. I've been on his track for years and have never set eyes on him yet.'

Clay is all too aware of his ancestry and tells Jones not to touch him with his filthy hands – 'I have royal blood in my veins.'

Holmes has one or two little scores of his own to settle with Clay, who, before being led away, bows respectfully low to Holmes.

James Windibank
The stepfather of jilted bride Mary Sutherland in 'A Case of Identity', James Windibank is 'a sturdy, middle-sized fellow, some thirty years of age, clean-shaven and sallow-skinned, with a bland, insinuating manner, and a pair of wonderfully sharp and penetrating gray eyes'; he wears a shiny top hat. Eager not to lose the income from his stepdaughter's shares if she marries, he pretends to be one Hosmer Angel and woos her, presumably with the collusion of her mother. Holmes sees through this ruse and Windibank narrowly escapes a thrashing with a riding crop.

John Turner
In 'The Boscombe Valley Mystery', Charles McCarthy is murdered by his landlord John Turner, who strikes Watson as a strange and impressive figure. 'His slow, limping step and bowed shoulders gave the appearance of decrepitude, and yet his hard, deep-lined, craggy features, and his enormous limbs showed that he was possessed of unusual strength of body and of character. His tangled beard, grizzled hair, and outstanding, drooping eyebrows combined to give an air of dignity and power to his appearance, but his face was of an ashen white, while his lips and the corners of his nostrils were tinged with a shade of blue.' It is clear to Watson at a glance that Turner is in the grip of some deadly and chronic disease.

Turner is also jealous of his daughter, who he forbids from marrying James McCarthy, the son of the man who had been blackmailing him. Holmes takes pity on the terminally ill man and presents enough evidence at the assizes to secure McCarthy's release (had been accused of murdering his father) and allowing Turner to die in his bed seven months later. The marriage had another impediment: McCarthy's previous marriage to a barmaid in Bristol, but this turns out to be a sham, clearing the way for every prospect that the son and daughter may come to live happily together in ignorance of the black cloud which rests upon their past.'

James Ryder

The upper-attendant at the Cosmopolitan hotel, James Ryder, learns of the Blue Carbuncle from the countess's maid, steals it, frames the plumber and is then stupid enough to feed it to a goose. When he meets Holmes, he says his name is John Robinson. Holmes sees through this immediately. Ryder is a little man – 'a shrimp' who, when accused almost faints and has to be revived with brandy.

He subsequently prostrates himself and clutches at Holmes's knees: 'For God's sake, have mercy!' he shrieks. 'Think of my father! Of my mother! It would break their hearts. I never went wrong before! I never will again. I swear it. I'll swear it on a Bible. Oh, don't bring it into court! For Christ's sake, don't!'

Eventually, when he has made a full confession, Holmes takes pity on him and throws him out.

Dr Grimesby Roylott

The stepfather of Helen and Julia Stoner in 'The Adventure of the Speckled Band', Dr Grimesby Roylott is impoverished and lives off his daughter's inheritance after failing to establish himself in practice in London. He is a violent man, involved in a series of brawls, two of which end in court. Immensely strong, with an uncontrollable temper, he is the terror of the village. At one point he hurled the local blacksmith over a bridge and and had to pay to hush it up. His only friends are the gypsies who he lets camp on the family estate. He has a passion also for animals from India, which he has sent over to him by a correspondent. A cheetah and a baboon wander freely over his grounds and are feared by the villagers almost as much as their master.

After Julia dies in mysterious circumstances Helen, fearing for her life, consults Holmes. He spots marks on her wrist where Roylott has grabbed her. When she leaves, Roylott turns up.

He is a huge man.

'His costume was a peculiar mixture of the professional and of the agricultural,' says Watson, 'having a black top-hat, a long frockcoat, and a pair of high gaiters, with a hunting-crop swinging in his hand. So tall was he that his hat actually brushed the cross bar of the doorway, and his breadth seemed to span across from side to side. A large face, seared with a thousand wrinkles, burned yellow with the sun, and marked with every evil passion, was turned from one to the other of us, while his deep-set, bile-shot eyes, and his high, thin, fleshless nose, gave him somewhat the resemblance to a fierce old bird of prey.'

He ridicules Holmes, but Holmes refuses to be intimidated. Roylott then gets his comeuppance when Holmes solves the murder and turns the swamp adder back on Roylott.

Colonel Lysander Stark aka Dr Becher

In 'The Adventure of the Engineer's Thumb', the mysterious Colonel Stark is 'a man rather over the middle size, but of an exceeding thinness'. Vincent Hatherley does not think he has ever seen so thin a man: 'His whole face sharpened away into nose and chin, and the skin of his cheeks was drawn quite tense over his outstanding bones. Yet this emaciation seemed to be his natural habit, and due to no disease, for his eye was bright, his step brisk, and his bearing assured.' He is plainly but neatly dressed, and nearer forty than thirty. He has a slight German accent and his house is full of German publications.

He has a female accomplice and a side-kick he introduces as Mr Ferguson, his 'secretary and manager'. Ferguson appears to be a morose and silent man but he is, at least, English. When the woman helps Hatherley to escape, Stark attempts to make a murderous attack on him. He returns the next day with Holmes, and they discover that Stark is, in fact, the infamous Dr Becher, who has now disappeared.

Sir George Burnwell

A notorious rake, Sir George Burnwell leads City banker Alexander Holding's son, Arthur, into bad ways, but even Holding *père* says: 'I have found myself that I could hardly resist the fascination of his manner. He is older than Arthur, a man of the world to his finger-tips, one who had been everywhere, seen everything, a brilliant talker, and a man of great personal beauty. Yet when I think of him in cold blood, far away from the glamour of his presence, I am convinced from his cynical speech and the look which I have caught in his eyes that he is one who should be deeply distrusted.'

Naturally, Holding's niece, Mary also falls for him. She helps him steal the beryl coronet, which is then mostly retrieved by Arthur. Holmes finds the missing piece and Mary runs off with Burnwell.

Jephro Rucastle

In 'The Adventure of the Copper Beeches', Miss Violet Hunter finds Jephro Rucastle, her new employer, a kind, good natured man. He is over forty-five and his wife – a silent, pale-faced woman – is much younger, not more than thirty. He is kind to her also in his bluff, boisterous fashion, and on the whole they seem to be a happy couple, apart from a few oddities, such as asking Violet to cut off her hair and sit with her back to the window. Violet says Rucastle tells her some of the funniest stories she has ever heard. Even when she finds him coming out of a mysterious locked room he is as merry and jovial as ever. He only turns nasty when Holmes and Watson arrive.

It turns out that Rucastle has imprisoned his daughter because she won't sign her inheritance over to him. She escapes. Rucastle is attacked by his own guard dog. He survives, but is a broken man 'kept alive solely through the care of his devoted wife'.

John Straker

By the time Holmes takes on the case of 'Silver Blaze', the villain of the story, John Straker, is already dead. Having taken a expensive mistress, he decides to nobble Silver Blaze, the favourite in the Wessex Cup, by nicking the tendon with a small knife. But the horse rears up and strikes him dead with its hooves.

Silas Brown at the Mapleton stables is also a bit of a baddie. He attempt to hide Silver Blaze until the race is over, but he is no match for Holmes.

Arthur Pinner aka Harry Pinner aka Beddington

In 'The Stockbroker's Clerk', Hall Pycroft is approached by Arthur Pinner, 'a middle-sized, dark-haired, dark-eyed, black-bearded man, with a touch of the sheeny about his nose'. Sheeny is a pejorative term for a Jew, though it may derive from the Yiddish word '*shayner*', which means 'beautiful' and is often used to describe a pious or traditional Jew, particularly one with a full beard. Pinner also 'had a brisk kind of way with him and spoke sharply, like a man who knew the value of time'.

In Birmingham, the man introducing himself as Harry Pinner has the same figure and voice, but is clean-shaven and has lighter hair. However, his second tooth on the left-hand side had been badly stuffed with gold – just like his brother's. Pycroft concludes he is the same man, who has merely shaved and donned a wig.

When Watson meets Pinner, he says: 'I had never looked upon a face which bore such marks of grief, and of something beyond grief – of a horror such as comes to few men in a lifetime. His brow glistened with perspiration, his cheeks were of the dull, dead white of a fish's belly, and his eyes were wild and staring.'

Pycroft concludes that he is ill and, soon after, Pinner tries to kill himself. It then becomes clear that he is the brother of Beddington, the famous forger and cracksman – now thief and murderer – who is assigned to keep Pycroft occupied while Beddington take Pycroft's place at Mawson & Williams. Thwarted by Holmes, Pinner will probably hang.

Hudson

In 'The *Gloria Scott*', when the villain Hudson arrives at the Trevors' country seat, Donnithorpe, he is a little wizened fellow with a cringing manner and a shambling style of walking.

'He wore an open jacket, with a splotch of tar on the sleeve, a red-and-black check shirt, dungaree trousers and heavy boots badly worn,' says Holmes. 'His face was thin and brown and crafty, with a perpetual smile upon it, which showed an irregular line of yellow teeth, and his crinkled hands were half closed in a way that is distinctive of sailors.'

The effect on the Justice of the Peace is instantaneous: 'As he came slouching across the lawn I heard Mr Trevor make a sort of hiccoughing noise in his throat, and, jumping out of his chair, he ran into the house. He was back in a moment, and I smelt a strong reek of brandy as he passed me.' It is more than thirty years since the two men last saw each other and, though Trevor has become a wealthy landowner, Hudson is still a poor seaman and attempts to blackmail his former friend.

Hudson is hired by Trevor, though the maids complain of his drunken habits and his vile language. Eventually Hudson goes off to find a second victim to blackmail. His fate is unclear.

Cunningham, father and son

In 'The Reigate Puzzle', old Cunningham is described by Colonel Hayter as 'our leading man about here' and 'a very decent fellow'. His son Alec is altogether a more suspect type – he claims to have been smoking a pipe in his dressing-gown when the coachman was killed. Visiting the Cunninghams', Watson says: 'The one was an elderly man, with a strong, deep-lined, heavy-eyed face; the other a dashing young fellow, whose bright, smiling expression and showy dress were in strange contrast with the business which had brought us there.'

Alec makes the mistake of mocking Holmes as a Londoner. He and his father are strong enough to wrestle Holmes to the ground, with Alec clutching at Holmes's throat with both hands and the elder Cunningham twisting his wrists. But they cannot disguise the guilt on their faces.

'Never certainly have I seen a plainer confession of guilt upon human countenances,' says Watson. 'The older man seemed numbed and dazed, with a heavy, sullen expression upon his strongly marked face. The son, on the other hand, had dropped all that jaunty, dashing style which had characterized him, and the ferocity of a dangerous wild beast gleamed in his dark eyes and distorted his handsome features.'

Alec thinks he can shoot his way out, but Inspector Forrester disarms him. After they are arrested, Holmes finds Cunningham senior 'tractable enough': 'When Cunningham saw that the case against him was so strong he lost all heart and made a clean breast of everything.'

His son, though, 'was a perfect demon, ready to blow out his own or anybody else's brains if he could have got to his revolver'.

Colonel James Barclay

The victim and the villain are one and the same in 'The Crooked Man'. During the Indian Mutiny, Corporal Henry Wood volunteers to fetch help but is betrayed to the enemy by Sergeant James Barclay, who wants to rid himself of a love rival. Barclay is then commissioned, marries the colour-sergeant's daughter and is promoted through the ranks. In the meantime, Wood who had been captured and tortured, is released a broken man. A life of hardship follows until one day he sees his former love and goes to visit her. When Barclay sees him, he collapses in terror, hits his head and dies.

Blessington aka Sutton

Dr Percy Trevelyan thinks his resident patient, Blessington, is his benefactor. Blessington has a weak heart and is in need of constant medical supervision. Otherwise, Trevelyan says: 'He was a man of singular habits, shunning company and very seldom going out. His life was irregular, but in one respect he was regularity itself. Every evening, at the same hour, he walked into the consulting-room, examined the books, put down five and three-pence for every guinea that I had earned, and carried the rest off to the strong-box in his own room.'

Trevelyan is then visited by a patient who purports to be a Russian nobleman: 'He was an elderly man, thin, demure, and commonplace,' says Trevelyan, 'by no means the conception one forms of a Russian nobleman.'

He arrives with 'a tall young man, surprisingly handsome, with a dark, fierce face and the limbs and chest of a Hercules'. However, when helping his elderly companion to a chair, he exhibits 'a tenderness which one would hardly have expected from his appearance'.

When Watson meets Blessington, he describes him as 'a singular-looking man, whose appearance, as well as his voice, testified to his jangled nerves. He was very fat, but had apparently at some time been much fatter, so that the skin hung about his face in loose pouches, like the cheeks of a blood-hound. He was of a sickly colour, and his thin, sandy hair seemed to bristle up with the intensity of his emotion. In his hand he held a pistol, but he thrust it into his pocket as we advanced.'

Count and his companion have come to kill him. They had robbed a bank together, but Blessington, aka Sutton, had turned Queen's evidence. Blessington is hanged by his fellow criminals, though they are then drowned escaping the country.

Latimer and Harold

The Greek interpreter Melas is hired by Latimer, 'a fashionably dressed young man'. When in a carriage together, he pulls out 'a most formidable-looking bludgeon loaded with lead from his pocket, and switching it backward and forward several times, as if to test its weight and strength. Then he placed it without a word upon the seat beside him'.

His accomplice Harold is 'a small, mean-looking, middle-aged man with rounded shoulders' who wears glasses – hardly the sort of man Sophy would have fallen for, one would have thought. Both Latimer and Harold are found dead in Budapest, possibly at Sophy's hand.

Joseph Harrison

Joseph Harrison, who steals a naval treaty from his brother-in-law, is 'a rather stout man who received us with much hospitality. His age may have been nearer forty than thirty, but his cheeks were so ruddy and his eyes so merry that he still conveyed the impression of a plump and mischievous boy.'

When trying to recover the treaty at night he wears a long black cloak thrown over his shoulders so that he can hide his face if necessary. He carries a long-bladed knife. And when confronted by Holmes, Harrison has a murderous look in his eye, but in the end listens to reason and gives up the treaty.

Holmes reports the matter to Scotland Yard, but assumes that Harrison will have fled, considering it better for the government and everyone else concerned if the matter never comes to court. The theft was purely opportunistic. It appears that Harrison had lost heavily on the stock market and was prepared to do anything to improve his fortunes.

Jack Stapleton aka Baskerville

When Watson first meets the naturalist Jack Stapleton, he does not take him for a murderer: 'He was a small, slim, clean-shaven, prim-faced man, flaxen-haired and lean-jawed, between thirty and forty years of age, dressed in a gray suit and wearing a straw hat,' says Watson. 'A tin box for botanical specimens hung over his shoulder and he carried a green butterfly-net in one of his hands.'

He and his 'sister' Beryl, who turns out to be his wife, live in Merripit House, near Baskerville Hall. Son of Rodger Baskerville, the black sheep of the family who disappeared in Central America, Stapleton is third in line to the Baskerville estate. He is also an embezzler, armed robber and failed school master. Additionally, he breaches his promise in the case of Laura Lyons. It is no great loss when he is drowned in Grimpen Mire.

Ted Baldwin and Black Jack McGinty

Although Moriarty is the dead hand in *The Valley of Fear*, he is only facilitating Ted Baldwin and other killers. When Baldwin first appears, he is 'just over fifty, with grizzled hair and moustache, and about the same height . . . dressed in a heavy grey suit with a reefer jacket, and . . . a short yellow overcoat and a soft cap'.

In Vermissa he is introduced as the boss of the Scowrers. Everyone is afraid of him and he is seen 'swaggering with the air of one who is the master'. He is a handsome, dashing young man, with 'fierce, domineering eyes and a curved hawk-bill of a nose' and wears broad-brimmed black felt hat.

Ettie is afraid of him but McMurdo is not, and offers to take him outside for a fight. Baldwin demurs, saying: 'I'll get even with you without needing to dirty my hands.'

But Baldwin is not all he is cracked up to be. The real boss is the Bodymaster of Vermissa Lodge, Black Jack McGinty. 'He had a rough, jovial disposition which formed a mask, covering a great deal which lay behind it. But apart from this popularity, the fear in which he was held throughout the township, and indeed down the whole thirty miles of the valley and past the mountains on each side of it, was enough in itself to fill his bar; for none could afford to neglect his good will.'

McGinty pulls a gun on McMurdo when he walks into his saloon. As well has having 'secret powers which it was universally believed that he exercised in so pitiless a fashion', he is a high public official, a municipal councillor, and a commissioner of roads, voted into office by those who expect favours in return. He appropriates taxes and public assets for his own uses, bribes auditors and terrorizes decent citizens who want to speak out against him.

The man himself is a 'tall, strong, heavily built man . . . a black-maned giant, bearded to the cheek-bones, and with a shock of raven hair which fell to his collar. His complexion was as swarthy as that of an Italian, and his eyes were of a strange dead black, which, combined with a slight squint, gave them a particularly sinister appearance.' He has black, thick eyebrows, a brown moustache and he keeps a cigar hanging at an acute angle from the corner of his mouth. 'All else in the man – his noble proportions, his fine features, and his frank bearing – fitted in with that jovial, man-to-man manner which he affected. Here, one would say, is a bluff, honest fellow, whose heart would be sound however rude his outspoken words might seem. It was only when those dead, dark eyes, deep and remorseless, were turned upon a man that he shrank within himself, feeling that he was face to face with an infinite possibility of latent evil, with a strength and courage and cunning behind it which made it a thousand times more deadly.'

McGinty is hanged, Baldwin spends ten years in prison, then comes after McMurdo, who flees to England. When he catches up with McMurdo, Baldwin is shot in the face with his own sawn-off shotgun.

Jonas Oldacre

In 'The Adventure of the Norwood Builder', retired builder Jonas Oldacre tries to fake his own death and frame John Hector McFarlane for murder to revenge himself on McFarlane's mother, his former fiancée who broke off the engagement when she heard that he had turned a cat loose in an aviary. 'He was more like a malignant and cunning ape than a human being,' she says, 'and he always was, ever since he was a young man.'

When Holmes eventually smokes him from his lair, Oldacre is a little, wizened man with 'an odious face – crafty, vicious, malignant, with shifty, light-gray eyes and white lashes'.

He is then arrested and it turn out that he has also being trying to swindle his creditors.

Abe Slaney

Chicago gangster Abe Slaney tracks down his former fiancée Elsie in Norfolk and contacts her using the 'dancing man' code. When she refuses to leave her husband and run away with him, there is a gunfight. Hilton Cubitt, her husband is killed, and Elsie is critically wounded.

According to Watson: 'He was a tall, handsome, swarthy fellow, clad in a suit of gray flannel, with a Panama hat, a bristling black beard, and a great, aggressive hooked nose, and flourishing a cane as he walked. He swaggered up the path as if the place belonged to him, and we heard his loud, confident peal at the bell.'

When arrested, he has 'blazing black eyes'. But when he hears that Elsie was injured, he is overcome with remorse. Though condemned to death, Slaney's sentence is commuted to penal servitude 'in consideration of mitigating circumstances, and the certainty that Hilton Cubitt had fired the first shot'.

Carruthers and Woodley

Two conmen from South Africa, Carruthers and Woodley try to cheat Miss Violet Smith out of her inheritance. She finds Woodley 'a most odious person. He was for ever making eyes at me – a coarse, puffy-faced, red-moustached young man, with his hair plastered down on each side of his forehead'. In conclusion, he is 'perfectly hateful'.

Carruthers is a much older man and more agreeable. A widower, he is a dark, sallow, clean-shaven and silent but has polite manners and a pleasant smile. He proposes marriage but she turns him down.

Woodley then tries to marry her by force with the aid of a white-bearded former priest named Williamson, but Carruthers has changed his mind and rides to her protection. He shoots Woodley and, when he is arrested, Holmes offers to give evidence on behalf of Carruthers in court.

James Wilder and Reuben Hayes

Wilder and Hayes conspire to kidnap Lord Saltire, the young son of the Duke of Holdernesse. Wilder is the duke's illegitimate son and works as his secretary.

'He was small, nervous, alert, with intelligent light-blue eyes and mobile features,' notes Watson, who opens the conversation in an incisive and positive tone.

Hayes is the duke's former coachman, who claims he had been treated badly and sacked on the word of a lying corn-chandler, a squat, dark, elderly gentleman who smokes a black clay pipe. Making his escape, Hayes is arrested in Chesterfield and faces murder charges. Wilder absconds to go to Australia.

Peter Carey and Patrick Cairns

Peter Carey is a successful seal and whaler fisher. But he quits the sea travels for a while and then settles in Sussex. He is a strict Puritan – a silent, gloomy fellow. He is also an intermittent drunkard, which turns him into a perfect fiend. He has been known to drive his wife and daughter out of doors in the middle of the night and flog them through the park until the whole village outside the gates is aroused by their screams. On another occasion he had savagely assaulted a vicar.

As captain of the *Sea Unicorn*, he had been a shipmate of the harpooner Patrick Cairns and is 'a man of remarkable appearance,' says Watson. 'A fierce bulldog face was framed in a tangle of hair and beard, and two bold, dark eyes gleamed behind the cover of thick, tufted, overhung eyebrows.' When he arrives at 221B, he salutes and stands sailor-fashion, turning his cap around in his hands.

While at sea he and Cairns had found Neligan's father adrift in a small boat off the Norwegian coast and took him on board with the tin box he was carrying. Later Cairns saw Carey throw Neligan's father overboard and figured he has done so for whatever was in the tin box. It is soon after this that Carey quits the sea.

Years later, Cairns tracks him down, believing that Carey could afford to pay him to keep his mouth shut. They get drunk. Carey has a murderous look in his eye but before he could unsheath his knife, Cairns grabs a harpoon and runs him through.

Charles Augustus Milverton

According to Holmes, Charles August Milverton is 'the worst man in London'. When he is due to arrive at 221B, Holmes asks: 'Do you feel a creeping, shrinking sensation, Watson, when you stand before the serpents in the Zoo, and see the slithery, gliding, venomous creatures, with their deadly eyes and wicked, flattened faces? Well, that's how Milverton impresses me. I've had to do with fifty murderers in my career, but the worst of them never gave me the repulsion which I have for this fellow.'

He is the king of the blackmailers, happy to ruin one life to scare others to pay up. When he is shot, Holmes and Watson do nothing to detain the assassin and happily become accessories to the crime.

Professor Coram

The villain here is not the perpetrator of the crime Holmes is investigating in 'The Adventure of the Golden Pince-Nez', that is Anna, who accidentally killed the professor's secretary Willoughby Smith and, having lost her glasses, finds refuge in the professor's bedroom. As a girl of twenty, she had married Coram, who was then fifty, in Russia. He then betrayed their revolutionary cell but has lived in safety in England ever since while others were hanged or, like her, sent to Siberia. While Coram goes unpunished, Anna dies at her own hand.

Don Juan Murillo aka Henderson

In 'The Adventure of Wisteria Lodge', deposed dictator Don Juan Murillo – the Tiger of San Pedro – is responsible for the deaths of Aloysius Garcia and Miss Burnet's husband, Victor Durando, and for drugging and imprisoning Miss Burnet. He is 'the most lewd and bloodthirsty tyrant that had ever governed any country with a pretence to civilization,' says Watson. 'Strong, fearless, and energetic, he had sufficient virtue to enable him to impose his odious vices upon a cowering people for ten or twelve years. His name was a terror through all Central America. At the end of that time there was a universal rising against him. But he was as cunning as he was cruel, and at the first whisper of coming trouble he had secretly conveyed his treasures aboard a ship which was manned by devoted adherents.'

Under the name Henderson, he lives with his children in High Gable, a country house near Esher. According to the police description, he has magnetic black eyes and tufted brows. Fearful of assassination, he walks everywhere with his body-guard manservant. They thwart an assassination attempt in England, but meet their end in Madrid.

Jim Browner

The antagonist of 'The Adventure of the Cardboard Box', Jim Browner is a drunken sailor, driven to murder by his spiteful sister-in-law and the infidelity of his wife. Though his revenge was blood-thirsty, when caught he is contrite and accepts his fate.

Giuseppe Gorgiano

Black Gorgiano is a Neapolitan gangster who initiated Gennero Lucca into the 'Red Circle'. According to Lucca's wife Emilia, Gorgiano is 'a devil and a monster . . . who had earned the name of "Death" in the south of Italy, for he was red to the elbow in murder'.

Unable to marry in their hometown of Posillipo, near Naples, Gennero and Emilia flee to Bari, where they wed, then head for New York. There Gennero goes to work for Tito Castalotte, who treats him like a son. Then, one day, Gennero brings Gorgiano home.

'He was a huge man,' says Emilia. 'Not only was his body that of a giant but everything about him was grotesque, gigantic, and terrifying. His voice was like thunder in our little house. There was scarce room for the whirl of his great arms as he talked. His thoughts, his emotions, his passions, all were exaggerated and monstrous. He talked, or rather roared, with such energy that others could but sit and listen, cowed with the mighty stream of words. His eyes blazed at you and held you at his mercy.'

Gorgiano had also fled to New York to avoid the Italian police.

He had begun a new lodge of the Red Circle there and Gennero was obliged to join. Then one day Gorgiano comes to the house, grabs Emilia, covers her in kisses and implores her to come away with him. She screams and Gennero rushes in to defend her, but Gorgiano knocks him out and flees.

A few days later, Gennero returns from a Red Circle meeting where Gorgiano had proposed raising funds by blackmailing prominent Italians. Castalotte has been approached but refused to pay up and Gennero is ordered to kill him.

Gennero and Emilia flee again to London, but Gorgiano follows. Gennero kills him and Emilia is taken to see the chief at Scotland Yard. Inspector Gregson says: 'If what she says is corroborated, I do not think she or her husband has much to fear.'

Hugo Oberstein

Colonel Valentine Walter steals the 'Bruce-Partington Plans' for £5,000 to cover his losses on the stock exchange. The brother of Sir James Walter, who has just died, he is 'a very tall, handsome, light-bearded man of fifty . . . His wild eyes, stained cheeks, and unkempt hair all spoke of the sudden blow which had fallen upon the household.' However, he denies killing Cadogan West, who had followed him to his rendezvous with the spy Hugo Oberstein. Walter maintains that Oberstein was the one who the dealt a fatal blow with a life-preserver. Nevertheless, Oberstein gets off with a comparatively light sentence of fifteen years, while Walter dies in prison after serving only a year.

Culverton Smith

In 'The Adventure of the Dying Detective', Culverton Smith is a plantation owner from Sumatra and an expert on tropical diseases who has already used this knowledge to kill his nephew.

He is a busy man with a high, petulant, penetrating voice. When Watson visits him he observes: 'I saw a great yellow face, coarse-grained and greasy, with a heavy, double-chin, and two sullen, menacing grey eyes which glared at me from under tufted and sandy brows. A high bald head had a small velvet smoking-cap poised coquettishly upon one side of its pink curve. The skull was of enormous capacity, and yet as I looked down I saw to my amazement that the figure of the man was small and frail, twisted in the shoulders and back like one who has suffered from rickets in his childhood.' He also has 'a malicious and abominable smile'.

When he is tricked into visiting Holmes and to confessing both the murder of his nephew and the attempted murder to Holmes, he is arrested.

Dr Shlessinger aka Henry Peters

When Lady Frances Carfax meets Dr Shlessinger in the Englischer Hof in Baden, he appears to be suffering from a tropical disease contracted in his missionary work and is nursed by his wife. According to the manager: 'He spent his day . . . upon a lounge-chair on the veranda, with an attendant lady upon either side of him. He was preparing a map of the Holy Land, with special reference to the kingdom of the Midianites, upon which he was writing a monograph.'

From the description of his 'jagged and torn' ear, Holmes identifies him as 'Holy' Peters, a notorious villain from Australia who had part of his ear bitten off in a saloon brawl. Peters's speciality is 'the beguiling of lonely ladies by playing upon their religious feelings'. The woman masquerading as his wife is an Englishwoman named Fraser, who is 'a worthy helpmate . . . a tall, pale woman, with ferret eyes'.

When he turns up at a pawn shop in London, he is 'a large, clean-shaven man of clerical appearance' and gives a false address. Then Holmes beards him in his lair and he is a big, clean-shaven bald-headed man with a large red face, pendulous cheeks 'and a general air of superficial benevolence which was marred by a cruel, vicious mouth'.

Holmes finds Lady Frances and Watson revives her, by which time Peters and Fraser have fled.

'If our ex-missionary friends escape the clutches of Lestrade,' says Holmes, 'I shall expect to hear of some brilliant incidents in their future career.'

Mortimer Tregennis

In 'The Adventure of the Devil's Foot', Mortimer Tregennis murders his sister and drives his two brothers insane by throwing the toxic Devil's-foot root on the fire in their cottage.

Tregennis is a thin, dark, bespectacled man, with 'a stoop which gave the impression of actual, physical deformity'. When Holmes and Watson first visit the vicarage where he lodges, they find him 'strangely reticent, a sad-faced, introspective man, sitting with averted eyes, brooding apparently upon his own affairs'. After the murder, he is still self-contained, but the twitching of his thin lips and the brightness of his dark eyes betray emotion.

Asked why he lives apart from his siblings, he says: 'We were a family of tin-miners at Redruth, but we sold out our venture to a company, and so retired with enough to keep us. I won't deny that there was some feeling about the division of the money and it stood between us for a time, but it was all forgiven and forgotten, and we were the best of friends together.'

But it seems that this was not the case and when Dr Sterndale realizes that Tregennis has killed his beloved Brenda, he returns and kills Tregennis the same way.

Von Bork

In 'His Last Bow', Holmes's adversary is 'a remarkable man who could hardly be matched among all the devoted agents of the Kaiser'. His cohort, the German ambassador Baron Von Herling, is 'a huge man, the secretary, deep, broad, and tall, with a slow, heavy fashion of speech which had been his main asset in his political career'.

Von Bork is a born sportsman. He matches the English at sailing, polo, driving four-in-hand, boxing . . . every game, even drinking. They think he is 'quite a decent fellow for a German'. But Holmes is not fooled and, posing as an Irish-American, he feeds Von Bork false information, then overpowers and arrests him.

Baron Adelbert Gruner

Before the beginning of 'The Adventure of the Illustrious Client', Holmes already knows of Gruner, whom he describes as 'the Austrian murderer'.

'Who could possibly have read what happened at Prague and have any doubts as to the man's guilt!' he says. 'It was a purely technical legal point and the suspicious death of a witness that saved him! I am as sure that he killed his wife when the so-called "accident" happened in the Splugen Pass as if I had seen him do it. I knew, also, that he had come to England and had a presentiment that sooner or later he would find me some work to do.'

He met Violet de Merville on a yachting trip in the Mediterranean and has the guile to present his own version of all the scandals that dog him.

Sir James Damery says: 'He has expensive tastes. He is a horse fancier. For a short time he played polo at Hurlingham, but then this Prague affair got noised about and he had to leave. He collects books and pictures. He is a man with a considerable artistic side to his nature. He is, I believe, a recognized authority upon Chinese pottery and has written a book upon the subject.'

To Holmes, this means he has a complex mind, making him more of a challenge. When he goes to Kingston to meet the baron, Holmes finds that: 'He is an excellent antagonist, cool as ice, silky voiced and soothing as one of your fashionable consultants, and poisonous as a cobra. He has breeding in him – a real aristocrat of crime, with a superficial suggestion of afternoon tea and all the cruelty of the grave behind it.' He is also 'A purring cat who thinks he sees prospective mice'. He even has 'little waxed tips of hair under his nose, like the short antennae of an insect. These quivered with amusement as he listened, and he finally broke into a gentle chuckle.'

Gruner boasts that he has used post-hypnotic suggestion to control Violet. But he is not above using violence on anyone who gets in the way of his plans.

According to his former mistress Kitty Winter, Gruner is no

coward, but he does have one fatal flaw. He writes down the details of all his love affairs in a leather-bound book. Because he is a 'precise, tidy cat of a man', this is easily found in a pigeon-hole in his desk.

When Watson goes to see Gruner, he finds that he lives in a beautiful house and grounds, indicating that he is a man of considerable wealth. The property, built by a South African gold king has a long winding drive, with banks of rare shrubs on either side that open out to a great gravelled square adorned with statues. The long, low house had turrets at the corners and, though an architectural nightmare, it is imposing in its size and solidity. A butler 'who would have adorned a bench of bishops' shows Watson in and a plush-clad footman ushers him into the baron's presence.

According to Watson: 'He was certainly a remarkably handsome man. His European reputation for beauty was fully deserved. In figure he was not more than of middle size, but was built upon graceful and active lines. His face was swarthy, almost Oriental, with large, dark, languorous eyes which might easily hold an irresistible fascination for women. His hair and moustache were raven black, the latter short, pointed, and carefully waxed. His features were regular and pleasing, save only his straight, thin-lipped mouth. If ever I saw a murderer's mouth it was there – a cruel, hard gash in the face, compressed, inexorable, and terrible. He was ill-advised to train his moustache away from it, for it was Nature's danger-signal, set as a warning to his victims. His voice was engaging and his manners perfect. In age I should have put him at little over thirty, though his record afterwards showed that he was forty-two.'

It is this handsome face that would be ruined by Kitty and her sulphuric acid, and his opportunist marriage prospects ruined by Holmes, who seizes the leather-bound book recording his pitiless love life.

Count Negretto Sylvius
The thief of the Mazarin Stone, Count Negretto Sylvius is, like

Colonel Sebastian Moran, out to shoot Holmes with an airgun – this one bought from a workshop in the Minories. Holmes has followed him there.

Sylvius is a 'famous game-shot, sportsman, and man-about town ... a big, swarthy fellow, with a formidable dark moustache shading a cruel, thin-lipped mouth, and surmounted by a long, curved nose like the beak of an eagle. He was well dressed, but his brilliant necktie, shining pin, and glittering rings were flamboyant in their effect.' His eyes are 'fierce, startled ... like one who suspects a trap at every turn' and then dark and murderous. He carries a revolver.

Holmes tells the count that he keeps a notebook containing 'every action of [your count's] vile and dangerous life', including 'the real facts as to the death of old Mrs Harold, who left you the Blymer estate, which you so rapidly gambled away ... and the complete life history of Miss Minnie Warrender [and] the robbery in the train de-luxe to the Riviera on February 13, 1892. Here is the forged cheque in the same year on the Credit Lyonnais.'

'No; you're wrong there,' says Sylvius, inadvertently admitting that the other charges were right.

Holmes likens his pursuit of Sylvius to the count's lion-hunting in Algeria. 'For the sport, the excitement, the danger?' asks the count.

'And, no doubt, to free the country of a pest,' says Holmes.

Sylvius is then joined by his partner in crime, the prize-fighter Sam Merton, 'a heavily built young man with a stupid, obstinate, slab-sided face'.

Holmes then tricks them into producing the stone and they are arrested.

Isadora Klein

In 'The Adventure of the Three Gables', Isadora Klein tries to force the elderly Mrs Maberley to leave home to gain access to and destroy her son Douglas's incriminating manuscript. Holmes says: 'She was, of course, the celebrated beauty. There was never a woman to touch her. She is pure Spanish, the real blood of the masterful Conquistadors, and her people have been leaders in Pernambuco for generations. She married the aged German sugar king, Klein, and presently found herself the richest as well as the most lovely widow upon Earth. Then there was an interval of adventure when she pleased her own tastes. She had several lovers, and Douglas Maberley, one of the most striking men in London, was one of them. It was by all accounts more than an adventure with him. He was not a society butterfly but a strong, proud man who gave and expected all. But she is the "*belle dame sans merci*" of fiction. When her caprice is satisfied the matter is ended, and if the other party in the matter can't take her word for it she knows how to bring it home to him.'

Broken hearted Maberley, fictionalizes their affair, and the possible publication of the novel threatens to impede her marriage to the Duke of Lomond, who is young enough to be her son. In the end, the manuscript is retrieved and destroyed. The only penalty Isadora pays is the price of a round-the-world trip for Mrs Maberley.

John Garrideb aka James Winter aka Morecroft aka 'Killer' Evans

Pretending to be a 'counsellor at law' from Moorville, Kansas, John Garrideb is 'a short, powerful man with the round, fresh, clean-shaven face characteristic of so many American men of affairs. The general effect was chubby and rather childlike, so that one received the impression of quite a young man with a broad set smile upon his face. His eyes, however, were arresting. Seldom in any human head have I seen a pair which bespoke a more intense inward life, so bright were they, so alert, so responsive to every change of thought. His accent was American, but was not accompanied by any eccentricity of speech.'

His clothes, though, are distinctly British, alerting Holmes to the fact that he has been in the UK for some time. Identifying him from Scotland Yard's files, Holmes reveals he is James

Winter, alias Morecroft, alias 'Killer' Evans, who had been imprisoned for shooting Rodger Prescott, a forger from Chicago. He had been spared the gallows when Prescott was shown to have been the aggressor. Thanks to Holmes and Watson, 'Killer' Evans is returned to prison.

Josiah Amberley

On seeing retired colourman Josiah Amberley leaving 221B, Watson calls him 'a pathetic, futile, broken creature'. When Watson sees him again in Lewisham, he says: 'He seemed to me like a man who was literally bowed down by care. His back was curved as though he carried a heavy burden. Yet he was not the weakling that I had at first imagined, for his shoulders and chest have the framework of a giant, though his figure tapers away into a pair of spindled legs.' Holmes also notes that Amberley has an artificial leg.

At the age of sixty-one, Amberley married a good-looking woman twenty years his junior: 'A competence, a wife, leisure – it seemed a straight road which lay before him,' says Holmes. 'And yet within two years he is, as you have seen, as broken and miserable a creature as crawls beneath the sun.'

But he has one hobby in life: chess. His latest opponent is a young doctor.

'The old story, Watson. A treacherous friend and a fickle wife,' says Holmes. But he soon changes his tune when he realizes that Amberley is playing him for a fool. After killing his wife and the doctor and disposing of their bodies, Amberley thinks he has got away with it. He goes to the police, then hires Holmes out of 'pure swank'.

'He felt so clever and so sure of himself', says Holmes, 'that he imagined no one could touch him. He could say to any suspicious neighbour, "Look at the steps I have taken. I have consulted not only the police but even Sherlock Holmes."'

Holmes thinks his incarceration is more likely to be in Broadmoor – the hospital for the criminally insane – than on the scaffold.

Chapter 16

Inspector Lestrade and Scotland Yard

In 1888, Scotland Yard badly needed a good detective: Jack the Ripper was on the prowl and the Criminal Investigation Department had failed to find him or come up with a firm suspect. Perhaps the follies of Inspector Lestrade and his less well known colleagues can show us why.

When Watson first moves into 221B Baker Street in *A Study in Scarlet* he is introduced to a Mr Lestrade, who calls three or four times in a single week. He is a 'little sallow, rat-faced, dark-eyed fellow' and later he is 'lean and ferret-like'. Holmes says he is a well-known detective who got himself into a fog recently over a forgery case. As Scotland Yarders, he and his colleague, Inspector Gregson, are the pick of a bad lot. They are both quick and energetic but shockingly conventional. Plus, they have their knives into one another; they are as jealous as a pair of professional beauties. Consulted on the Lauriston Gardens mystery, Holmes says: 'There will be some fun over this case if they are both put upon the scent.'

But he says he cannot really be bothered to take on the case himself because Lestrade and Gregson will take all the credit. Then he changes his mind and agrees to go to Lauriston Gardens: 'I may have a laugh at them, if I have nothing else.'

When he arrives, he says to Gregson, who appears to be Lestrade's boss: 'With two such men as yourself and Lestrade upon the ground, there will not be much for a third party to find out.'

Lestrade is in charge of the investigation. At the scene of the crime he finds no clues, but Holmes has already found enough to solve the case. When they move the victim's body and a wedding ring rolls across the floor, Lestrade concludes that a woman has been there. And when he finds the word 'RACHE' written in blood on the wall he rubs his hands in a pompous and self-satisfied manner. He concludes that the victim was writing the name 'Rachel', but died before he could finish it. When Holmes laughs, Lestrade says: 'You may be very smart and clever, but the old hound is the best, when all is said and done.'

Gregson and Lestrade then watch Holmes take measurements, collect dust and minutely examine the scene with a magnifying glass with 'considerable curiosity and some contempt'. They are then incredulous when Holmes gives a detailed description of the perpetrator, explains how the crime was committed and quashes Lestrade's suggestion that a woman named Rachel had anything to do with it. Later Holmes explains to Watson that by studying such details the skilled detective differentiates himself from those of the Gregson and Lestrade mould.

While Gregson arrests the wrong man, Lestrade becomes even more perplexed.

'The assurance and jauntiness which generally marked [Lestrade's] demeanour and dress were, however, wanting,' says Watson. 'His face was disturbed and troubled, while his clothes were disarranged and untidy.'

He had come to consult Holmes but when he sees Gregson already there, he is embarrassed and stands in the centre of the room, fumbling nervously with his hat; however, Lestrade is on the right track – he had been following Stangerson and found him dead.

Though he has retrieved the pills that have caused the death, Lestrade adopts the injured tone of one who suspects he is being laughed at when Holmes feeds them to the dog. He and Gregson are far from satisfied with Holmes's assurance that there will be no more murders and are unimpressed by Holmes's new handcuffs, though Jefferson Hope, the guilty man disguised as a cabbie, is on the way up to the flat. Fortunately, in the succeeding scuffle Lestrade proves his worth. 'It was not until Lestrade succeeded in getting his hand inside his neckcloth and half-strangling him that we made him realize that his struggles were of no avail,' says Watson.

Lestrade then takes over the cab to drive the culprit to the police station and later, gives Watson access to his notebook so he could copy out Hope's statement. Gregson and Lestrade are miffed that Hope dies before he could be hanged but, as Holmes predicted, they get the credit for his arrest. Nevertheless, Holmes concludes that when Gregson, Lestrade and another colleague, Inspector Athelney Jones 'are out of their depths – which, by the way, is their normal state – the matter is laid before me'.

In 'The Boscombe Valley Mystery' a Miss Turner 'retained' Lestrade – that is, as Herefordshire has no criminal investigation department she asked the chief constable to call for help from the Metropolitan Police. When Lestrade is perplexed by the case, he again summons Holmes, who on the way assures Watson that they may hit on obvious facts that are by no means obvious to Mr Lestrade.

When they arrive in Ross, they are met by a lean, ferret-like man, furtive and sly-looking: 'In spite of the light brown dust-coat and leather-leggings which he wore in deference to his rustic surroundings,' says Watson, 'I had no difficulty in recognizing Lestrade, of Scotland Yard.'

To Lestrade, the case is as plain as a pikestaff. But Miss Turner has heard of Holmes and he can not refuse a lady. She immediately chides Lestrade because Holmes gives her hope and when she leaves, Lestrade upbraids Holmes for raising the girl's expectations, calling him 'cruel'. Nevertheless, Lestrade generously offers Holmes every assistance while dismissing his deductions and inferences. 'I find it hard enough to tackle facts, Holmes,' he says, 'without flying away after theories and fancies.'

Holmes leads Lestrade through the investigation clue by clue, then gives him a detailed description of the culprit.

Lestrade laughs, then shrugs his shoulders. 'I am a practical man,' he says, 'and I really cannot undertake to go about the country looking for a left-handed gentleman with a game-leg. I should become the laughing-stock of Scotland Yard.'

In private, Holmes dismisses Lestrade as an imbecile.

In 'The Adventure of the Noble Bachelor', Lestrade, who is already dealing with the case, has no objection to Lord St Simon hiring Holmes. Lestrade thinks the jilted Flora decoyed the runaway bride and laid some terrible trap for her. After dragging the Serpentine, he turns up at 221B 'attired in a pea-jacket and cravat, which gave him a decidedly nautical appearance, and he carried a black canvas bag in his hand'. He admits being flummoxed and Holmes generously offers him a drink and a cigar, but Lestrade grows angry when Holmes says he has already cracked the case. He condemns Holmes for not being very practical with his deductions and inferences – and even accuses him of making 'two blunders'. One of them concerning a note. Holmes congratulates him. Lestrade gets up triumphantly, but Holmes points out that Lestrade is looking at the wrong side: what is of interest is what is written on the back of a hotel bill.

Lestrade does not see the significance. 'I've wasted time enough,' he says 'I believe in hard work and not in sitting by the fire spinning fine theories.' Then he challenges Holmes to see who gets to the bottom of the matter first.

Ever magnanimous, Holmes gives Lestrade another hint – 'Lady St Simon is a myth.'

'Lestrade looked sadly at my companion,' says Watson. 'Then he turned to me, tapped his forehead three times, shook his head solemnly, and hurried away.'

When the missing bride turns up and explains what happened, Holmes says: 'Nothing could be more natural than the sequence of events as narrated by this lady, and nothing stranger than the result when viewed, for instance, by Mr Lestrade, of Scotland Yard.' After all, 'friend Lestrade held information in his hands the value of which he did not himself know'.

Lestrade makes his first visit to Dartmoor taking an unsigned warrant to Holmes in *The Hound of the Baskervilles*. When he arrives he is 'reverential'.

'He had learned a good deal since the days when they had first worked together,' says Watson. 'I could well remember the scorn which the theories of the reasoner used then to excite in the practical man.'

As they stake out Merripit House, Holmes asks him if he is armed.

'As long as I have my trousers I have a hip-pocket,' says Lestrade, 'and as long as I have my hip-pocket I have something in it.'

However, confronted with the hound, Lestrade gives out a yell of terror and throws himself face down on the ground. But, he is ready with the brandy flask to thrust between the baronet's lips when the hound is dead. This comes in handy again when Beryl Stapleton needs reviving.

Lestrade is on hand to arrest Moriarty gang member Colonel Moran in 'The Adventure of the Empty House', but, in the letter Holmes left for Watson at the Reichenbach Falls, he directs the arrests of Moriarty's gang to Inspector Patterson, via a blue envelope inscribed 'Moriarty' in pigeonhole 'M', which contains all Patterson needs to convict them. Despite giving him the crdit for arresting the Moriarty gang, Lestrade says to Holmes: 'It's good to see you back in London, sir.'

Holmes replies highhandedly: 'I think you want a little unofficial help. Three undetected murders in one year won't do, Lestrade. But you handled the Molesey Mystery with less than your usual – that's to say, you handled it fairly well.'

Lestrade does at least have the forethought to bring candles so they can see their prisoner and Holmes allows Lestrade to take the credit for the arrest.

'I congratulate you!' says Holmes. 'With your usual happy mixture of cunning and audacity, you have got him.'

'Got whom, Mr Holmes?' asks Lestrade.

'The man that the whole force has been seeking in vain

– Colonel Sebastian Moran, who shot the Honourable Ronald Adair,' announces Holmes.

In 'The Adventure of the Norwood Building', Lestrade immediately jumps to the most obvious yet incorrect conclusion and arrests John Hector McFarlane. But he does give McFarlane half-an-hour to tell Holmes his side of the story. Lestrade is then puzzled that Holmes heads for Blackheath when the crime took place in Norwood. But by now he knows better than to question the great detective. When McFarlane is taken into custody, Lestrade stays on to find out what else he can learn. Holmes, too, has become more tolerant and encourages Lestrade to add 'imagination to your other great qualities'. However, Holmes begins to fear that, for once, Lestrade is right.

As the case progresses, things get worse. Lestrade even sends a wire saying: 'Important fresh evidence to hand. McFarlane's guilt definitely established. Advise you to abandon case.'

Again Lestrade is triumphant. But Holmes turns Lestrade's fresh evidence – a well-marked thumb-print – on its head and uses it to prove that McFarlane is innocent. Lestrade even allows Holmes to set fire to straw in the upstairs landing, though his face grows red and angry, and he says: 'I don't know whether you are playing a game with us, Mr Sherlock Holmes . . . If you know anything, you can surely say it without all this tomfoolery.'

But when he smokes out Oldacre, Holmes once again gives all the credit to Lestrade.

In 'The Adventure of Charles Augustus Milverton', Lestrade arrives at Baker Street to ask for Holmes's help in finding a killer. On this occasion, Holmes turns him down. So, at the beginning of 'The Adventure of the Six Napoleons', Lestrade adopts another strategy and turns up pretending there is nothing on his mind. Holmes sees through his ruse immediately, but they now have a mutual understanding.

'In return for the news which Lestrade would bring, Holmes was always ready to listen with attention to the details of any case upon which the detective was engaged,' says Watson.

Lestrade then involves Holmes in every aspect of the case,

while Holmes invites Lestrade to dine at Baker Street and avail himself of the sofa until they are ready for their late night foray to Chiswick. Again Lestrade shows his true mettle in the arrest.

When Holmes smashes the last bust to reveal the black pearl of the Borgias, Lestrade joins Watson in a spontaneous round of applause. And Lestrade is fulsome in his praise.

'I've seen you handle a good many cases, Mr Holmes,' he says, 'but I don't know that I ever knew a more workmanlike one than that. We're not jealous of you at Scotland Yard. No, sir, we are very proud of you, and if you come down tomorrow, there's not a man, from the oldest inspector to the youngest constable, who wouldn't be glad to shake you by the hand.'

In 'The Adventure of the Second Stain', Inspector Lestrade is investigating the murder of Eduardo Lucas. He has matured and Watson remarks on his 'bulldog features'. Lestrade chuckles with delight when he thinks he has bested the great detective by already working out why the blood stain on the carpet does not match that on the floor.

'The official police don't need you, Mr Holmes, to tell them that the carpet must have been turned round,' says.

When the first report concerning he discovery of the ears in 'The Adventure of the Cardboard Box' appears, the *Daily Chronicle* refers to Lestrade, who is in charge of the case, as 'the very smartest of our detective officers'. He has, of course, already contacted Holmes to ask for help. In this story Lestrade is 'as wiry, as dapper, and as ferret-like as ever' and observes that string has been tarred, but does not see the significance of a crucial knot. He thinks the two ears sent in a parcel are a medical student's practical joke and he is amazed when Holmes uncovers a double murder. He does his duty by arresting Jim Browner, and sends Holmes a full account.

In 'The Adventure of the Bruce-Partington Plans', Lestrade – now, surely, one of Scotland Yard's most trusted detectives – is sent to investigate. Again he fulfils his narrative purpose by articulating the most obvious inference, only to be pooh-poohed by Holmes. Lestrade personally supervises the examination of the underground carriage while Holmes works out that the body they find had been thrown from on top. And again Lestrade is in on the arrest.

In 'The Disappearance of Lady Frances Carfax', Holmes strolls to Scotland Yard to have a word with 'friend Lestrade' and later sends a note to him to ask for a warrant.

Holmes visits Lestrade again in 'The Adventure of the Three Garridebs' to go through Scotland Yard's photographic records. Lestrade does not appear in time for the arrest, but Holmes asks Watson to give the Yard a call after they have subdued the villian of the piece, 'Killer' Evans.

Tobias Gregson

It is Tobias Gregson, Lestrade's boss, who invites Holmes to help in the Lauriston Gardens mystery. While Holmes acknowledges that 'Gregson is the smartest of the Scotland Yarders', he goes on to say: 'He knows that I am his superior, and acknowledges it to me; but he would cut his tongue out before he would own it to any third person.'

Gregson is a tall, white-faced, flaxen-haired man who carries a notebook. He greets them at the scene of the crime and says he has left everything untouched.

'Except that!' says Holmes, pointing at the pathway. 'If a herd of buffaloes had passed along, there could not be a greater mess.'

Inside Gregson rubs his hands in a self-satisfied way that reminds Holmes of the death of Van Jansen in Utrecht in 1834. When he asks Gregson if he knows the case, Gregson admits he does not.

In *A Study in Scarlet*, Gregson gets a chapter to himself called: 'Tobias Gregson Shows What He Can Do'. What he does is arrest Arthur Charpentier and vault up the stairs at Baker Street 'pompously rubbing his fat hands and inflating his chest'. Even so, Holmes is gracious enough to offer him a cigar and a whisky and water. Gregson then makes fun of Lestrade's efforts to track down Stangerson, 'who had no more to do with the crime than the babe unborn'. When Gregson outlines his theory, Holmes says: 'Well done . . . Gregson, you are getting along. We shall make something of you yet.'

Then Lestrade turns up to announce that Stangerson is dead. At the news, Gregson leaps from his chair, upsetting what was left of his whisky and soda.

When Holmes draws his own conclusion, Gregson grows impatient.

'Look here, Mr Sherlock Holmes,' he says, 'we are all ready to acknowledge that you are a smart man, and that you have your own methods of working. We want something more than mere theory and preaching now, though . . . Can you name the man who did it?'

Lestrade concurs. Then, thanks to the Baker Street Irregulars, the culprit Jefferson Hope turns up at 221B.

Gregson is not called on again until 'The Greek Interpreter'. Even then at Scotland Yard, it was more than an hour before Holmes and Watson could get Inspector Gregson to complete the legal formalities which would enable them to enter the house in Beckenham.

In 'The Adventure of Wisteria Lodge', Gregson turns up at Baker Street with Inspector Baynes of the Surrey Constabulary. Despite past encounters, Watson bills Gregson as 'an energetic, gallant, and, within his limitations, a capable officer'. Gregson and Baynes are after a statement from Holmes's client, John Scott Eccles, though Holmes suspects they want to arrest Eccles, who tells his tale. This agrees with the facts, concedes Gregson in a 'very amiable tone'.

In 'The Adventure of the Red Circle', Holmes finds Gregson, muffled in a cravat and greatcoat, leaning against the railings outside the flats in Howe Street, where a signal lamp has been was spotted. They greet each other like old friends.

'I'll do you this justice, Mr Holmes, that I was never in a case yet that I didn't feel stronger for having you on my side,' says Gregson.

Knowing that the Mafioso Gorgiano was inside, Gregson

'climbed the stair to arrest this desperate murderer with the same absolutely quiet and businesslike bearing with which he would have ascended the official staircase of Scotland Yard'. Leverton from the famous American Pinkerton Agency tries to push past him, but Gregson firmly elbows him back: London dangers were the privilege of the London force. Finding the flat, Gregson goes in first and discovers Gorgiano dead.

When Holmes summons Emilia Lucca, Gregson tries to arrest her, but Holmes persuades him to listen to her story and Gregson changes his mind.

Mr Leverton of Pinkerton's
In 'The Adventure of the Red Circle', Gregson is accompanied by Mr Leverton of Pinkerton's American Agency.

'The hero of the Long Island cave mystery?' says Holmes. 'Sir, I am pleased to meet you.'

He is a quiet, businesslike young man, with a clean-shaven, hatchet face, who flushed at the words of commendation. When Holmes tells him of the signals, Leverton claps his hands together in vexation and says: 'He's on to us.'

He tries to pass Scotland Yard's Gregson on the stairs but is pushed aside. When they find their quarry dead, it is Leverton who identifies the corpse. And after Emilia Lucca has told her story, Leverton says: 'I don't know what your British point of view may be, but I guess that in New York this lady's husband will receive a pretty general vote of thanks.'

Athelney Jones
Athelney Jones makes his first appearance in *The Sign of the Four*. Holmes introduces himself during the investigation of the murder of Bartholomew Sholto at Pondicherry Lodge.

'It's Mr Sherlock Holmes, the theorist,' says Jones. 'Remember you? I'll never forget how you lectured us all on causes and inferences and effects in the Bishopgate jewel case. It's true you set us on the right track track; but you'll own now that it was more by good luck than good guidance.'

'It was a piece of very simple reasoning.'

'Oh, come, now, come! Never be ashamed to own up . . .'

Jones was out in Norwood on another case and was at the police station when the message arrived. He is there for the 'stern facts . . . no room for theories,' he says.

'This is hardly a case for me to theorize over,' says Holmes.

Jones then seeks to consult him privately while trying to weave a net around Thaddeus. When Holmes offers a fact that doesn't fit his theory, Jones is adamant.

'"Confirms it in every respect," said the fat detective pompously,' notes Watson. 'With great activity, considering his bulk, he sprang up the steps and squeezed through into the garret . . .'

Holmes is sure he will find something up there – 'he has the occasional glimmerings of reason'. Indeed, Jones finds the trap door to the roof partly open and announces triumphantly: 'You see! Facts are better than reason.' He is somewhat crestfallen when told that Holmes had opened the trap door himself.

Nevertheless, Jones arrests Thaddeus, though Holmes says he will clear him of the charge.

'Don't promise too much, Mr Theorist,' scoffs Jones.

To prove his point, Holmes then gives a full description of the true culprits. Jones merely sneers. Holmes and Watson decide to do a little more investigation on their own. 'Then I shall study the great Jones's methods and listen to his not too delicate sarcasms,' says Holmes.

Jones goes on to arrest the gatekeeper, the housekeeper and the Indian servant.

While searching for the *Aurora*, in the case of *The Sign of Four*, Holmes decides to do without the help of the police.

'I shall probably call Athelney Jones in at the last moment,' he tells Watson. 'He is not a bad fellow, and I should not like to do anything which would injure him professionally.'

In fact, Jones's misreading of the case is a positive advantage as it is bound to find its way into the press and lead the culprits into believing they can make their getaway safely. Indeed, the morning paper carries a story about the case and the 'energetic' Athelney Jones, lauding his 'well-known technical knowledge and his powers of minute observation'. Later the *Standard* praises his 'energy and sagacity' and expects further arrests any moment.

But Jones then turns up at 221B a very different person from the 'brusque and masterful professor of common sense who had taken over the case so confidently at Upper Norwood,' says Watson. 'His expression was downcast, and his bearing meek and even apologetic.'

When told Holmes is not in, he mops his face with a red bandanna handkerchief and accepts half a glass of whisky and soda while he waits. It transpires that Thaddeus Sholto has an alibi.

'It's a very dark case, and my professional credit is at stake,' he says. 'I should be very glad of a little assistance.'

Jones then praises Holmes, even saying he would make a most promising officer. Then, when an aged sailor turns up, Jones puts his broad back against the door to prevent him from leaving. The sailor, of course, turns out to be Holmes. Jones is delighted by this turn of events and praises Holmes's acting.

At Holmes's request, Jones orders a police launch, then Holmes insists that Jones dines with them. As a guest, 'Athelney Jones proved to be a sociable soul in his hours of relaxation and faced his dinner with the air of a bon vivant,' says Watson.

After toasting their success, Jones joins Holmes and Watson in the pursuit of the *Aurora*. He mans the searchlight, yells for the *Aurora* to stop and is on hand to arrest Jonathan Small. He then believes that he deserves a pull on Holmes's flask, saying: 'Well, I think we may all congratulate each other.'

Watson remarks: 'It was amusing to notice how the consequential Jones was already beginning to give himself airs on the strength of the capture.'

Jones is angry with Small for throwing the treasure overboard and, though he listens to Small's story, Jones is impatient to get him safely stowed in chokey. Jones, naturally, gets all the credit, though Holmes points out that he did arrest the Indian servant,

Small's inside man, and was due 'the undivided honour of having caught one fish in his great haul'.

In 'The Red-Headed League', a Peter Jones of Scotland Yard turns up, who Holmes says Watson knows and makes references to Sholto and the Agra treasure. He is also bulky and breathes heavily when they are in the cellar. This is surely Athelney Jones and the 'Peter' is a slip of Watson's (or Conan Doyle's) pen (the confusion possibly caused by Peter Jones, the name of the new department store that opened in Sloane Square in 1877).

'You may place considerable confidence in Mr Holmes,' says Jones loftily. 'He has his own little methods, which are, if he won't mind my saying so, just a little too theoretical and fantastic, but he has the makings of a detective in him. It is not too much to say that once or twice, as in that business of the Sholto murder and the Agra treasure, he has been more nearly correct than the official force.'

Excusing Jones' presence, Holmes tells Watson: 'He is not a bad fellow, though an absolute imbecile in his profession. He has one positive virtue. He is as brave as a bulldog and as tenacious as a lobster if he gets his claws upon anyone.'

He has also arranged for an inspector and two officers to be waiting at the front door as Holmes requested. Jones himself made a grab for the skirts of the coat of the villain's accomplice as he disappears down the hole. The fabric tears but with police at the front door he cannot get away. Jones then conducts the villain to the police station. And that is the last we hear of Athelney – or Peter – Jones.

Alec MacDonald and White Mason

When Holmes and Watson meet Inspector Alec MacDonald of Scotland Yard in *The Valley of Fear*, MacDonald had yet to attain the national fame that he would later achieve. The story is set in the late 1880s, when he is still a young but trusted member of the detective force. He had already distinguished himself in several cases.

'His tall, bony figure gave promise of exceptional physical

strength,' says Watson, 'while his great cranium and deep-set, lustrous eyes spoke no less clearly of the keen intelligence which twinkled out from behind his bushy eyebrows. He was a silent, precise man with a dour nature and a hard Aberdonian accent. Twice already in his career had Holmes helped him to attain success . . .'

His accent, Watson notes, becomes more Aberdonian when he loses himself in argument.

MacDonald has a profound respect for Holmes, and enough talent to recognize Holmes's genius, though he is suspicious of Holmes's obsession with Moriarty. Holmes, not prone to friendship, is tolerant of the big Scot and smiles at the sight of him when MacDonald comes to consult him over the murder in Birlstone House. Holmes calls him 'friend MacDonald' and frequently addresses him as 'Mr Mac'.

He has great sandy eyebrows that bunch into a yellow triangle when he concentrates. When he professes ignorance of Jonathan Wild, Holmes administer him: 'Mr Mac, the most practical thing that you ever did in your life would be to shut yourself up for three months and read twelve hours a day at the annals of crime.'

MacDonald been called in on the Valley of Fear case by local officer White Mason, who asks him to bring Holmes and describes the case as 'a snorter'. Holmes concludes Mason is no fool and Watson says: 'White Mason was a quiet, comfortable-looking person in a loose tweed suit, with a clean-shaved, ruddy face, a stoutish body, and powerful bandy legs adorned with gaiters, looking like a small farmer, a retired gamekeeper, or anything upon earth except a very favourable specimen of the provincial criminal officer.'

Mason is thrilled to have Holmes on the case, and when Holmes deduces that the sawn-off shotgun is American, Watson says: 'White Mason gazed at my friend as the little village practitioner looks at the Harley Street specialist who by a word can solve the difficulties that perplex him.'

However, he needs reassurance from MacDonald before he

allows an amateur near the scene of the crime. 'I have worked with Mr Holmes before,' says MacDonald. 'He plays the game.'

Like Holmes, MacDonald is ponderous and methodical, refusing to be rushed to conclusions. In contrast, White Mason comes up with theories that Holmes finds unconvincing. But MacDonald is frustrated by Holmes' obtuse methodology. 'You get to your point, I admit,' he says, 'but you have such a deuced round-the-corner way of doing it.'

Then when Holmes reveals that the alleged victim is still alive, MacDonald loses his temper. 'And how long have you been playing this trick upon us, Mr Holmes?' he asks. 'How long have you allowed us to waste ourselves upon a search that you knew to be an absurd one?'

'Not one instant, my dear Mr Mac,' says Holmes. 'Only last night did I form my views of the case.'

Inspector Bradstreet
In 'The Man with the Twisted Lip', Inspector Bradstreet is on duty in Bow Street when Holmes calls to unmask the beggar Hugh Boone. Holmes knows Bradstreet well. He is tall and stout and a uniformed officer who wears a peaked cap and frogged jacket. He complains that Boone is a dirty scoundrel. It is all they can do to make him wash his hands and Bradstreet cannot wait until the case is settled so that Boone will be forced to take a regular prison bath. After Holmes has washed the sleeping Boone's face to reveal Neville St Clair, he leaves Bradstreet to take care of the paperwork. Bradstreet then insists that St Clair give up begging.

Inspector Bradstreet reappears a newspaper reporter in 'The Adventure of the Blue Carbuncle', when he wrongly arrests Horner, the plumber, at the Hotel Cosmopolitan for stealing a jewel.

In 'The Adventure of the Engineer's Thumb', Inspector Bradstreet, now of Scotland Yard, accompanies Holmes, Watson, a plain-clothes man and a hydraulic engineer to Eyford, only to find the house that they are looking for has gone up in smoke.

Inspector Gregory

Holmes has received a telegram from Inspector Gregory at the beginning of the 'Silver Blaze', inviting him to join the investigation. Watson says he is a 'tall, fair man with lion-like hair and beard and curiously penetrating light blue eyes . . . a man who was rapidly making his name in the English detective service'.

Holmes grants that he is 'an extremely competent officer', but goes on to say that, 'Were he but gifted with imagination he might rise to great heights in his profession.'

Gregory has, of course, arrested the wrong man. However he does have enough imagination to anticipate Holmes' needs and gets him a photograph of John Straker before Holmes asks for it.

Inspector Forrester

While Holmes is convalescing in Reigate, Inspector Forrester visits him to seek his advice. Forrester is a smart, keen-faced young fellow. We are not informed of how – or if – he is related to Mrs Cecil Forrester, Miss Morstan's employer.

Forrester enjoys Holmes' puzzlement at the scrap of a note found in the murdered coachman's hand. Then he becomes little more than Holmes's messenger boy. But he is on hand to arrest the Cunninghams.

Inspector Lanner

In 'The Resident Patient', Lanner is at the scene of the crime when Holmes turns up and apologizes for intruding. Lanner is convinced that Blessington's death is a suicide and, when Holmes suggests it is murder, he cries: 'Impossible!' But Holmes insists and advises him to arrest the page. He hurries away to make enquiries and arrest the page, while Holmes identifies the rest of the gang involved. Unlike other policemen, Lanner follows Holmes' reasoning and identifies Blessington as the bank robber Sutton. Holmes then leaves Lanner to wield the sword of justice and avenge the murdered man, though the killers are drowned when trying to escape by steamer, which sinks.

Inspector Forbes

In 'The Naval Treaty', Inspector Forbes is in charge of the investigation. He suspects the commissionaire's wife and has her searched.

According to Watson, Forbes is a 'small, foxy man with a sharp but by no means amiable expression'.

He is decidedly frosty himself when he learns the Holmes is on the case. 'I've heard of your methods before now, Mr Holmes,' said he tartly. 'You are ready enough to use all the information that the police can lay at your disposal, and then you try to finish the case yourself and bring discredit on them.'

Holmes says that out of his last fifty-three cases, his name has appeared in only four. The police had taken the credit in the other forty-nine.

In that case, 'I'd be very glad of a hint or two,' says the detective, changing his manner. 'I've certainly had no credit from the case so far.'

When the culprit, Joseph Harrison, flees, Holmes wires full particulars to Forbes, who can then, presumably, take full credit for catching him.

Inspector Martin

In 'The Adventure of the Dancing Men', Inspector Martin of the Norfolk Constabulary is on the case. He is pleasantly surprised when Holmes turns up and has the good sense to let Holmes do things in his own way, contenting himself with noting down the results. Watson says he is 'trim'.

The country policeman is amazed that, after a quick examination of the house and garden, Holmes announces that the case is almost completely solved. Martin listens quietly when Holmes explains how he deciphered the code. Later, he deftly slips the handcuffs on to the criminal Slaney's wrists while Holmes holds a gun to Slaney's head.

Stanley Hopkins

Inspector Hopkins is in charge of the investigation into the death of Peter Carey in 'The Adventure of Black Peter'. He calls on Holmes after failing to make any headway with the case and berates himself for not asking for help earlier.

'It's my first big chance, and I am at my wit's end,' he says. 'For goodness' sake, come down and lend me a hand.'

The young detective says that he knows Holmes's methods and tries to apply them, but after a week he has still made no progress. When Holmes points out that the 'C.P.R.' in Carey's notebook might mean Canadian Pacific Railway, Hopkins swears between his teeth and in frustration strikes his thigh with his clenched hand.

Hopkins is a man of action and grabs the collar of John Hopley Neligan, who is breaking into Carey's cabin. But Holmes is not happy. 'Stanley Hopkins's methods do not commend themselves to me,' says Holmes. 'I am disappointed in Stanley Hopkins. I had hoped for better things from him.'

Nevertheless, he invites Hopkins to breakfast at Baker Street the following morning. Hopkins arrives promptly and is still convinced of his case against Neligan, until Holmes points out that he could not have done it. When Holmes tries to arrest the harpooner Patrick Cairns, Hopkins comes to Holmes's assistance. 'It seems to me that I have been making a fool of myself from the beginning,' says Hopkins. 'I understand now, what I should never have forgotten, that I am the pupil and you are the master.'

In 'The Adventure of the Golden Pince-Nez', the young Stanley Hopkins, 'a promising detective, in whose career Holmes had several times shown a very practical interest', turns up at Baker Street at midnight, asking for his help. Holmes immediately furnishes him with a cigar, and hot water and lemon. Hopkins in 'an ecstasy of admiration', is astonished by Holmes's powers of deduction. After Holmes solves the mystery, he says to Hopkins: 'I congratulate you on having brought your case to a successful conclusion.'

In 'The Adventure of the Missing Three-Quarters', Hopkins recommends that Cyril Overton take his case to Holmes. And in 'The Adventure of Abbey Grange', Hopkins writes to Holmes asking, again, for his help.

'Hopkins has called me in seven times, and on each occasion his summons has been entirely justified,' Holmes says to Watson. 'I fancy that every one of his cases has found its way into your collection . . .' In fact, they haven't. He only appears in four stories.

From the handwriting, Holmes deduces that Hopkins is agitated, but believes that he will live up to his reputation. Thanks to Holmes, Hopkins recovers the missing silver from the pond. Holmes lets him believe the Randall gang were responsible, until they are arrested in New York. Hopkins is invited to stay for dinner, but goes him go off in search of another gang of burglars while Holmes and Watson tie up the case. When they let Crocker go free, Holmes says: 'I have given Hopkins an excellent hint, and if he can't avail himself of it I can do no more.'

Inspector Baynes

In 'The Adventure of Wisteria Lodge', Inspector Baynes of the Surrey Constabulary arrives at Baker Street with Inspector Gregson. But after taking a statement from Eccles, Gregson then drops out of the case, leaving it to Baynes.

Watson says: 'The country detective was a stout, puffy, red man, whose face was only redeemed from grossness by two extraordinarily bright eyes, almost hidden behind the heavy creases of cheek and brow.' He takes a delight in his work.

When Baynes produces the note that he found in a dog-grate, Holmes says: 'I must compliment you, Mr Baynes, upon your attention to detail in your examination of it' – though Holmes goes on to add 'a few trifling points'.

Holmes asks if Baynes objects to him collaborating, saying he finds him 'very prompt and business-like'.

'Highly honoured, sir, I am sure,' says Baynes.

When Holmes wants a list of large country houses in the area to limit their search, he telegrams Baynes, telling Watson: 'No doubt Baynes, with his methodical mind, has already adopted some similar plan.'

Baynes then gives Holmes a detailed tour of Wisteria Lodge. Afterwards, Holmes says: 'I must congratulate you, Inspector, on handling so distinctive and instructive a case. Your powers, if I may say so without offence, seem superior to your opportunities.'

Watson notes: 'Inspector Baynes's small eyes twinkled with pleasure.'

As Holmes and Watson ramble around the area they occasionally come across Baynes: 'His fat, red face wreathed itself in smiles and his small eyes glittered as he greeted my companion. He said little about the case, but from that little we gathered that he also was not dissatisfied at the course of events.'

But then Baynes goes and does the inevitable – arrests the wrong man. Holmes points out the error. 'I assure you I speak for your good,' says Holmes.

Watson notes: 'It seemed to me that something like a wink quivered for an instant over one of Mr Baynes's tiny eyes.'

'We agreed to work on our own lines, Mr Holmes,' says Baynes. 'That's what I am doing.'

Baynes is as devious as Holmes. He is also after Henderson and later tells Holmes: 'I arrested the wrong man to make him believe that our eyes were off him. I knew he would be likely to clear off then and give us a chance of getting at Miss Burnet.'

'You will rise high in your profession. You have instinct and intuition,' says Holmes. These are not qualities that Holmes usually commends.

Baynes flushes with pleasure. But he is way ahead of the great detective. He has had plain-clothes men waiting at the police station all week. Holmes then has to ask Baynes who Henderson really is. Baynes knows – Don Murillo, the Tiger of San Pedro. He has already made a full investigation of the deposed dictator.

While Watson still thinks a good lawyer can get Don Murillo off, Baynes is adamant this will not happen. Later he turns up at Baker Street with confirmation that Don Murillo and his manservant have been killed in Madrid.

Inspector Morton
Outside 221B in the fog, Watson bumps into 'an old acquaintance, Inspector Morton of Scotland Yard, dressed in unofficial tweeds. He asks how Holmes is. When told Holmes is very ill, Watson glimpses a look of exultation in his face. Morton is clearly in on the plot.

Inspector Bardle
In 'The Adventure of the Lion's Mane', Inspector Bardle of the Sussex Constabulary investigates. According to Holmes, he is 'a steady, solid, bovine man with thoughtful eyes'. He is deferential towards Holmes's 'immense experience' and asks him whether he should make an arrest. Holmes recommends against it, but the 'burly, phlegmatic man was sorely troubled in his mind'.

Edmunds
In 'The Adventure of the Veiled Lodger', Holmes says that years before he was consulted over the mauling at Abbas Parva by a 'worried young Edmunds of the Berkshire Constabulary', whom he judged 'a smart lad'. He was a thin, yellow-haired man who was later sent to Allahabad. They smoked a pipe or two over the mauling, but got no further.

Inspector MacKinnon
After Holmes and Barker had taken Amberley to the police station in 'The Adventure of the Retired Colourman', Holmes returns with 'a smart young police inspector' – MacKinnon. Although Scotland Yard had passed Amberley on to Holmes, MacKinnon asserts that they would have got there all the same.

'Don't imagine that we had not formed our own views of this

case, and that we would not have laid our hands on our man,' he says. 'You will excuse us for feeling sore when you jump in with methods which we cannot use, and so rob us of the credit.'

When Holmes says that he intends to take no credit, MacKinnon seems considerably relieved. Then Holmes has to take him through the whole case and MacKinnon concedes that Holmes's handling of the case is 'masterly'.

Carrying the story, the *North Surrey Observer* says: 'The remarkable acumen by which Inspector MacKinnon deduced from the smell of paint that some other smell, that of gas, for example, might be concealed; the bold deduction that the strong-room might also be the death-chamber, and the subsequent inquiry which led to the discovery of the bodies in a disused well, cleverly concealed by a dog-kennel, should live in the history of crime as a standing example of the intelligence of our professional detectives.'

'MacKinnon is a good fellow,' Holmes concludes.

Other policemen are also mentioned. There is Sam Brown of the Yard in *The Sign of the Four*; 'my friend Algar of the Liverpool force'; Inspector Montgomery in 'The Adventure of the Cardboard Box'; Inspector Hill in 'The Adventure of the Six Napoleons'; William Hargreave of the New York Police Bureau in 'The Adventure of the Dancing Men'; Youghal of the CID in 'The Adventure of the Marazin Stone' and Merivale of the Yard in 'The Adventure of Shoscombe Old Place'.

The question remains: are all these irredeemably dumb and interfering policemen really necessary? In 'The Five Orange Pips', Holmes says: 'I shall be my own police. When I have spun the web they may take the flies, but not before.'

Bibliography

H.W Bell (ed.), *Baker Street Studies* (London: Constable & Co, London, 1934).

William S. Baring-Gould (ed.), *The Annotated Sherlock Holmes* (London: John Murray, 1968).

Arthur Conan Doyle, *Arthur Conan Doyle on Sherlock Holmes* (London: Favil Press, 1981).

Arthur Conan Doyle, *The Case-Book of Sherlock Holmes* (London: John Murray, 1927).

Arthur Conan Doyle, *The Complete Stories of Sherlock Holmes* (Ware: Wordsworth Library Collection, 2007).

Arthur Conan Doyle, *Memories and Adventures* (London: John Murray, 1930).

Owen Dudley Edwards, *The Quest for Sherlock Holmes* (Harmondsworth: Penguin Books, 1984).

Alistair Duncan, *Close to Holmes* (London: MX Publishing, 2009).

Joseph Green and Ridgway Watt, *Alas, Poor Sherlock* (Beckenham: Chancery House Press, 2007).

Michael Harrison, *The London of Sherlock Holmes* (Newton Abbot: David & Charles, 1972).

Michael Harwick and Mollie Harwick, *The Sherlock Holmes Companion* (London: John Murray, 1962).

Roger Johnson and Jean Upton (eds), *Back to Baker Street: An Appreciation of Sherlock Holmes & London* (London: The Sherlock Holmes Society of London, 1994).

Leslie S. Klinger (ed.), *The New Annotated Sherlock Holmes* (New York City: W.W. Norton & Company, 2005).

Jon Lellenberg, Daniel Stashower and Charles Foley (eds), *Arthur Conan Doyle: A Life in Letters* (London: HarperPress, 2007).

Christopher Lindsey, *Sherlock Holmes and a Question of Science* (Leatherhead: Hadley Pager Info, 2006).

Andrew Lycett, *The Man Who Created Sherlock Holmes: The Life and Times of Sir Arthur Conan Doyle* (London: Weidenfeld & Nicolson, 2007).

Ben Macintyre, *The Napoleon of Crime: The Life and Times of Adam Worth, the Real Moriarty* (London: Flamingo, 1998).

Russell Miller, *The Adventures of Arthur Conan Doyle* (London: Harvill Secker, 2008).

Andrew Norman, *Arthur Conan Doyle: Beyond Sherlock Holmes* (Stroud: Tempus, 2007).

Reginald Pound, *The Strand Magazine 1891–1950* (London: Heinemann, 1966).

Brian W. Pugh, *A Chronology of the Life of Sir Arthur Conan Doyle* (London: MX Publishing, 2009).

Christopher Redmond, *A Sherlock Holmes Handbook* (Toronto: Simon & Pierre, 1993).

Nick Rennison, *Sherlock Holmes: The Unauthorized Biography* (London: Atlantic Books, 2005).

Ransom Riggs, *The Sherlock Holmes Handbook: The Methods and Mysteries of the World's Greatest Detective* (Philadelphia: Quirk Books, 2009).

Alvin E. Rodin, *The Medical Casebook of Dr Arthur Conan Doyle: From Practitioner to Sherlock Holmes and Beyond* (Malabar, Florida: Robert E. Krieger Publishing Company, 1984).

David Sinclair, *Sherlock Holmes's London* (London: Robert Hale, 2009)

David Sinclair, (ed.) *The Uncollected Stories of Arthur Conan Doyle* Newcastle upon Tyne: Cambridge Scholars Publishing, 2009).

Index